HISTORIC BATTLEFIELDS IN
500
WALKS

Thunder Bay Press
An imprint of Printers Row Publishing Group
9717 Pacific Heights Blvd, San Diego, CA 92121
www.thunderbaybooks.com • mail@thunderbaybooks.com

This book was conceived, designed, and produced by
The Bright Press, an imprint of The Quarto Group,
The Old Brewery, 6 Blundell Street, London N7 9BH
www.quarto.com

Thunder Bay Press
Publisher: Peter Norton
Associate Publisher: Ana Parker
Editor: Dan Mansfield

The Bright Press
Publisher: James Evans
Editorial Director: Isheeta Mustafi
Managing Editor: Jacqui Sayers
Art Director: James Lawrence
Designer: Tony Seddon
Cover design: Emily Nazer
Picture Researcher: Jenny Quiggin
Project Editor: Kath Stathers
Senior Editor: Sara Harper

Library of Congress Control Number: 2022938732

ISBN: 978-1-6672-0049-1

Printed in Singapore

26 25 24 23 22   1 2 3 4 5

HISTORIC
BATTLEFIELDS
IN
500
WALKS

Hiking routes and rambles through the
world's most iconic battlegrounds

STEVE FALLON

THUNDER BAY
P · R · E · S · S

San Diego, California

CONTENTS

INTRODUCTION

Since earliest times, war has brought out both the worst and the best in humans. Greed, irredentism, empire-building, and vengeance have wreaked havoc on nations, cultures, and people, changing the course of history more often than not in the wrong direction. But at the same time, the intense, very focused emotions that cause human beings to attack and kill one another have created heroes celebrated for their bravery, Samaritans praiseworthy for their generosity and exemplars of self-sacrifice. In *Historic Battlefields in 500 Walks*, we will encounter a cast of characters that include both monsters and saints.

This book is composed of six chapters that look at battles, conflicts, and uprisings across six continents arranged chronologically from the very distant past—ten millennia before the birth of Christ—to the end of the Vietnam War in 1975. It is designed to help you travel through time and space using your imagination, your own two feet, or a combination of both. Armchair travelers content to experience battles from the sidelines will find the book just as informative as those eager to get up and go.

The 500 walks vary in length. Some are snippets designed to whet your appetite, while the slightly longer entries describe an important battle or skirmish and sketch a possible walk on or around the site. The longest ones describe the confrontations in more detail and contain definable routes, walk descriptions and, in some cases, maps. We hope the book inspires you to seek out history and follow in the writers' footsteps—but only up to a point. Bear in mind that the walk descriptions do not contain all the information you would need to trace the route itself. Instead, they are merely suggestions of interesting places from where to start, with a sense of the right route to take.

ANCIENT HISTORY
10,000 BC–AD 499

Examine pictorial evidence of prehistoric tribal
warfare and then move forward to the end of the
fifth century AD, relying on ancient legends and
myths as much as hard facts to uncover the past.

Hunter-Gatherer Group Warfare

ARNHEM LAND, NORTHERN TERRITORY, AUSTRALIA

Learn about the original hunter-gatherers of Australia and their possible group warfare on a guided walk around the rock galleries of Arnhem Land.

◆ **LENGTH**
Route dependent on tour

◆ **START**
Injalak Arts in Gunbalanya

◆ **TYPE OF WALK**
Guided day walk as part of an art tour

◆ **WHEN TO GO**
During the dry season, May to October

For thousands of years, the Australian Aborigines have been documenting their lives and observations through forms of rock art. Yet among all their imagery, it is rare to find art that depicts battles and combat. However, among the wild terrains of Arnhem Land—an area of Indigenous-owned land in the Northern Territory of Australia—there are paintings of people that seem to be engaged in fighting, suggesting that tribal warfare did sometimes occur.

A walk around these rock-art galleries gives an insight into what the Aborigine people have experienced throughout their long history in the area, which dates back more than 10,000 years.

While here, take in the lush green wetlands and the rare wildlife that thrive in this part of the world. A permit is required to enter Arnhem Land. Inquire at Injalak Arts in Gunbalanya to learn more about the arts and culture directly from the local Indigenous guides to whom these lands belong.

RIGHT In places, Arnhem Land looks exactly as it has for thousands of years.

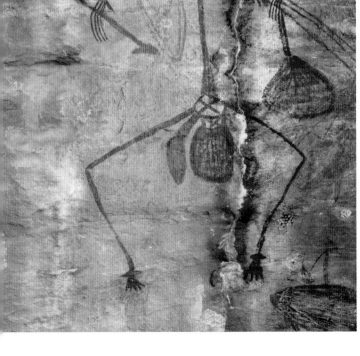

Nataruk Massacre
NATARUK, KENYA

Meander around Lake Turkana's placid shores to discover possible evidence of human warfare: nearly thirty skeletons, including women and children, have been found at this site which dates back approximately 10,000 years. They all show evidence of blunt trauma that could only have come from other human beings.

Archers on the Wall
COVA DEL ROURE, SPAIN

Walk through the underground maze of Cova del Roure, near Valencia, to discover ancient cave paintings that show archers in battle with other warriors. These skirmishes were recorded as long as 10,000 years ago and preserved on grotto ceilings and walls, a testament to humans' warlike nature as far back as hunter-gatherer days.

LEFT A rare example of Aboriginal rock art showing weapons.

Talheim Death Pit

TALHEIM, GERMANY

Discovered in 1983, the Talheim Death Pit is an ancient mass grave measuring 25 feet by 3 feet, containing thirty-four adult and child skeletons believed to be villagers slaughtered by other community groups around 7,000 years ago. It was the first ever discovery of Stone Age bodies showing signs of severe trauma, which suggest the killings may be the result of organized violence. As the initial such find from the early Neolithic period in Europe, the uncovering of this mass grave was of specific interest to archaeologists. The site can be reached by a short walk from the center of Talheim, along Hauptstraße toward the river.

Expansion of Egyptian Empire

JEBEL BARKAL, KARIAMA, SUDAN

Around the year 1450 BC, the Egyptian pharaoh Thutmose III pushed his armies south along the Nile to take control of much of what is today Sudan. Fast-forward 3,500 years or so and, after a short climb to the flat summit of the Jebel Barkal, you can look down on a clutch of pyramids, temple columns, and ceremonial walkways, half-buried by sand, marking the southern limit of this expansion.

RIGHT The 3,000-year-old ruins at Jebel Barkal mark the southern limit of the Egyptian Empire's expansion under Pharaoh Thutmose III.

Sargon of Akkad Defeats Uruk

AHWAR, IRAQ

Wander through the marshlands where one of the world's first great emperors conquered tribe after tribe.

◆ **DISTANCE**
1 mile

◆ **START**
Molla Fadhel
Sakrani Tomb

◆ **TYPE OF WALK**
A stroll past marshlands
and inlets with vistas,
wildlife, and birds

◆ **WHEN TO GO**
Avoid the middle of the
day; early morning or late
afternoon is best

Sargon of Akkad is considered by some historians to be the first emperor. Sumerian scripts tell of how he "broke the walls" of Ur, Uruk, Umma, Eridu, Lagash, and many more cities as he consolidated control over the region around 2400 BC (although exact dating is impossible). One particularly vivid quote says that after conquering these southern enemies, Sargon "washed his weapons in the sea" as he'd reached the coast and there were no further cities to conquer.

The ruins of Ur and Uruk still exist today, rising out of the parched desert that once was fertile ground. Though modern borders now divide this valley, the entire region is where Sargon waged his wars and created an empire.

Walkers will enjoy the roads that skirt the marshlands of what, centuries ago, was once Sargon's empire. It's an area full of birds, with little hint of the dramatic warfare. Locals cut reeds and carry them on hand-poled boats to reach shore. Keep an eye out for flamingos, which not only feed here but raise their young here, too.

RIGHT There is little sign in this reedy marshland that this was once the battleground of Sargon of Akkad.

Cerro Sechín and the Ancient War Sacrifices

CASMA VALLEY, PERU

In the Casma Valley, 168 miles north of Lima, Cerro Sechín is an archaeological site which belongs to the pre-Incan era of Peru. It is one of the most studied sites for the depiction of warfare and sacrifices in the culture between 1800 and 900 BC. A walk around the site is an instructive learning experience.

The Lagash-Umma Dispute

MESOPOTAMIA, IRAQ

In ancient Sumer, well-documented battles broke out between the Umma and Lagash peoples. Though precise details are still debated today, carved stone stelae depicting the battle show a man holding a basket of men in one hand, evidence of captives. Today, the site exists in modern Iraq. Those who visit will find a barren desert with ample room to wander amid excavated and unexcavated structures.

LEFT This stone relief, now in the Louvre, shows Sargon of Akkad in front of a Tree of Life.

Siege of Megiddo

TEL MEGIDDO NATIONAL PARK, HAIFA, ISRAEL

Imagine biblical battles between ancient civilizations at the top of this *tel*, or historic settlement mound.

DISTANCE
0.5 mile

START
Museum

TYPE OF WALK
Around ruins

WHEN TO GO
All year

ABOVE RIGHT Archaeologists have uncovered objects dating back more than 4,000 years.

RIGHT Tel Megiddo's hilltop location was both its strength, and ultimately, its downfall.

Megiddo's strategic hilltop location at the crossing through the Carmel Mountains between the ancient region of Canaan (which is today Israel, Palestine, Lebanon, and parts of Syria and Jordan) and Egypt and Mesopotamia gave it an importance far beyond its size. According to the New Testament, it was the site of Armageddon (*Har-Megiddo*), the final battle between God's forces and Satan, and archaeologists claim it's also the site of at least thirty battles between the ancient Israelites and their opponents dating back over 4,000 years to the Neolithic era.

The seven-month Siege of Megiddo, in 1479 BC, came when the Canaanites were fighting Pharaoh Thutmose III, one of the greatest military strategists of ancient Egypt. Each army had around 1,000 chariots and 10,000 infantry. However, the Canaanites retreated uphill to Megiddo and Thutmose built a moat and stockade encircling it, eventually forcing its occupants to surrender. The victory gave Thutmose control over northern Canaan and a base to launch campaigns into Mesopotamia.

The area is now a national park and UNESCO World Heritage Site. Start at the excellent museum which navigates the vast history and uses models to re-create Megiddo's original structures. Then pass through a fifteenth-century BC Canaan gate and follow footpaths around the ruined fortifications, temples, palaces, tombs, and water tunnels. As you do so, imagine the various occupants that inhabited the site from 4000 to 400 BC.

Battle of Megiddo

TEL MEGIDDO NATIONAL PARK, HAIFA, ISRAEL

Another important battle that took place at Tel Megiddo was in 609 BC when King Josiah of Judah was defeated by Pharaoh Necho II and Judah subsequently became a vassal state of Egypt. Walk to the southern lookout point to imagine the fierce clash of chariots and foot soldiers on the plains below.

Battle of Kadesh

HOMS, SYRIA

Around 1274 BC, Egyptian pharoah Ramses II was taken by surprise due to the duplicity of Hittite spies. More than 6,000 chariots fought each other as first the Hittites, then the Egyptians, took the lead. At one point Ramses himself battled hand-to-hand. Today, the site can be visited as Tell al-Nabi Mando. Climb the *tell*—Arabic for mound—to get a bird's-eye view of the site, then go down and meander around the site's remaining structures.

Siege of Troy

HISARLIK, ÇANAKKALE PROVINCE, TURKEY

Walk through the iconic site of Troy—proof
of the importance of myth to the human experience.

◆ **DISTANCE**
1 mile

◆ **START**
Archaeological site
ticket office

◆ **TYPE OF WALK**
Easy and well-marked

◆ **WHEN TO GO**
All year; there are less
crowds midweek

ABOVE LEFT Walk around the site
that gave us the legend of the
Trojan horse.

LEFT Ruins here date back to
3000 BC.

Few battles from ancient times resonate to the same degree as
the siege of Troy, in the middle of the thirteenth century BC,
when the Mycenaean Greeks attacked what was then one of the
largest towns in the Aegean region. Alas, everything we know
about the Trojan War—from the abduction of the beautiful
Helen by Paris to the famous wooden horse used by the Greeks
in their surprise incursion—comes from Homer, who described it
in detail in his epic poems the *Iliad* and the *Odyssey* based on
myths written half a millennium after the event. Excavations
begun in the late nineteenth century do show evidence of
widespread destruction and mass slaughter around 1250 BC.

The archaeological site, added to UNESCO's World Heritage
list in 1998, tops an artificial mound. From the ticket booth, walk
1,650 feet west, past the model Trojan horse, and begin a
counterclockwise circular tour via the boardwalk that will lead
you past the nine stages of the city's development, from 3000 BC
to AD 500. Most of what remains, including the impressive
two-story palace complex, dates from what is known as Troy VI,
which ended with what is believed to have been the Trojan War.

13

Battle of Mount Gilboa

GILBOA SCENIC ROAD,
BEIT SHE'AN, ISRAEL

During this twelfth-century BC battle between the Philistines of Crete and the biblical Israelites, King Saul and 10,000 troops retreated to the peaks of Mount Gilboa. But they were attacked by 15,000 Philistines, resulting in a crushing defeat; Saul's three sons fell first and Saul died by falling on his sword as his army fell apart. The curving 11-mile-long Gilboa Scenic Road follows the mountainous ridges from where great hikes lead to stunning viewpoints overlooking the battlefield below in Jezreel Valley, while on Mount Shaul (Saul) a trail has Hebrew plaques describing biblical events.

14

Sea Peoples Raid Egypt

MEDINET HABU, NEAR WEST BANK,
LUXOR, EGYPT

Though no records indicate where the Sea Peoples came from, they were seafaring raiders of Mediterranean coastal cities between 1276 and 1176 BC, especially Egypt. In 1176 BC the last great Egyptian pharaoh, Ramses III, defeated the Sea Peoples, who subsequently vanished from history. Walk around Medinet Habu's mortuary temple of Ramses III, Luxor's second-largest ancient Egyptian complex after Karnak, to see the highly detailed hieroglyphics telling the story of the battle, including Ramses III showing off his prisoners of war to the god Amun.

15

Dynasties of China: Battle of Muye

XINXIANG, HENAN, CHINA

The Battle of Muye (*ca.* 1046 BC) is one of the pivotal points in Chinese history, when the Shang dynasty was overthrown, leading to the ascent of the Zhou dynasty, which became the longest existing dynasty in Chinese history, surviving almost 800 years. Not much evidence from this battle remains visible; however, you can walk along the Yellow River, and visit a modern re-creation of the Tong Pass, the mountain pass which the Zhou forces would have had to cross to get to Muye for the decisive battle.

16

Decline of the Olmec Civilization

SAN LORENZO TENOCHTITLÁN,
VERACRUZ STATE, MEXICO

The Olmec culture thrived along Mexico's Gulf coast from about 1200 to 400 BC. It reached its heyday with the city now known as San Lorenzo Tenochtitlán, center of commerce, religion, and political power. Some historians believe its demise was brought on by environmental disruptions. The archaeological site has yielded a treasure trove of artifacts, and can be easily visited in half a day.

RIGHT The mortuary temple of Ramses III at Medinet Habu houses spectacular hieroglyphics.

17

Siege of Lachish

**TEL LACHISH NATIONAL PARK,
NEAR KIRYAT GAT, ISRAEL**

After Jerusalem, Lachish was considered Judea's second most important fortified city as it guarded the main route from Egypt. In 701 BC while King Hezekiah revolted against Assyria, it was besieged and captured by Sennacherib, king of Assyria. Modern excavations have revealed a fierce battle; 1,500 skulls, hundreds of arrowheads, and a stone and dirt ramp built to storm the city wall have been uncovered. Visitors can walk around the remains of Hezekiah's gateways and palace-fort, while a path climbs up to the top of the *tel*, or artificial mound.

18

Siege of Sardis

SARDIS, MANISA PROVINCE, TURKEY

Expansion of the first Persian empire came fast under Cyrus the Great, but his first major prize came in 547 BC with the conquest of the powerful Lydian kingdom, which paved the way for further expansion southward into Lycia. Details of the battle are scant, but Herodotus writes that during the battle Cyrus placed his camels in front of his warriors; the Lydian horses, not used to the smell, bolted. At Sardis, follow the more recent 60-foot-long Roman road past Byzantine shops to a third-century AD synagogue. Jews are believed to have settled here as early as 547 BC, presumably with Cyrus.

Sieges of Xanthos

KINIK, ANTALYA PROVINCE, TURKEY

Lycia flourished on Turkey's southwest Mediterranean coast from roughly 1200 BC to AD 400. The legacies of this unique culture include stunning funerary monuments and the Lycian League, the first democratic union of city-states. The capital, Xanthos, is today an important archaeological site with a host of Lycian and Greek ruins. Xanthos had a checkered history; when besieged by clearly superior enemy forces of both the Persians in 540 BC and again by the Romans under Brutus in 42 BC, the city's population committed mass suicide. To view the battlefield (now filled with polytunnels), climb to the top of the amphitheater.

Early Roman Wars

ROME, ITALY

In 508 BC, Lars Porsena's Etruscan army approached Rome from behind the Janiculum, a hill to the west of the city, taking the Romans by surprise. Seeing their enemy approach, the Romans crossed into the city to seek safety via the Sublician Bridge. Roman hero Horatius Cocles came up with an ingenious plan—he and two friends removed the bridge's *sublicae*, or wooden planks, thereby demolishing the bridge and impeding the enemy's access to the city. Take a stroll around the lively Testaccio district and then cross the modern bridge to bustling Trastevere.

ABOVE LEFT The ruins of Sardis, where the smell of camels was used to scare the horses.

ABOVE From the top of the amphitheater at Xanthos, you can look over the former battlefield.

Adena People

CRIEL MOUND, SOUTH CHARLESTON, WEST VIRGINIA

In 500 BC, the Adena culture inhabited much of what is now the state of Ohio. It was known for its custom of making burial mounds, some of which contained skeletons with evidence of battle wounds; other studies indicate some bodies, possibly captives, were buried alive. Many mounds have been destroyed, but one of the best preserved is the Criel Mound in South Charleston, where you can walk to the top, circle the grassy park, and then head to the river. Squint and try to imagine a vast, fertile valley, with hunter-gatherers cultivating squash and sunflowers.

Battle of Marathon

MARATHON, EAST ATTICA, GREECE

The plain surrounding the town of Marathon, northeast of Athens, was the site of this celebrated battle in which Persian forces unsuccessfully tried to subjugate Greece in 490 BC. As a sign of honor, the 192 men killed here were buried in a collective tomb, a 33-foot-high tumulus south of the town. It was from here that a courier ran to Athens to announce the victory which gave the name to the long-distance running race. Walk around the burial mound; a short distance to the north is a replica of the Ionic Trophy of Marathon erected by the Athenians to commemorate their win.

23

Battle of Thermopylae

PASS OF THERMOPYLAE, GREECE

Thermopylae is a strategic mountain pass in northern Greece linking a north-south passage along the Balkan peninsula's east coast. In 480 BC a Greek force moved to prevent the Persian army from getting through. During three days of battle, a small force led by Sparta's King Leonidas I blocked the only road by which the massive Persian army could pass. But a local resident betrayed them. Leonidas and 300 Spartans held their ground until the last man fell. The pass is now crossed by a highway, with Leonidas on one side and a visitor's center on the other.

24

Peloponnesian Wars

CORINTH, GREECE

Athens and Sparta were the two most powerful states in ancient Greece. From 431 to 404 BC, they were at war with each other, known as the Peloponnesian Wars. Eventually, the majority of power shifted to Sparta, where democracy was replaced by an oligarchy of Athenians who were in alliance with Sparta. A major naval battle took place off Corinth. A walk along the beaches in Corinth, between the Historical and Folklore Museum and the Ancient Port of Lechaeum, looks out over where the battle would have been fought.

ABOVE A walk along the Corinth beachfronts, past the statue of Pegasus, looks out over where the Peloponnesian Wars would have been fought.

LEFT The tumulus outside Marathon where casualties of the battle in 490 BC were buried.

Magadha and Vajji War

BIHAR, INDIA

Walk between temples on the Falgu River
where dynasties once battled over jewels.

DISTANCE
8 miles

START
Mahabodhi Temple, Gaya

TYPE OF WALK
Leisurely day walk
(one way)

WHEN TO GO
Visit between October
and March to avoid the
monsoon and the heat
of summer

RIGHT The Mahabodhi Temple
where Buddha is reputed to have
attained enlightenment.

The story of the Magadha and Vajji War of 484 to 468 BC,
between the Haryanka dynasty of Magadha and the Vajji
confederacy, has different origin stories depending on which
religion you read.

While not strictly a religious war, the Haryanka dynasty was
predominantly Buddhist and the Vajji confederacy a mix of Jain
and Buddhist faith. According to Buddhist texts, the war was
fought because the Vajjians stole Ajatashatru, king of the
Haryanka's share of the riches of a diamond mine. Jain sources,
however, state that the fight was over a divine necklace which
Ajatashatru wanted as a gift for his queen. He demanded that
the Vajjians give it to him, and when they refused, he decided to
take it by force.

The battle was fought in the modern state of Bihar along
the Ganges River on the Nepali border. But this walk is in
Gaya, around 56 miles south of the Ganges, where you can
stroll along the Falgu River and visit Buddist, Jain, and Hindu
temples, including the ancient Mahabodhi Temple complex, a
UNESCO World Heritage Site where the Buddha is said to
have attained enlightenment.

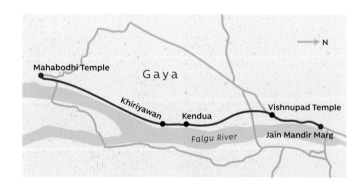

26

Gauls Settle Etruscan Territories

MARZABOTTO, ITALY

The Etruscan city of Kainua, near present-day Marzabotto, served as an important commercial hub between the Etruscan settlements of the Tyrrhenian Sea and the northern city-states. Its importance declined during the fourth century BC when the Gauls swept into the Po Valley, capturing Etruscan territory. A 10.5-mile circular route from Marzabotto meanders through hornbeam and oak woods, passing ancient ruins, including a necropolis, two temples, and private houses.

Romans Hold Off the Gauls

ROME, ITALY

Explore the smallest of Rome's seven hills,
where the Gauls' sacking of the city was rebuffed.

◆ **DISTANCE**
1.6 miles

◆ **START**
Colosseum

◆ **TYPE OF WALK**
City stroll

◆ **WHEN TO GO**
All year

LEFT The ruins of the Roman Forum stand tall in the center of Rome.

BELOW LEFT Stairs lead up to the Piazza del Campidoglio, which marks the top of the smallest of Rome's seven hills.

All roads in ancient Rome converged at the Campidoglio, or Capitoline Hill, the smallest of Rome's seven hills. Lying at the center of religious and political power, the Capitoline symbolized the heart of the empire, and its hilltop temple dedicated to Jupiter, the king of the gods, was ancient Rome's most important religious site.

On July 18, 390 BC, the Gauls attacked and crushed the Romans at the confluence of the Allia and Tiber Rivers; they advanced toward Rome, sacking the city as they went.

Legend says that when the Gauls subsequently attacked the Capitoline at night, a loud flock of sacred geese that inhabited the Temple of Jupiter squawked and shrieked, their deafening clucking and hissing echoing throughout the city and alerting consul Marcus Manlius Capitolinus to the Gauls' presence, thereby saving the city from capture.

Start this walk from the Colosseum and head northwest up Via dei Fori Imperiali, admiring the ruins of the Roman Forum. When you reach Piazza Venezia, turn left and keep an eye out for some steps leading up to the Campidoglio. Pass the former site of the Temple of Jupiter and continue south, ending your walk at the circular Temple of Hercules Victor in Piazza della Bocca della Verità, by the Tiber.

Battle of Allia River

ROME, ITALY

This famous battle took place on the banks of the Tiber River where it meets the Allia River, between the Romans and the Gauls in 387 BC. The latter surprised the Romans, who had little time to mount an attack, and they were soundly defeated. Some Roman soldiers, weighed down by their armor, drowned trying to swim away from the superior Gauls. Start your walk at the nature reserve just behind the Salaria Padel Club. You can walk north, following the river, as far as you can go, checking out the river, the farmland, some stores, and fields.

BELOW The Moshan Scenic Area in Wuhan provides beautiful walks, layered with history.

China's Warring States

WUHAN, HUBEI PROVINCE, CHINA

Beginning in the fifth century BC, ancient China was a collection of warring states, with powerful warlords constantly battling for supremacy. At the end of the Warring States era, the most powerful endured and formed China's first united dynasty—the Qin dynasty—in 221 BC. There are many places in China where you can learn more about the Warring States, yet none so condensed and beautiful as the Moshan Scenic Area in Wuhan. Take a walk along Dong Lake and view historical landmarks before visiting the Hubei Provincial Museum with the largest collection of artifacts from the Warring States era.

LEFT Standing stones add to the landscape on a walk around the site of the Battle of Granicus.

30

Battle of Granicus

NEAR BIGA, ÇANAKKALE PROVINCE, TURKEY

Fought in 334 BC, this was the first of three major battles fought between Alexander the Great of Macedon and the Persian Achaemenid Empire. The three accounts of the battle provided by ancient historians, including Plutarch, contradict one another as to strategy and tactics, but the result was an overwhelming Macedonian victory. The exact location of the battlefield is unknown, but it is thought to have been on the plain just east of the Granicus River (now the Biga Stream). You can follow the course of the Biga for a 12-mile stretch between the villages of Çavuşköy and Karabiga.

31

Battle of Issus

GULF OF ISSUS, ANATOLIA, TURKEY

The second great battle of Alexander the Great's conquest of Asia Minor was fought by the Gulf of Issus, north of the city of Iskenderun ("Alexandria" in Turkish). After the Persians' defeat at Granicus, the Achaemenid king Darius III took personal command of his army. He gathered reinforcements and led his men in a surprise march behind the Hellenics' advance to cut their supply line. This forced Alexander to countermarch, setting the stage for the battle. The site is at a mound under excavation called Kinet Höyük, where there's an impressive Hellenistic theater and the remains of a huge Roman aqueduct.

Battle of Sentinum

NEAR SASSOFERRATO, MARCHE, ITALY

From this peaceful trail you can see the site where the Romans defeated the Gauls and Samnites, leading them to gain control of central and northern Italy.

◆ **DISTANCE**
12 miles

◆ **START**
Montelago

◆ **TYPE OF WALK**
Long-distance trail

◆ **WHEN TO GO**
All year

ABOVE RIGHT The archaeological site at Sentinum is full of interesting details.

RIGHT The peaceful walking trail from Montelago to Monte Strega.

Legend says that moments before the Battle of Sentinum of 295 BC began, a doe chased by a wolf appeared on the battlefield. The doe is said to have bolted toward the Gauls, who immediately killed it, while the wolf headed in the direction of the Romans, who saw it as a divine message from the gods. The battle did indeed end with Roman victory and was to change the history of the country, with Rome gaining control of central and northern Italy.

From Montelago you can walk through meadows and woodland to the summit of Monte Strega, from where you can admire the possible site of the battle between the Romans and the extraordinary coalition of Samnites, Etruscans, Umbrians, and Senone Gauls. The tribal alliance broke up and its peoples were defeated by the Romans.

From Monte Strega, return to Montelago and head east to Regedano, from where you can walk to the Archaeological Park of Sentinum, which lies between the Marena Torrent and the Sentino River. The site houses several Roman remains, including two roads with visible ruts, a foundry used for casting metal, and two thermal bath houses with caldarium, tepidarium, and frigidarium dating back to the first and second centuries AD. Every year, on the last weekend of July, you can watch a historical reenactment of the battle.

Great Wall of China

CHINA

Originally, the Great Wall of China was many small sections of wall built to keep out invaders. But, in 220 BC, the first emperor, Qin Shi Huang, began the process of linking up all these sections to create one long, impregnable barrier. Many of the oldest sections were built from wood and rammed earth, but as building techniques developed, so did the wall, invariably using local materials, such as granite or marble, found in the hills and valleys it crossed. Today the wall stretches about 13,000 miles. Walking the entire length could take twenty months, but shorter walks can be planned between many of the gates, taking in the views of the wall snaking into the distance.

34

Battle of Tagus River

PROVINCE OF GUADALAJARA, SPAIN

Many are familiar with the story of Hannibal and his march across the European Alps with his war elephants during the Second Punic War. However, his first major victory was the Battle of the Tagus in 220 BC, between the cities of Driebes and Illana in Spain's Guadalajara province, where the Carthaginian general's troops, including 40 war elephants, were largely outnumbered. His success created the legend of Hannibal and his elephants. Re-create his victory with a full day's walk between Driebes and Illana, crossing the Tagus from the north of both towns. As you pass Castillo de Vállaga along the river, you can picture elephants wading across.

35

Battle of Trasimene

LAKE TRASIMENE, UMBRIA, ITALY

In June 217 BC, having crossed the Alps and defeated the Roman army in two battles already, Hannibal was sweeping south through Italy. He tactically drew the Romans to Lake Trasimene, ready to ambush his enemy. On the misty morning of June 21, as the Romans entered the valley, Hannibal's troops attacked, beginning a three-hour battle that saw the massacre of 15,000 Roman soldiers and the death of Roman consul Gaius Flaminius. A 10-mile circular trail from Tuoro sul Trasimeno traces key historic moments, and there's also a small museum dedicated to the battle.

Battle of Cannae
CANNE DELLA BATTAGLIA, ITALY

The Roman city of Cannae in Apulia was the site of one of the worst defeats in Roman history, when in 216 BC Hannibal used a full pincer movement to surround and then slaughter Roman troops. You can walk around the archaeological site of Cannae, today known as Canne della Battaglia, which sheds light on Hannibal's presence in Italy during the Second Punic War. Sitting on a hill in the Ofanto Valley, the site also houses a museum displaying archaeological finds, with illustrative panels describing the tactical maneuvers that led to the Carthaginians' victory.

37

Battle of Gaixia
GUZHEN COUNTY, ANHUI, CHINA

A conclusive and fiercely fought battle during the Chu–Han War, Gaixia (203 BC) determined the fall of the Qin dynasty of ancient China and the beginning of the Han dynasty. Immerse yourself in this era of Chinese history with a walk around Hangu Pass, a gateway separating the upper Yellow River and Wei valleys. Here, warrior Liu Bang (who later became Emperor Gauzo of the Han dynasty) advanced eastward on his way to winning the war.

LEFT Hannibal defeated the Romans at Cannae, which now offers pleasant views across the Ofanto Valley.

Battle of Cynoscephalae

NEAR VÓLOS, THESSALY REGION, GREECE

The Battle of Cynoscephalae was fought in the rugged hills northwest of Athens in 197 BC. The battle was a decisive Roman victory and marked the end of the Second Macedonian War. The Macedonians suffered heavy losses when they were surrounded by the Roman legion. They raised their spears in surrender, a signal the Romans either did not understand or chose to ignore, and 8,000 men were killed and 5,000 captured. To get a closer look at the probable site, scramble up the Cynoscephalae Hills north of Vólos.

Battle of Magnesia

MANISA, MANISA PROVINCE, TURKEY

In 190 BC, King Antiochus III of the Seleucid Empire tried to project his power and authority into Hellenistic Greece, but his attempts were thwarted by the Roman Republic. The Battle of Magnesia ad Sipylum (now Manisa in Turkey) was a decisive victory for Rome. As a result, Antiochus was forced to renounce all territorial claims, pay reparations, surrender his war elephants, and furnish hostages, including his son. The battle site is probably below Mount Sipylus, in what is now the Spil Dağı National Park, which offers excellent trekking through its rugged landscape.

Battle of Pydna

PYDNA, CENTRAL MACEDONIA REGION, GREECE

The Battle of Pydna, in 168 BC, between Rome and Macedon broke the back of Macedonian power and led to the empire's eventual annexation. Macedonian casualties were extremely high and the Macedonian king and commander Perseus was captured while fleeing. The battle was probably fought at what is now the village of Katerini, 15 miles southwest of Pydna. Another 25 miles southwest is Mount Olympus National Park, a biosphere reserve around an iconic peak with excellent hiking routes, caves, and a waterfall.

Han-Xiongnu War

XINZHOU, CHINA

China's continuous conflicts with neighboring tribes led to the staged construction of the Great Wall of China. The wall's Yanmen Pass was a pivotal location in the Han–Xiongnu War (133 BC to AD 89), between the Han Empire and the nomadic Xiongnu confederation, a powerful Mongolic tribe at the time. In this war, General Wei Qing led 30,000 men to battle through the Yanmen Pass and returned victorious. One of the steepest passes on the Great Wall, a walk along this section offers an insight into the conditions of battle as well as spectacular views.

RIGHT The Yanmen Pass remains an impressive defensive structure.

42

Servile War

CAPUA, ITALY

In the last of the Servile War series of slave rebellions against the Roman Republic, seventy gladiators escaped their slavery as entertainment in the city of Capua, and fought their way to begin the third and final Servile War. Walk around the city of Capua, starting at the amphitheater—the first gladiator school, where the war was fomented. Known as Alter Roma (the "other Rome"), you'll encounter Roman bridges, squares, and statues all around.

Third Servile War

ITALY

The Appian Way was once used to display crucified gladiators, but today offers a chance to see remains of the Roman Empire.

◆ **DISTANCE**
230 miles or 9 miles

◆ **START**
Rome, Italy

◆ **TYPE OF WALK**
Choice of day walk in Rome, or multi-day itinerary for the full length

◆ **WHEN TO GO**
Avoid hot summer days by visiting in the spring or fall

LEFT The Appian Way stretches 230 miles from Rome to Brindisi.

RIGHT Ruins of the Roman Empire line the length of the Appian Way.

The Appian Way is an epic, long-distance Roman road that stretches 230 miles between Rome and the port of Brindisi, an important political and trade route that played a tragic role in the Third Servile War.

At the end of the Third Servile War, the final uprising of the slaves against their Roman masters, the slave leader Spartacus launched the full strength of his forces against the legions and was defeated. Around 6,000 escaping survivors, including gladiators, were crucified in a public display along this important Roman thoroughfare.

With enough planning and time, it is possible to walk the full length of the Appian Way. However, for those visiting Rome who would like to sample just a small section, start at the Via Appia Antica Regional Park Visitor Center just two miles south of the Colosseum, and walk a nine-mile route which finishes at Castelli Romani Regional Park. You will encounter ruins of the Roman Empire all along the walk.

44

Julius Caesar's Invasion of Britain

EBBSFLEET, KENT, ENGLAND

Why the Romans first came to Britain is unknown, but it may have been revenge against the Celtic Britons for supporting the Gauls in the wars with Julius Caesar. Caesar himself came first in 55 BC in a badly planned visit. His more successful foray came the following year, when he subjugated a local warlord and set up his first client king. In 2010, a 16-foot-wide ditch was discovered at Ebbsfleet in Kent during road repairs. Ongoing excavations suggest it was part of a large fort protecting Caesar's ships in Pegwell Bay where the Romans landed. Just a half-mile north is Pegwell Bay Country Park, a seafront wetland with excellent walking and hiking trails.

45

Siege of Alesia

ALISE-SAINTE-REINE, BURGUNDY, FRANCE

In 52 BC, forces under Julius Caesar besieged the town of Alesia defended by Vercingetorix in what was to be the last of the battles between Rome and Gaul. Roman troops erected a series of fortifications, including two walls encircling the city. Vercingetorix eventually surrendered and was executed. The story is retold (slightly differently) in *Asterix and the Chieftain's Shield* by René Goscinny and Albert Uderzo. The battle site was above modern Alise-Sainte-Reine where the MuséoParc Alésia has battle artifacts and displays as well as a reconstruction of the Roman siege lines. An easy walk two miles south leads to the remains of the Gallo-Roman city that developed after the battle.

46

Luling Rebellion

KUNMING, YUNNAN, CHINA

For a very short period (AD 23–29) during the Han dynasty of China, one of the emperor's consorts established a competing Xin dynasty. A peasant uprising movement, known as the Luling Rebellion, fought against this new dynasty, and, with victory at the Battle of Kunyang, restored the Han dynasty. The place of the battle, Kunyang, is now a neighborhood of the city of Kunming in the Yunnan province. Not much of this rebellion or the Xin dynasty was documented. However, Kunming is a culturally rich city to visit, and you can walk around the Kunyang neighborhood and contemplate how history is shaped by the people who engage with it.

47

Battle of Teutoburg Forest

TEUTOBURG FOREST, GERMANY

As one of the successful revolts against Roman rule in Germania, the Battle of Teutoburg Forest, in AD 9, is well remembered in the region. Local Germanic chief Arminius (Hermann in German) ambushed three Roman legions, preventing them from advancing further to the northeast. With marked trails, the forest is a great destination for a day hike. At the top of the hill is a monument dedicated to Arminius and the battle, Hermannsdenkmal, and on the way back down you can explore rock formations that would have made perfect ambush points.

Roman Invasion of Britain

RICHBOROUGH, KENT, ENGLAND

Explore the remains of the settlement at Richborough that was crucial to the Roman colonization of Britain.

◆ **DISTANCE**
1.3 miles

◆ **START**
Ticket office/museum

◆ **TYPE OF WALK**
Easy to moderate

◆ **WHEN TO GO**
All year

Although Julius Caesar visited Britain in 55 BC and again the following year, prompting the Roman Senate to declare celebrations for 20 days, the actual occupiers arrived in AD 43 with Claudius leading an invasion force of 40,000 men. They made landfall at today's Richborough, about 1.8 miles inland in the east Kent marshes on an important sea channel with a sheltered harbor. They built fortifications but encountered no local resistance.

Their fortifications developed into the major port of Rutupiae, which would later boast an amphitheater and an 82-foot-tall monumental marble arch, one of the largest in the empire. It was also the starting point of Watling Street, a major road that led to London and beyond, which facilitated trade and the subjugation of Celtic tribes farther afield.

Now an English Heritage site, Richborough is a wonderful place to visit and very evocative of the past. Its well-marked paths lead past ditches and defenses, the remains of Rutupiae fort, massive city walls, the plinth of the monumental arch, and the start of Watling Street. The amphitheater is 500 yards to the southwest.

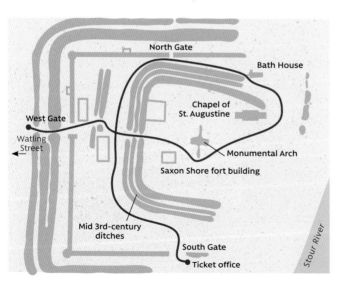

North Gate
Bath House
Chapel of St. Augustine
West Gate
Watling Street
Monumental Arch
Saxon Shore fort building
Mid 3rd-century ditches
South Gate
Ticket office
Stour River

ABOVE RIGHT The remains of the Roman fort show the meticulous building style of the Romans.

RIGHT The ruins of the Rutupiae fort at Richborough mark where the Romans first landed in Britain.

Defeat of Boudicca

COLCHESTER, ESSEX, ENGLAND

Walk around the moat of Colchester's Norman castle, built on the site of a Roman temple that Boudicca burned to the ground.

◆ **DISTANCE/TIME**
Two hours

◆ **START**
Castle drawbridge

◆ **TYPE OF WALK**
Easy

◆ **WHEN TO GO**
All year

After the Roman invasion and the establishment of the province of Britannia, Prasutagus, the head of the Iceni tribe in East Anglia, was made a "client king" of the Romans. When he died in AD 60, his kingdom was meant to be shared between the emperor Nero and Prasutagus's two daughters from his wife, Boudicca. Instead, Nero took all the property and when Boudicca resisted she was flogged, and her daughters raped.

Boudicca went on the warpath, taking control of Camulodunum (today's Colchester) and burning everything to the ground, including a temple dedicated to the emperor Claudius. She then headed for Londinium (London), where she did the same.

An estimated 80,000 Iceni and other tribespeople were killed and Boudicca is thought to have poisoned herself to avoid capture.

Colchester, which is the oldest recorded town in Britain, is dominated by a Norman castle built in around 1076 on the foundations of the temple dedicated to Claudius. Have a walk around the one-time moat of the castle keep—once the largest in Britain, though only two stories high today—and then enter and climb to the first floor for such unmissable exhibits as the Fenwick Treasure, a hoard of Roman jewels thought to have been buried during Boudicca's revolt.

ABOVE The Norman castle, built in 1076, dominates the city of Colchester.

LEFT Explore inside the castle, which contains Roman jewels.

50

Siege of Masada
DEAD SEA, ISRAEL

The last resistance to Roman rule in Judea was crushed in AD 73 on this isolated desert plateau. Jewish zealots had earlier overcome the Roman garrison here; the Roman legion surrounded Masada and used a battering ram to breach the wall of the fortress. When they entered, the Romans discovered the defenders—960 men, women, and children—had committed mass suicide. Nowadays the site is easily reached by cable car. Otherwise follow the well-maintained and historical Snake Path (built around 35 BC), which wends its way up the plateau's east side and takes 45 minutes to an hour.

51

Dacian Wars
SARMIZEGETUSA, ROMANIA

Dacia was a small kingdom in the modern region of Romania that existed during the rule of the Roman emperor Trajan (AD 98–117). It twice went to war with the Roman Empire and the kingdom's capital, Sarmizegetusa Regia, was destroyed and rebuilt by the Romans. The city's ruins are a good example of the cultural crossover between Dacia and the Roman Empire. Head a little further east and hike in the Grădiştea Muncelului-Cioclovina Natural Park, where several Dacian fortress ruins and archaeological sites are dotted around the area.

52

Hadrian's Wall
NORTHERN ENGLAND

Begun in AD 122 by the Roman emperor Hadrian, Hadrian's Wall was built as a defensive fortification against the "wild" northern barbarians; it crosses England from the North Sea to the Irish Sea. In its heyday, the wall would have been teeming with life with military settlements, barracks, forts, and small castles. Today, much of the wall lies in ruins. The official Hadrian's Wall Path is an 84-mile route managed by Britain's National Trust. It links Newcastle upon Tyne in the east with Bowness-on-Solway in the west; a long-distance, multi-day route that is favored by many keen walkers.

53

Demise of Monte Albán
OAXACA, OAXACA STATE, MEXICO

Monte Albán is the city from which the ancient Zapotecs once ruled Oaxaca. It flourished from about 500 BC to AD 850 when, for reasons unknown, its eventual abandonment began. By AD 1000, the city's population had dropped to less than a fifth of its peak and was deserted. A UNESCO World Heritage Site, this is one of the most culturally rich archaeological sites in Mexico where you can walk around the remains of temples, palaces, and tall stepped platforms with wonderful 360-degree views.

RIGHT Explore the Zapotec city of Monte Albán and wonder what caused its demise.

Battle of Chibi

YANGTZE RIVER, CHINA

Among many battles between warlords in third-century China, the naval battle of Chibi (AD 208–209) is notable for the fact that trickery won the day. Allied forces from the south feigned a defection, but filled their "defecting" ships with kindling and oil, which they sent into the fleet of northern warlord Cao Cao, setting it ablaze. The battle happened around the Wu Gorge section of the Yangtze, which is lined with plunging cliffs that display a metallic red hue and are served by wonderful, vertiginous walking paths.

RIGHT The many well-preserved pyramids and structures of Tikal bring the mysteries of the past into the present.

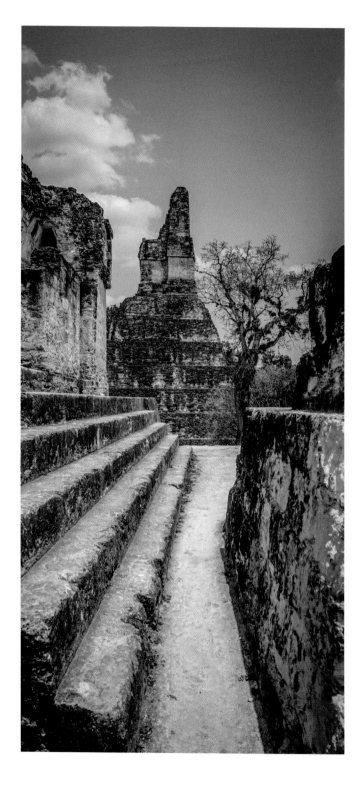

The Fall of Tikal

TIKAL, GUATEMALA

Set in toucan-filled jungle, the ruins of Tikal still enthrall.

♦ **DISTANCE**
2.5 miles

♦ **START**
Entry gate

♦ **TYPE OF WALK**
An up-and-down walk
with lots of stair-climbing
in a mix of forest and
open fields

♦ **WHEN TO GO**
Sunrise if possible, or
early in the day

BELOW The pyramids of Tikal rise
from the surrounding jungle.

Few Maya sites are more grand or more mystical than that of
Tikal, in the Petén region of Guatemala.

Used as a location for *Star Wars Episode IV: A New Hope*, this
gem of the Petén is still giving up its secrets even today, but some
of the turbulent history is in plain view, recorded in the stone
stelae for all to see.

Originally Tikal's ruling class were Maya. But in AD 378, the
city was attacked and conquered by invaders from northern
Mexico, most likely from Teotihuacán, a culture markedly
different. Tikal's ruler Chak Tok Ich'aak I, also known as Great
Jaguar Paw, was put to death by the new ruler, monuments were
smashed, and the ruling class was either killed or overthrown.
From then on, the city was ruled by Teotihuacán.

From the main entry gate, walk first to the Central Acropolis
to view Chak Tok Ich'aak I's pyramid. From there, continue to
Temple V, one of Tikal's most famous edifices. Though you can't
climb Temple V, you can climb the structure facing it. Lastly, visit
the "Lost World" (Mundo Perdido) before returning.

ABOVE The five-mile walking trail in Slovenia takes you through battlefields from the Roman Empire.

56

Battle of the Milvian Bridge

ROME, ITALY

The Battle of the Milvian Bridge in AD 312 saw the victory of Constantine I, who went on to become the sole ruler of the Roman Empire (his enemy Emperor Maxentius drowned in the Tiber). The bridge still stands, having been repaired several times between the fifteenth and the nineteenth centuries. The well-preserved ruins of Maxentius's imperial villa are found along the long-distance walking route of the Appian Way. Located between the second and third miles from Rome, it comprises three buildings: the palace, the circus of Maxentius, and the mausoleum.

57

Battle of the Frigidus

VIPAVA VALLEY, PRIMORSKA PROVINCE, SLOVENIA

In this battle in AD 394, the army of the Roman emperor Theodosius the Great and a contingent of Goths faced the usurper Eugenius and his forces in the eastern region of Roman Italy. Despite having placed a statue of Jupiter on the edge of the battlefield, the rebels were soundly defeated, and Theodosius was able to restore unity to the Roman Empire. The battle took place along the Vipava River in today's Slovenia; the *bora* wind that blows in the valley contributed to Eugenius's defeat. Follow the Vipavska Cesta, a five-mile trail that links the towns of Ajdovščina and Vipava.

Pyramids of the Moche

TRUJILLO, PERU

The Moche civilization is believed to have been South America's first empire; it existed 800 years before the Inca. The two pyramids, Huaca del Sol and Huaca de la Luna near Trujillo at the base of the Cerro Blanco caldera, served as high political and religious sites. Wall paintings and carvings of military campaigns, religious rituals, and bloody sacrifices as well as scenes of everyday lives are found here. A walk around the grounds visiting the excavated areas of the pyramids is a good way to understand this little-known culture.

BELOW The pyramids at Trujillo are thought to have been built by South America's first civilization.

Siege of Aquincum

BUDAPEST, HUNGARY

The most complete Roman civilian town in Hungary, Aquincum, was built around AD 100 and had paved streets and sumptuous single-story houses, complete with courtyards and sophisticated drainage and heating systems. It was named the seat of the Roman province of Pannonia Inferior in AD 106, and a *colonia* a century later. But it came under barbarian attack and was largely destroyed by the middle of the fourth century. By the time the Huns invaded the region in AD 409, it was all but deserted. The Aquincum Archaeology Park, with its museum and nearby civil amphitheater in northern Buda, can be visited and walked around all year.

Sack of Rome

ROME, ITALY

On the night of August 24, AD 410, the Visigoths entered Rome through the Salarian Gate, near the Horti Sallustiani, or Gardens of Sallust, a private complex of gardens adorned with pavilions, fountains, statues, and baths that had once belonged to the private villa of Roman historian and statesman Sallust. The city was ransacked and pillaged for three consecutive days, and the villa, whose ruins can be seen in Piazza Sallustio, was badly damaged. From here, stroll southwest to Palazzo Altemps and the Capitoline Museums, which house famous statues once displayed in the gardens, passing Trinità dei Monti, home to the 46-foot-high obelisk that also once belonged to the villa.

BELOW Visit the sumptuous Gardens of Sallust, used by the Visigoths to launch an attack on Rome.

Sack of Timgad

TIMGAD (THAMUGADI), ALGERIA

Sitting between fertile mountain valleys and Saharan trade routes, the city of Timgad in northern Algeria was founded by the Roman emperor Trajan around 100 BC, and fast became an important military and trade center. But its wealth attracted interest and in the fifth century it was sacked by the Vandals and fell into decline. Today, this vast site is one of the planet's most complete Roman towns, yet it remains almost totally unknown to the wider world. Strolling the empty cobbled streets today, the silence is so complete you can sense the spirits of the past.

62

Siege of Arles

ARLES, FRANCE

In AD 425, the Visigoths laid siege to the beautiful French Mediterranean city of Arles, but were driven away by Roman Legionnaires. Today, Arles is home to a rich collection of Roman monuments; marked walking routes lead you around the key sites.

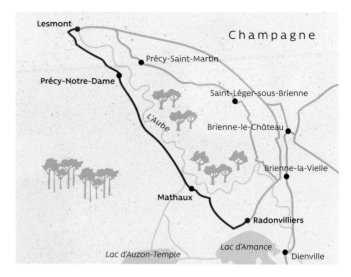

Lesmont

Champagne

Précy-Saint-Martin

Précy-Notre-Dame

Saint-Léger-sous-Brienne

L'Aube

Brienne-le-Château

Brienne-la-Vielle

Mathaux

Radonvilliers

Lac d'Auzon-Temple

Lac d'Amance

Dienville

Battle of the Catalaunian Plains

PARC NATUREL RÉGIONAL DE LA FORÊT D'ORIENT, CHAMPAGNE, FRANCE

Pass through small communes and charming churches in this region where Attila the Hun once fought.

◆ **DISTANCE**
7 miles

◆ **START**
Lesmont, near Troyes

◆ **TYPE OF WALK**
Leisurely half-day walk

◆ **WHEN TO GO**
Outside the winter
season, between
April and October

LEFT Follow the pretty river
L'Aube in search of the battle
site where the Roman Empire
defeated Attila the Hun.

Attila the Hun, whose Latin name *Flagellum Dei* means "Scourge of God," fought this battle in AD 451 against a mixed Roman and Visigoth alliance under Aetius and Theodoric I. This battle was one of the most decisive that Attila had launched against the Roman Empire. The Romans defeated the Hun forces and consequently stopped the Hunnic invasion of Europe.

Historical accounts mention that the battle took place in Gaul, which is modern-day France, although the exact location has never been confirmed. Many researchers believe it to be near the town of Troyes in the Champagne region. The nearby Parc naturel régional de la Forêt d'Orient has some great scenic hiking paths.

Paintings of the battle depict a river running through the plain, possibly the Aube River in the park. Follow the river from Lesmont all the way to the pretty lake at Radonvilliers in search of the real Catalaunian Plains. You'll pass small communes with charming wooden houses and varying styles of churches en route.

EARLY MIDDLE AGES
500–1099

Explore the Early Middle Ages as the character
of warfare transforms, with more defined tactics,
the increased role of cavalry and artillery, and
the emergence of the castle.

Siege of Amida

DIYARBAKIR, TURKEY

The city of Amida (now Diyarbakır) was part of the Byzantine Empire when it found itself under siege from the Persian king Kavadh I in 502. Despite having no actual troops in the town to help them, the citizens held off the siege for three months. Eventually, though, Kavadh's troops found a way over the thick basalt walls of the city and, once inside, set about brutally slaughtering the townsfolk. Although a local priest succeeded in persuading Kavadh to call off the slaughter, the city was still plundered and the survivors rounded up and taken to Persia as slaves. The basalt walls still stand and, between the Mardin and Urfa gates, it's possible to walk along them.

Battle of Vézeronce

VÉZERONCE-CURTIN, ISÈRE, FRANCE

In the Early Middle Ages, much of what is now western Europe was ruled over by the Franks. One of their great leaders was King Clovis. At his death in 511, his kingdom was split between his four sons, who frequently banded together as they sought to expand their empire further still. At the Battle of Vézeronce in 524, one of Clovis's sons, Chlodomir, was killed. This united the other brothers in a quest for revenge and they surged to victory. A helmet thought to be from this skirmish was discovered in 1871 in a peat marsh near Saint-Didier-de-Bizonnes. Hike up the nearby peak of La Cochette for views over the former Frankish territory.

ABOVE Relec Abbey, in Brittany, was built on the spot where the Battle of Brank Haleg might have taken place.

LEFT The view from La Cochette takes in much of Frankish territory, including where the Battle of Vézeronce was fought.

Battle of Brank Haleg

RELEC ABBEY, BRITTANY, FRANCE

For the Celtic people of Brittany, history and legend are often one and the same. One of the most important battles in ancient Breton history—and one that may just be a legend—took place in the early sixth century between two regional but rival kings: Conomor, a bloodthirsty tyrant who murdered six of his wives, and the other a good king, possibly Judual, who wished to unite the fiefdoms of Brittany. Five centuries later, Relec Abbey was built at the site where the battle took place and a marked four-hour hike loops through the surrounding countryside.

Vandalic War

TUNIS, TUNISIA

Wander through the ruins of Carthage, which date back to the times when the Romans ousted the Vandals from the area.

◆ **DISTANCE**
3 miles

◆ **START**
Carthage Archaeological Site

◆ **TYPE OF WALK**
Easy

◆ **WHEN TO GO**
All year; avoid summer

ABOVE RIGHT The ancient ruins of Carthage overlooking Tunis.

RIGHT The ruins at Carthage date back to the Punic and Roman periods.

The Vandalic War was fought in the early sixth century across North Africa (but largely in today's Tunisia) between forces of the Byzantine (or Eastern Roman) Empire and the Vandalic Kingdom of Carthage. It was the first of Emperor Justinian I's wars to recapture the Western Roman Empire, lost a century before.

Both the Battle of Ad Decimum, in September 533, and the Battle of Tricamarum, three months later, pitted Byzantine forces under General Flavius Belisarius against Gelimer, king of the Vandals—who had extended their kingdom from Germany to as far as North Africa in the fifth century.

In the first battle, fought "at the tenth milestone" along the coastal road south of Carthage, Belisarius routed the unprepared Vandals and captured the city. In the second, fought 30 miles west of Carthage, the outnumbered Byzantines managed to gain the upper hand and eliminated the power of the Vandals once and for all.

The exact battle sites are unknown, so concentrate on the UNESCO-listed Carthage Archaeological Site, in an eastern suburb of Tunis. It contains ruins dating back to the Punic and Roman periods and includes a number of limestone "cannonballs," projectiles from Carthaginian arsenals. There's an easy three-mile loop around the park.

Battle of Taginae

GUALDO TADINO,
UMBRIA, ITALY

In the summer of 552, the Byzantine army invaded Taginae, putting an end to Ostrogoth power in the Italian peninsula. From the Church of San Antonio di Rasina, walk along the ancient Flaminian Way (now SS3) to reach the former site of Taginae.

The Fall of Teotihuacán

MEXICO STATE, MEXICO

Explore the mysteries of the ancient city of Teotihuacán
from its mile-long central avenue.

◆ **DISTANCE**
2.5 miles

◆ **START**
Teotihuacán Cultural
Museum

◆ **TYPE OF WALK**
Easy stroll, best done in
the morning before it
gets too hot

◆ **WHEN TO GO**
All year

ABOVE RIGHT Teotihuacán's
Pyramid of the Sun is one of the
tallest ancient buildings found
in Mexico.

RIGHT Restoration work at the
site gives a strong indication of
its original appearance.

When a city's history is pieced together from its ruins, there is
always a level of mystery about its origins, and so it is with
Teotihuacán—even its name is not its own but was given to the
site by the Aztecs who discovered it in the 1400s; it translates as
"the place the gods were created."

Signs of civilization here date back as far as 150 BC, but the
city reached its zenith around AD 400–500 with evidence of
running water, a working sewer system, and a population of up to
175,000. Who lived here is still debated, but scholars all agree it
was the leading city of its time, attracting migrants from the
south and trading far and wide.

Around AD 550 it was sacked and burned and left to fall into
ruin. The reasons behind the fire are another of this great site's
mysteries. Scholars originally thought invaders burned the city to
the ground. However, new research suggests that the burning was
limited to buildings associated with the ruling class; so cultural
and class tensions may have led to its demise.

Starting from the Teotihuacán Cultural Museum, this walk is
a counterclockwise loop around the ruins, taking in the mile-
long Calzada de los Muertos (Avenue of the Dead), which
includes the soaring Pyramid of the Sun—one of the tallest
ancient buildings in Mexico.

Battle of the Volturnus

VOLTURNO RIVER, NEAR CAPUA, ITALY

In 554, the Byzantine army, led by General
Narses, defeated a combined force of Franks
and Alemanni, signaling a triumphal moment
for the Byzantines in Italy. Alemanni chieftain
Butilinus set up camp along the banks of the
river Volturno, forming a wall on one side and
fortifying the other bank. Narses attacked,
slaying Butilinus and slaughtering virtually all
his men. You can walk the Via Francigena
pilgrimage route, crossing the river plain,
passing through rolling hills carpeted with
olive groves and vineyards.

BELOW The earthworks at Hinton Hill could be
where a decisive battle formed modern Britain.

Battle of Deorham

HINTON HILL, NEAR DYRHAM, SOUTH GLOUCESTERSHIRE, ENGLAND

The Battle of Deorham pitted West Saxons
against the Romano-British kings of
Cirencester, Gloucester, and Bath in 577.
According to the *Anglo-Saxon Chronicle*
entry for that year, all three of these kings
were killed and their cities occupied. The battle
confirmed the supremacy of Anglo-Saxon
Wessex in southern England and brought the
permanent cultural and ethnic separation of
Wales to the north and Cornwall to the south.
Deorham is thought to be Dyrham in south
Gloucestershire. The site could be the
earthworks around Hinton Hill, an easy walk
just over a mile to the north of the town.

Battle of Salsu River

NORTH KOREA

One of history's most lethal battles occurred on the Salsu River (now the Cheongcheon) in 612. Korean forces lured advancing Sui troops into a shallow river basin which, unbeknown to the Sui, had the flow cut off by a dam upstream. Once the troops were crossing, the dam was opened, drowning thousands of soldiers. The survivors, scrambling to higher ground, were slaughtered by Korean troops. Records state that of the 300,000 Sui, only 2,700 survived. Today, the Cheongcheon is deep within North Korea and offers placid spots to walk and enjoy the view.

Battle of Baekgang

GEUM RIVER, SOUTH KOREA

Few naval defeats have been as clear-cut as that of the Battle of Baekgang in 663, where 170 ships of the Silla–Tang alliance defeated 400 Japanese ships in the lower reaches of the Geum River. It was such a commanding victory that it forced Japan to withdraw entirely and established Silla–Tang dominance over Baekje. Today it's a scenic spot with a number of walks and riverside trails. The Ecorium in Seocheon is a nice starting spot for a walk that skirts the riverside and then crosses over to the Geum River Estuary Bank.

BELOW A peaceful riverside walk on the Geum Estuary belies the fierce fighting that took place here.

Battle of the Masts
FINIKE, ANTALYA PROVINCE, TURKEY

The Battle of the Masts off ancient Phoenix (today's Finike) in 654 was a crucial naval conflict between Muslim Arabs and the Byzantine fleet. In rough seas, the ships on both sides—either bearing the Christian cross or Muslim crescent on their masts—were arranged in lines and lashed together, leading to close, hand-to-hand combat. The Muslim victory paved the way for Arab expansion in the Mediterranean. Today it's hard to conjure up images of the fighting while wandering along Finike marina and its yachts, but that is where it took place.

Arab Siege of Constantinople
ISTANBUL, TURKEY

The first attempt by the Arabs to seize Constantinople in 674 was a momentous Byzantine victory. After four decades of defeats by Muslim armies, the successful defense of the city saved both the Byzantine Empire and Europe from Muslim rule. According to Byzantine accounts, there was constant fighting around the Golden Gate, a triumphal arch built in the fourth century AD and later incorporated into the massive city walls as the Fortress of the Seven Towers. You can walk along a five-mile stretch of the Theodosian Walls; the fortress stands at the southern end.

Battle of Roncevaux Pass
RONCESVALLES, FRENCH–SPANISH BORDER

In 778, the Frankish leader Charlemagne set out to conquer northern Spain, which he had been told was sympathetic to his cause. However, this proved not to be the case, and as he returned to France through the Roncevaux Pass in the Pyrenees, his rearguard was ambushed and annihilated by a guerrilla force of Basques. This battle was the inspiration for the oldest surviving work of French literature, *The Song of Roland*—a knight killed in the battle. Many long-distance hikes cross this pass, or it's a short walk from Roncesvalles village.

Sack of Lindisfarne
HOLY ISLAND, BERWICK-UPON-TWEED, NORTHUMBERLAND, ENGLAND

In 793, the monastery on the Holy Island of Lindisfarne, just off the Northumberland coast, was attacked by Vikings. Many of the monks were killed or captured in the raid, which is seen as the start of the sustained Danish invasion of England, which lasted for centuries. An easy but lengthy nine-mile circular tour of the island, which is connected to the mainland by a narrow causeway passable only at low tide, leads past the ruins of the priory and Lindisfarne castle.

RIGHT A nine-mile walk around Lindisfarne takes in the island's castle.

The Tiwanaku Empire

LA PAZ DEPARTMENT, BOLIVIA

Near Lake Titicaca, Tiwanaku was the capital of a pre-Incan empire whose influence extended across the central Andes in its AD 50–900 heyday. Walk past the ruins of a pyramid and a temple complex to a sunken patio lined with scores of stone heads representing conquered rivals.

Fall of Aguateca

PETEXBATUN, GUATEMALA

Aguateca, protected by a ravine and outcropping with a commanding view of the river valley below, fell to invading forces in about 800. A valuable archaeological site for its artifacts that were abandoned, visiting Aguateca involves a river ride and jungle trek.

RIGHT A stela from El Ceibal that escaped destruction.

The Fall of El Ceibal

PETÉN, GUATEMALA

Feel the majesty of the jungle as you explore the ruins of this lost city.

◆ **DISTANCE**
2 miles

◆ **START**
Entrance gate

◆ **TYPE OF WALK**
Well-marked trail, with some hills and ravines in thick jungle

◆ **WHEN TO GO**
All year

BELOW A hike through the jungle leads to this destroyed temple.

El Ceibal, located on the banks of the Río de la Pasión, was defeated and conquered by neighboring Dos Pilas in 735, and—humiliatingly—the city's ruler was forced to be a vassal to the victor, Ucha'an K'in B'alam.

Even more dismaying to the fallen king was that Ucha'an K'in B'alam is recorded by neighboring cities as having destroyed the stelae of El Ceibal, even going so far as to have scribes chip off the glyphs on the monuments. It wasn't enough to defeat the city; he erased its memory. Much of El Ceibal's early history has thus been lost forever.

Today, El Ceibal can be reached by boat or by car. The site has three main sections, each of them separated by trails through thick jungle. Some unexcavated ruins are deep in the jungle and require a bit of hill climbing on a rough, sometimes muddy, rocky trail, which goes out all the way to the river. Another jungle trail leads to a round platform structure that is called the Observatory. Jungle flowers, birds, butterflies, and lizards are easy to spot, though there are mosquitoes as well.

Danevirke: The Danish Wall

DANNEWERK, SCHLESWIG-HOLSTEIN, GERMANY

Spot remaining sections of Danevirke, a wall built by Vikings to keep the Saxons out, on an easy walk from the town center.

◆ **DISTANCE**
From 2.5 miles

◆ **START**
Haithabu-Dannewerk

◆ **TYPE OF WALK**
Leisurely walk

◆ **WHEN TO GO**
All year

ABOVE RIGHT Sections of the wall can be spotted over a 19-mile stretch.

RIGHT It's a pleasant walk from the Viking houses of Haithabu-Dannewerk to the Danish Wall.

The Danevirke, possibly one of the least known of all ancient walls, is considered one of the world's best-preserved Viking-age sites. Built upon the foundations of a previously existing Nordic Iron Age fortification, its construction consists of earthworks, trenches, and sea barriers that stretch over 19 miles.

Originally thought to have been built by the Vikings as a defensive wall to keep out the Saxons and the Slavs from invading Denmark, later research suggests it may also have served as a protection to the trade route along the river Eider.

Throughout the years, the wall has been the site of border conflicts between Denmark and Germanic lands. In 1864, during Denmark's war with Prussia, the possession of the wall was ceded to Prussia, which has left the wall on the German side of the border today.

For the best experience of the Danevirke, now a designated UNESCO World Heritage Site, take a walk around the reconstructed Viking-era houses of Haithabu-Dannewerk, and along sections of the wall dotted in the surrounding landscape on a route that leads to the Danevirke Museum.

Offa's Dyke
WALES-ENGLAND BORDER

Offa, the Anglo-Saxon king of Mercia (central England), ordered the construction of Offa's Dyke in the eighth century as a defensive barrier from neighboring kingdoms. Parts of the large rampart and ditch have been incorporated into a long-distance walking trail, totaling 177 miles, that roughly follows the border between England and Wales.

Battle of Jengland
GRAND-FOUGERAY, BRITTANY, FRANCE

When the Bretons broke an agreed truce with
the Frankish kingdom, then ruled by Charles
the Bald, Charles sought an alliance with the
Saxons to fight back. With this additional help,
his forces outnumbered the Bretons four-to-
one, but it was not enough. At the battle in
Grand-Fougeray in 851, the Bretons surprised
the Franks with a javelin assault from a
distance, breaking up the ranks of the Franks.
The victory secured the independence of
Brittany in the Treaty of Angers, drawing the
border as we still know it today, marked by
the river Vilaine, which has many walks
along its banks.

Battle of Hafrsfjord
HAFRSFJORD, NORWAY

Around 872, King Harald Fairhair's Viking
forces defeated an allied force of the chieftains
of Hordaland, Rogaland, Agder, and Telemark
in a naval conflict on the Hafrsfjord, the
ultimate battle that unified Norway. Or was it?
All knowledge of this battle comes from the
legends recorded by Snorri Sturluson, and no
evidence or other documentation has ever been
found to confirm that the battle took place.
There's a promenade that leads around the edge
of Hafrsfjord to three giant swords planted on
the headland as a monument to the battle.

Battle of Edington
EDINGTON, WILTSHIRE, ENGLAND

By 878, Danes had settled in the coastal areas
of east and northeast England, and the Viking
Great Army of Scandinavian warriors moved
in to conquer Wessex. Only the decisive victory
of Alfred the Great and his army at Edington
helped save Anglo-Saxon independence. The
Anglo-Saxon Chronicle names the battle site as
Ethandun, but it's now thought to be the
present-day town of Edington in Wiltshire.
King Alfred's Tower is an eighteenth-century
folly, 21 miles southwest of Edington. From
here an eight-mile walk through fields takes
you to "Egbert's Stone," where Alfred is said to
have rallied his troops before the battle.

Polish–Veletian Wars
SANTOK, POLAND

The Confederacy of the Veleti had been at war
with the Duchy of Poland since 963. With
ambitions to drive out the Veleti once and for
all, Poland's ruler, Mieszko I, allied with the
Duchy of Bohemia in 967. He then pulled
back his ground troops to lure the Veleti troops
into a trap. Encircled by the Bohemian cavalry,
the Veleti surrendered, thus ending the war. The
battle is believed to have happened around the
village of Santok, where you can walk up to
the reconstructed medieval guard tower for
sweeping views of the area.

RIGHT Three giant swords at Hafrsfjord mark the site
of the battle that claims to have unified Norway.

Battle of Bạch Đằng

BẠCH ĐẰNG RIVER NEAR
HA LONG BAY, VIETNAM

In 938, when a powerful Chinese fleet of warships sailed into the mouth of the Bạch Đằng, the Vietnamese employed a defense mechanism of fixing wooden stakes into the banks of the river, grounding the attacking fleet. This gave the Vietnamese forces a chance to attack the Chinese army and win the battle. The victory is considered a turning point in Vietnam gaining independence from Chinese rule. Take a short walk near the river around the Thủy Nguyên district of Hai Phong City to find monuments to the battles celebrating Vietnamese victory.

Rise and Fall of Toltec

TULA DE ALLENDE,
HIDALGO STATE, MEXICO

The Toltec were a fiercely militaristic, pre-Columbian culture based at Tula, Mexico, which thrived from about 900 to 1150. Not much is known about Toltec culture as the Aztec narratives relate what are now thought to be mythological, not historical, events. Tula was ransacked by neighboring tribes around 1170 and went into decline. An easy walk of just over a mile north of the center leads to the main Toltec ceremonial site perched on a hilltop. The highlight is standing atop a five-tier pyramid face-to-face with fearsome 15-foot-high stone warrior figures.

ABOVE Stand face to face with stone warrior figures at the ancient site of Toltec.

Battle of Lechfeld
LECHFELD, BAVARIA, GERMANY

Known for their ability to ride and shoot—a common Christian prayer during the tenth century was "Save us, O Lord, from the arrows of the Hungarians"—the Magyar tribes pillaged their way across Europe, reaching as far as Spain and southern Italy. But in 955 they were stopped dead in their tracks at Lechfeld, south of Augsburg in Bavaria, by the German king Otto I. There are many locations associated with the battle in the greater Augsburg area, linked by walking trails. The 955 Information Pavilion in Königsbrunn gives a great overview of the battle site and has maps of the trails.

Battle of Fýrisvellir
GAMLA UPPSALA, SWEDEN

It is a tale of family feuds, when Styrbjörn the Strong, who suspected that his father had been poisoned by his uncle, King Eric, in 985 launched a naval attack on Eric's kingdom in revenge. Unable to break Eric's defenses by sea, Styrbjörn set fire to his own boats as a signal to his men that he was going to fight to the death, and marched them to the plain of Fýrisvellir where the two forces met. King Eric made a sacrifice to the Norse god Odin in the hope of victory. In the bloody battle that followed, Eric's forces killed all of Styrbjörn's troops, including Styrbjörn himself, gaining Eric the title "the Victorious." Walk around the archaeological site at Gamla Uppsala, where some believe the three royal mounds represent the gods Odin, Thor, and Freyr.

BELOW The Royal Mounds at Gamla Uppsala, which possibly represent Odin, Thor, and Freyr.

Battle of Maldon

NORTHEY ISLAND, MALDON, ESSEX, ENGLAND

Cross the causeway on the Blackwater Estuary where
Vikings and Anglo-Saxons once battled.

◆ **DISTANCE**
2 miles

◆ **START**
Maeldune Heritage
Centre

◆ **TYPE OF WALK**
Easy

◆ **WHEN TO GO**
All year

ABOVE RIGHT A statue
commemorates Byrhtnoth, the
Anglo-Saxon who chose to fight
the Vikings to the last stand.

RIGHT It's possible to cross to
Northey Island on a causeway—
depending on the tide.

Maldon, on the muddy Blackwater Estuary, was one of only two towns in Essex—Colchester was the other—at the start of the first millennium and particularly susceptible to Viking raids. In a major attack in 991, the Anglo-Saxons were defeated at the Battle of Maldon. We know of this event from a 325-line fragment of an Anglo-Saxon poem describing the battle.

The Vikings sailed up the Blackwater and anchored at tiny Northey Island, where they were met by Alderman Byrhtnoth and his men. At the time, some preferred paying off the Viking invaders with land and wealth; others like Byrhtnoth preferred fighting to the last stand. At low tide, the Blackwater leaves a land bridge from Northey to the main shore; the Viking commander asked Byrhtnoth to allow his troops onto the shore for formal battle. Byrhtnoth did so and was killed.

You can walk from the Maeldune Heritage Centre, with good displays on the battle, along to the waterfront, the Hythe, and past Promenade Park to the larger-than-life Statue of Byrhtnoth. From there continue along the beach to a plaque marking the place of battle and the start of the Northey Island Causeway, accessible depending on the tide.

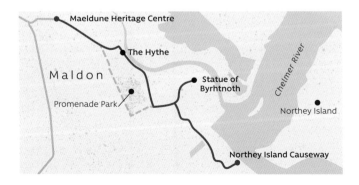

The Decline of Chichén Itzá

YUCATÁN STATE, MEXICO

One of the great Mesoamerican city-states, Chichén Itzá was a major power for a thousand years.

DISTANCE
1.5 miles

START
Main entrance

TYPE OF WALK
Easy stroll, best done in the morning before it gets too hot

WHEN TO GO
All year

Emerging around 600, the imposing city of Chichén Itzá on the Yucatán peninsula, in what is now southeast Mexico, was one of the great centers of ancient Maya culture. At its zenith, as many as 50,000 people are believed to have lived here.

Maya power in Chichén Itzá began to decline around 800–900 and some sources suggest the city was subsequently sacked, looted, and conquered by Toltec warriors who stamped their own mark on it. Others argue that climatic forces—specifically a series of severe droughts—were ultimately more significant factors. Either way, Chichén Itzá remained occupied to varying extents until the 1500s, when Spanish conquistadors arrived, captured the site, and later turned it into a cattle ranch.

Walk from the main entrance to the Temple of Kukulcán (also known as El Castillo), Chichén Itzá's iconic pyramid, then loop west past the column-lined Temple of the Warriors, Cenote Sagrado—a water-filled sinkhole, believed to be the entrance to the underworld, into which offerings and human sacrifices were thrown—and one of the largest surviving ancient ball courts, which saw fierce contests, sometimes to the death.

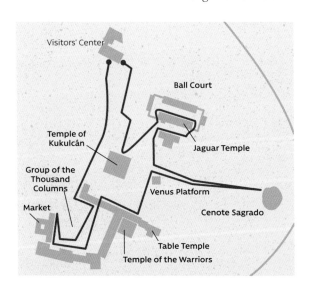

Visitors' Center

Ball Court

Temple of Kukulcán

Jaguar Temple

Group of the Thousand Columns

Venus Platform

Market

Cenote Sagrado

Table Temple

Temple of the Warriors

ABOVE RIGHT The beautiful Cenote Sagrado, once believed to be the entrance to the underworld.

RIGHT The Temple of Kukulcán dominates the Chichén Itzá site.

Chichén Viejo
YUCATÁN STATE, MEXICO

Chichén Viejo, the older section of the (accessible) Chichén Itzá site, underlines the scientific and technological advances that made the Maya city-state so powerful. Head south from the main entrance to find an observatory known as El Caracol ("The Snail"), as well as tombs and funerary structures.

Siege of Durham

DURHAM, ENGLAND

In 1006, Malcolm II had recently become the king of Scotland and, as was customary at the time, he went on a raid to prove his warring prowess. He and his army laid siege to Durham, then a fairly new settlement built on a curve in the river and only accessible by land from one direction. But the son of the aeldorman of Durham, Uhtred the Bold, managed to raise a force of Northumbrians and Yorkshiremen who roundly defeated the Scottish invaders. There is a footpath that follows the river all around its meandering curve, atop which, on the site of that early settlement, sits Durham Cathedral.

Battle of Svolder

ØRESUND, SWEDEN

Legendary for being the largest naval battle of the Viking era, the Battle of Svolder took place in 999 when King Olaf Tryggvason was sailing home from an expedition. His fleet was ambushed by an alliance of the King of Denmark, the King of Sweden, and the Jarl of Lade, who captured his ships one by one until Olaf jumped off his own ship in order to flee. The intensity and chaos of the battle have been captured in numerous paintings, many of them painted from the waterfront footpath that looks out over the waters of Øresund toward Skanör beacon.

Battle of Clontarf

CLONTARF AND DRUMCONDRA, COUNTY DUBLIN, IRELAND

Viking domination in Ireland ended at the Battle of Clontarf, north of Dublin, in 1014. Here, the forces of Brian Boru, High King of Ireland, defeated a Norse–Irish alliance of the King of Dublin (delightfully named Sigtrygg Silkbeard), the King of Leinster, and a Viking army from abroad. The battle only lasted a day, but losses on both sides were high and most of the leaders—including Brian Boru—were killed. Stroll around St. Anne's Park in Clontarf, the supposed battle site, and then walk west to Luke Kelly Bridge in Drumcondra, where the Vikings fell as they fled back to Dublin.

Battle of Assandun

ASHINGDON, ESSEX, ENGLAND

When Edmund Ironside, the son of Saxon King Ethelred the Unready, acceded to the throne, he resolved to gain back from the Danes all that his father had lost. But he met his match at the Battle of Assandun in 1016, when he was defeated by the Danes, led by Canute. The battle, which effectively concluded the Danish conquest of England, was probably fought on a hill in Ashingdon, Essex. From here, walk to the Church of St. Andrew, thought to have been erected as Ashingdon Minster as a sign of thanks by Canute in 1020.

Battle of Stiklestad

STIKLESTAD, NORWAY

In 1030, Christian King Óláfr Haraldsson of Norway was riding with 3,600 of his men to a farm at Stiklestad when he engaged in a battle with an army of peasants and farmers. Óláfr was killed in the battle, which has been credited as the beginning of Norway's conversion to Christianity, and he was later canonized to become Norway's patron saint. At Stiklestad, the National Cultural Center was created to preserve the heritage of St. Olaf. Walk around the center's medieval farm, which includes a reconstructed Viking longhouse.

LEFT Gaze out to sea from Skanör beach across the waters where a Viking sea battle once raged.

99

Battle of Stamford Bridge

EAST YORKSHIRE, ENGLAND

In 1066, just prior to marching south for the Battle of Hastings, the English army under Harold II surprised and defeated Norwegian invaders. The current Stamford Bridge is slightly downstream from its medieval predecessor, but cross it and head south through the village to follow the route of Harold's attack.

Battle of Hastings

BATTLE, EAST SUSSEX, ENGLAND

Wander around the exact field where the course of England's history was changed forever.

◆ **DISTANCE**
31 miles

◆ **START**
Pevensey Castle

◆ **TYPE OF WALK**
Three to four days through low level countryside

◆ **WHEN TO GO**
All year

ABOVE LEFT The ruins of the Battle Abbey church, which is said to have been built where King Harold fell.

LEFT The approach to the gatehouse of Pevensey Castle.

Perched at the end of a long narrow ridge, Battle Abbey was built on the very spot where on October 14, 1066, William of Normandy won the English crown by defeating and killing England's King Harold Godwinson.

Fighting on foot in tightly packed ranks, the English army occupied a strong defensive position up on the ridge. Initially they held firm, but eventually they were worn down by relentless Norman attacks, and Harold, possibly wounded in the eye by an arrow, was cut down and killed.

It would take William five years to complete his conquest of England, but Hastings was a decisive moment. The English had lost not only their leader but also their best chance to stop the invasion in its tracks.

A long-distance marked route, the 1066 Country Walk, goes from Pevensey Castle to the town of Rye, following in the footsteps of the invading Normans. There are ten wooden sculptures to look out for along the route.

The walk takes in the site of the battle where you can see the very slopes where the fighting took place. The abbey which was built on the site is now a ruin that can be explored. Tradition has it that the high altar in the abbey's church marked the place where Harold fell.

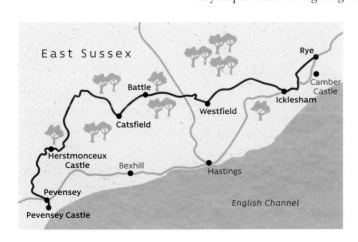

Siege of Polonnaruwa

POLONNARUWA, SRI LANKA

One of the greatest of Sri Lanka's medieval kingdoms, Polonnaruwa was a capital of the Chola dynasty. In 1070, the Sinhalese King Vijayabahu I laid siege to Polonnaruwa and pushed the Cholas out. Today this vast site, which is littered with temples and statues, all shaded by leafy, tropical trees, invites exploration on foot. Start at the southern end of the complex and walk slowly northward, being sure to take in the famed ruins around the Quadrangle, but also explore quieter corners of the parklike grounds where the only observers might be curious monkeys.

BELOW The vast site of Polonnaruwa has plenty for the visiting walker to discover.

Battle of Manzikert

MANZIKERT, TURKEY

The Byzantine Empire and the Great Seljuk Empire of Iran fought for control over eastern Anatolia in the Battle of Manzikert of 1071. Led by Romanos IV Diogenes, the Byzantines were wrong-footed by the Seljuks' tactic of avoiding battle and then further suffered due to insubordination in the ranks. Romanos was captured by the Seljuks, whose leader, Alp Arslan, set him free for a ransom and a marriage alliance betweeen his son and Romanos's daughter. The battle, which ruined Romanos's credibility, has a monument in the Battle of Manzikert National Historic Park, a pleasant area for a leisurely walk.

Siege of Antioch

ANTAKYA, HATAY PROVINCE, TURKEY

The siege of Antioch (now Antakya) took place during the First Crusade as the Crusaders made their way to Palestine through Syria. It culminated in the Battle of Antioch in 1098, in which Frankish forces defeated the Seljuk Turks. A walk of just under two miles northeast from the center brings you to what the Crusaders were trying to recapture—the cavelike Church of St. Peter, one of the earliest places where the newly converted followers of Jesus Christ met and prayed secretly. When Antioch fell, the Crusaders added a new facade as well as the narthex, the narrow vestibule along the west side of the church.

First Crusade

JERUSALEM, ISRAEL

The First Crusade reached Jerusalem in June 1099, and the month-long siege of the Old City began. On July 15, the Crusaders breached the northern wall (10 feet wide and 50 feet high) of the outer fortifications and made their way into the city through the Citadel (Tower of David). Then began the massacre of large numbers of resident Jews and Muslims, many of whom had sought shelter in the Al-Aqsa Mosque and in the Dome of the Rock on the Temple Mount. Stroll around Jerusalem's walled Old City, measuring just a square mile, and then proceed to the Temple Mount, which can be visited but requires planning in advance.

MIDDLE AGES
1100–1499

Witness the rise of city-states, increased military
strength, and religious schism and intolerance that
bring renewed conflict and destruction to virtually
every corner of the globe.

Jin-Song Wars
RUNAN COUNTY, HENAN, CHINA

This is a tale of friends becoming foes. Although previously allied, the Song and the Manchurian Jin dynasty engaged in a series of conflicts when the stronger Jin refused to give up captured lands to Song as had previously been negotiated. The two former allies went to war, from 1125 to 1234. The Song and the Mongols joined forces at the Siege of Caizhou (1233–1234) and finally conquered the Jin forces. Take a stroll in Tianzhong Mountain Culture Park among the traditional buildings and statues of notable figures from these and other ancient dynasties.

Siege of Lisbon
LISBON, PORTUGAL

The 1147 siege of Lisbon was one of the few Christian victories in the Second Crusade against the Moors. The success of the operation played a pivotal role in the Reconquista. The political center of Lisbon then was the hilltop Castelo São Jorge and this is where you should start a walking tour of this elegant city. From the castle, follow the steep, pebbled streets downhill, through the oldest part of Lisbon, to the large riverside plaza known as the Praça do Comércio, from where you can almost picture medieval battleships sailing up the Tejo (Tagus) River.

BELOW Walk in the steps of the Crusaders on the Horns of Hattin in Israel.

Battle of Legnano
LEGNANO, ITALY

The Battle of Legnano in 1176 played a vital role in the Holy Roman Empire's attempt to gain power over northern Italy. The Lombard league defeated Emperor Frederick Barbarossa, making this his last attempt to dominate Italy. From the Castello Visconteo, which houses a triptych depicting the battle, walk northwest to the Monument to the Warrior of Legnano, a bronze statue depicting a soldier raising his sword to symbolize the league's victory. On the last Sunday of May, the Palio of Legnano sees a historical pageant and horse race. Today, Legnano is mentioned in the Italian national anthem, a reminder of this important victory over foreign powers.

Battle of the Horns of Hattin
TIBERIAS, ISRAEL

Kurûn Hattîn, an extinct twin-peak volcano, is famous for the July 1187 battle between the Crusaders and forces of Saladin, the Muslim sultan of Egypt and Syria. After a fierce conflict, the 20,000 Crusaders were driven up the Horns of Hattin and were defeated by the 30,000-strong Muslim army. Saladin went on to capture Jerusalem in October 1187. Along well-marked hiking trails up the 1,070-foot-high horns are traces of walls and large stones of the Crusader defense line, plus excellent views of the Tiberias plains and the Sea of Galilee beyond.

Battle of Dan-no-ura
SHIMONOSEKI STRAIT, JAPAN

This final battle in a long conflict between the losing Taira and the victorious Minamoto clans was fought in 1185 in the waters between Honshu and Kyushu, two of the four major islands of Japan. Tidewaters played a key part in the outcome, first favoring the Taira, but then later in the day helping the Minamoto to victory; they went on to form Japan's first shogunate, based in Kamakura. Walk from the Dannoura battlefield site in Mimosusogawa Park up to the Hinoyama ropeway (like a cable car), where you can ride to the top and see beautiful views of the hills and water.

Battle of Arsuf
TEL ARSUF, APOLLONIA NATIONAL PARK, HERZLIYA, ISRAEL

The ancient Mediterranean city of Arsuf (now Apollonia) dates to the sixth century BC and underwent various occupations. In 1187, it was captured by the Muslims, but fell again to the Crusaders in the 1191 Battle of Arsuf with forces led by Richard I of England, who defeated a larger Ayyubid army led by Saladin. Today's clifftop Apollonia National Park features the remains of a city moat, a Crusader fortress, and a Roman villa. There are walking trails and terrific views southward to Herzliya from the coastal path.

Pillage of Sigtuna
SIGTUNA, UPPLAND, SWEDEN

The Karelians, people of the Baltic Finnic ethnic group, pillaged and burned the town of Sigtuna in 1187. As Sigtuna was the most important city of medieval Christian Sweden, this event was documented in the fourteenth-century Eric Chronicles as "Sweden then suffered serious harm." In the thirteenth century, the jarl of Sweden, Birger Magnussen, decided to build a defense for Sigtuna and began the construction of a fortress, the Tre Kronor castle, just outside Sigtuna. The area around the fortress is today's Stockholm. A walk around Sigtuna is a walk around old Sweden; the town's Stora Gatan is Sweden's oldest street, dating back to the tenth century.

Attack on Albi
ALBI, TARN, FRANCE

In the twelfth and thirteenth centuries, Albi, like many towns in southern France, was a Cathar town. This put it at odds with the Catholic Church, which regarded Cathars as heretics. In 1209, Pope Innocent III launched a "crusade" against the Cathars, the Albigensian Crusade. The city of Albi was attacked and, over a twenty-year period, the Cathars were wiped out. Follow the Cathar trail around the city and its stunning UNESCO World Heritage religious buildings, which include one of the grandest cathedrals in southern France.

RIGHT The French town of Albi was at the heart of the Catholic Church's crusade against the Cathars.

Siege of Carcassonne

CARCASSONNE, FRANCE

The walls of this huge, fortified town encase a network of lesser fortifications, a town, and the castle itself. Over the eons Carcassonne has played witness to numerous battles and sieges, notably in 1209 when after a short siege the pope's representative captured the city and expelled the Cathars. This was then followed by numerous skirmishes and battles between France, England, and Aragon over ownership of the town. The site was spectacularly restored in the nineteenth century by the architect Eugène Viollet-le-Duc, and a thrilling day can be spent walking the old streets and heading to hillside viewpoints.

<114>

The Cathar Castles of Lastours
LASTOURS, AUDE, FRANCE

Scramble between the romantic ruins of four Cathar castles strung along a rocky crag in the Pyrenean foothills.

◆ **DISTANCE**
4 miles

◆ **START**
Lastours campsite

◆ **TYPE OF WALK**
Half-day strenuous walk

◆ **WHEN TO GO**
April–October

ABOVE RIGHT Despite their age and location, the ruins of the Cathar castles still leave plenty to explore.

RIGHT The four castles were built along an impressive mountain crag that now makes for a spectacular walking route.

Built on the wealth of nearby iron mines, the four castles and small village of Lastours became centers of Cathar belief in the Middle Ages. And, as with all Cathar settlements, this put Lastours under the disapproving gaze of the Catholic clergy in Rome. In the Albigensian Crusade (1209–1229), the castles were attacked and many of the Cathar residents put to their deaths. Lastours succombed in 1210.

This three-hour walk begins from the campsite on the edge of Lastours village and heads first to the nearby viewpoint over the castles before a steep descent down to the valley floor and then a short, sharp climb up to the ragged, shark's-tooth ridge that the four Lastours castles are strung out along. The return is by the same path, which is clearly marked all the way.

While the castles themselves are the main interest of this hike, an unexpected attraction is the view toward the snow-blanketed Pyrenees mountains a short way to the south.

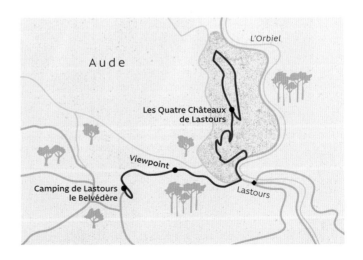

L'Orbiel

Aude

Les Quatre Châteaux
de Lastours

Viewpoint

Camping de Lastours
le Belvédère

Lastours

Third Crusade
AIGUES-MORTES, FRANCE

Bathed in southern light and washed through with the tang of salty sea breezes, Aigues-Mortes is a perfectly preserved example of medieval military architecture that, in the thirteenth century, was used as a point of departure for the Crusades. There are some superb, easy walks around the Camargue marshes that surround the town. Bring binoculars for a closer view of the famed flamingos.

116

Defensive Structure, Morlaix

LOCQUÉNOLÉ, BRITTANY, FRANCE

Over time, many defensive structures have been built along the banks of the river Morlaix in Brittany. One of the more mysterious sites is Castel-an-Trébez. Today it is just a raised mound of unknown date surrounded by forest. A delightful riverside walk runs from the village of Locquénolé to the site.

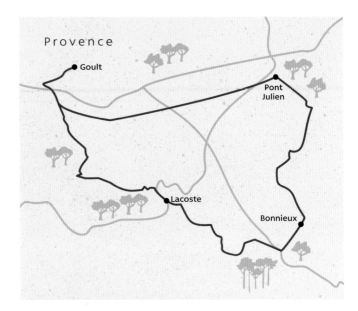

Route of the Third Crusade

BONNIEUX, PROVENCE, FRANCE

March confidently in the footsteps of the Knights Templar
through the olive-studded countryside of rural Provence.

◆ **DISTANCE**
20 miles

◆ **START**
Vieille Église (Old Church),
Bonnieux

◆ **TYPE OF WALK**
Two days on footpaths
and country roads

◆ **WHEN TO GO**
March–May or
September–October

Bonnieux has been inhabited since prehistoric times and the position of the village, on old trade and pilgrimage routes, means it has seen many armies pass by; some friendly, some a little less so. There are two churches in the village; the older one, in the upper part of the village, was built in the twelfth century and it was from the doors of this church that the Knights Templar set off on the Crusades. Although this walk doesn't take you all the way to Jerusalem, it does offer two days of gentle hiking through idyllic countryside.

Day one of the walk takes four and a half hours and meanders from Bonnieux to the honey-colored village of Lacoste, which is set around a small castle from where there are views over the surrounding Luberon countryside. Heading through light woodland along the Chemin de Font Pourquière, you'll come to the larger town of Goult, where you can spend the night. Day two is a six-hour walk back to Bonnieux. This starts out following the Calavon cycle path to the 2,000-year-old Roman bridge, Pont Julien. From here a countryside trail turns south and leads back to Bonnieux.

LEFT The Old Church crowns the town of Bonnieux in Provence.

RIGHT Begin your walk on the streets which the Knights Templar trod as they set out on the Crusades.

Battle of Mohi

MUHI, BORSOD-ABAÚJ-ZEMPLÉN COUNTY, HUNGARY

Circumnavigate a mound planted with huge wooden crosses at this memorial to those who died at this crucial battle.

◆ **DISTANCE**
1.8 miles

◆ **START**
Car park

◆ **TYPE OF WALK**
Easy

◆ **WHEN TO GO**
All year

RIGHT Crosses line the mound built as a memorial to the Battle of Mohi, where 10,000 Hungarians were killed.

The thirteenth-century Mongol invasion of Europe started in the 1220s and continued for two decades. As it arrived late in the Kingdom of Hungary, it created a false sense of security. Reality struck in 1241 when the Mongols raced through Hungary, virtually burning it to the ground and killing an estimated one-third of the population. The attacks culminated at Mohi (now Muhi) near the Sajó River in northeast Hungary, where the troops of Mongol leader Batu Khan engaged those of Hungary's King Béla IV. Hungary lost around 10,000 men and was soundly defeated. Hungary's—and Europe's—future appeared doomed.

Then, in a simple twist of fate, Ögedei Khan, the heir of Genghis Khan and supreme Mongol ruler, died suddenly. The Mongol advance into Europe and march to the "Great Sea" (Atlantic Ocean) was stalled and never regained momentum.

The Battle of Mohi National Memorial is an artificial earthen mound such as the defenses King Béla IV would have erected prior to the battle, constructed on the battlefield site. Walk around the two concentric walkways that lead up the mound and are lined with crosses. Enter the mound through one of the subterranean gates and move into the innermost chamber where wreaths have been laid to honor the dead.

Battle of Zhongdu

BEIJING, CHINA

After more than a century under the Jin dynasty, the Mongols under Genghis Khan breached the Great Wall in 1213 and ravaged northern China. Two years later they attacked and defeated the capital Zhongdu (now Beijing). The Mongols completed their conquest of China in 1279. You can walk the Badaling section of the wall, 50 miles northwest of Beijing.

Siege of Avignon

AVIGNON, PROVENCE, FRANCE

King Louis VIII of France besieged the city of Avignon in 1226 as part of the Albigensian Crusade. It followed a series of political disputes and attacks between the king and the city. The heavily fortified walls of Avignon made the siege difficult, and even the besiegers were having issues with supplies. Both sides suffered poor conditions and were eager to agree to terms, which gave Avignon the opportunity to negotiate better conditions for its surrender. Walk along the city walls beside the river toward the Palais des Papes for a glimpse of King Louis VIII's vision of the city during the siege.

Siege of Montségur

MONTSÉGUR, ARIÈGE, FRANCE

Perhaps the most spectacular of all the Cathar castles that dot the eastern side of the Pyrenees, Montségur castle sits atop a thumb-shaped pinnacle of rock that can be reached via a superb half-day hike with Pyrenean views all the way. In 1242, the castle, which at the time was sheltering several hundred soldiers and civilians, was attacked by around 10,000 royal troops. This culminated in a siege lasting nine months, and when the castle finally fell most of its Cathar occupants were burned alive and the fortress destroyed.

RIGHT Montségur castle, in the French Pyrenees, is a spectacular site with fabulous views.

Battle of the Neva

UST-IZHORA, RUSSIA

A stroll along the river at Ust-Izhora takes you past a statue of Prince Nevsky and the site of his first victory.

◆ **DISTANCE**
Various options

◆ **START**
Anywhere by the river in Ust-Izhora

◆ **TYPE OF WALK**
Leisurely stroll

◆ **WHEN TO GO**
May–September

ABOVE LEFT A statue of Prince Alexander stands at the confluence of the Neva and Izhora Rivers.

LEFT At the time of the battle the Neva River was an important trade route.

One summer's day in 1240, a fleet of naval ships led by Birger Jarl of Sweden, carrying an army of Swedish, Norwegian, Finnish, and Tavastian troops, sailed up the Neva River and camped at the confluence of the Neva and Izhora Rivers with the aim of mounting an attack.

Prince Alexander Yaroslavich of Novgorod got wind of the attack and managed to stop the invasion around the settlement of Ust-Izhora, just a little upstream from the site of the future St. Petersburg, preventing a possible takeover.

As no official accounts of the battle exist outside Russian chronicles, it is unclear whether the invasion was part of Christian Sweden's attempt to expand to northwestern Russia and to convert the Orthodox Novgorodians to western Christianity, or simply an attempt to control the river, as the Neva served as an important trade route at the time.

It is, however, the battle which gained Prince Alexander his nickname of "Nevsky" for his first significant victory in battle and his success in destroying Birger Jarl's army.

There is a museum dedicated to the battle in Ust-Izhora, which is worth a visit after a short leisurely walk along the St. Petersburg side of the river, where a statue of Nevsky greets visitors at the confluence.

Battle on the Ice

VARNJA, ESTONIA

The Northern Crusades, aiming to convert the Orthodox Novgorod Republic to Roman Catholicism, arrived to wage war in April 1242. Alexander Nevsky, however, lured the Catholic forces onto the frozen waters of Lake Peipus, where his troops attacked the Crusader knights from the sides as they drew closer to the center of the lake. As the knights retreated, the ice began to collapse under the weight of the horses and the heavy armor, resulting in great losses. Take a walk along the southern shores of the lake between Varnja and Kolkja to look over the site where this battle was fought.

Battle of Lewes

EAST SUSSEX, ENGLAND

Enjoy the views of the South Downs National Park, where Simon de Montfort became the temporary ruler of England.

◆ **DISTANCE**
3 miles

◆ **START**
Spital Road

◆ **TYPE OF WALK**
Short but hilly

◆ **WHEN TO GO**
All year

When King Henry III reneged on an agreement to share power with a council of barons, his brother-in-law, Simon de Montfort, led a rebellion against him.

In May 1264, the rebels marched on Henry's army at Lewes and deployed on the high ground above the town. Before the rest of the royal forces had formed up, the king's son, Prince Edward, had led his mounted knights on an impetuous charge. They scattered the inexperienced troops on de Montfort's left wing but then made the mistake of pursuing them off the battlefield. By the time Edward's knights returned, the main part of the Royalist army had been driven back through Lewes and defeated. Both Edward and Henry were forced to surrender.

The victory left de Montfort as de facto ruler of England, and the parliament he later summoned—the first to include townsmen—is seen as an important step in the development of parliamentary democracy.

Spital Road next to Lewes Prison leads up to Landport Bottom, an attractive stretch of open downland with lovely views where the initial fighting took place. From here, loop back down into the historic town. Lewes Castle, where Edward was based, and the ruins of Lewes Priory, where he and his father took refuge before surrendering, are both open to visitors.

LEFT A memorial to the battle sits in the grounds of Lewes Priory.

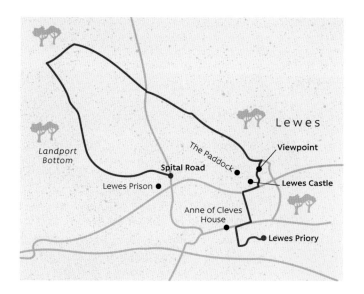

Lewes

Landport Bottom

The Paddock

Spital Road

Viewpoint

Lewes Prison

Lewes Castle

Anne of Cleves House

Lewes Priory

Battle of Largs
AYRSHIRE, SCOTLAND

Take the coastal path south out of Largs and you'll soon come to "the Pencil," a 70-foot-high monument commemorating the battle fought here in 1263 when part of a Norwegian invasion fleet was blown ashore, and the men sent to rescue them were defeated by the Scots.

Battle of Evesham
WORCESTERSHIRE, ENGLAND

Trapped in a loop of the river Avon, Simon de Montfort's outnumbered baronial army was slaughtered by Prince Edward's Royalists. De Montfort himself was literally cut to pieces. Just to the north of the town a marked trail takes you over the general area where the battle was fought in 1265.

LEFT Prince Edward was based at Lewes Castle before the battle.

Battle of Benevento
BENEVENTO, CAMPAGNA, ITALY

On the morning of February 26, 1266, the forces of Charles of Anjou and King Manfred of Sicily, the illegitimate son of Holy Roman Emperor Frederick II, came face-to-face at Benevento, northeast of Naples. Despite a promising start, Manfred's cavalry was soon overwhelmed, and he suffered heavy losses. His supporters were quick to desert him, leaving him to ride into the fray to meet a swift and brutal death. You can walk the Via Francigena, an ancient pilgrimage route, starting in Benevento and snaking your way northwest toward Rome.

Conquest of Shewa
ADDIS ABABA, ETHIOPIA

A historical region of today's Ethiopia, the Sultanate of Shewa was a Muslim kingdom in an otherwise largely Christian region that survived for almost 400 years until it was conquered in 1278 and absorbed into the Sultanate of Ifat. Today, the dynamic capital of Ethiopia, Addis Ababa, sits roughly in the center of what was once Shewa. For an inspiring view out across the city and the surrounding highlands, do the half-day climb up Mount Entoto (10,000 feet). As well as the views, there are also some interesting churches and monasteries.

Collapse of the Pagan Empire
BAGAN, MYANMAR (BURMA)

The most powerful empire in Burmese history, the Pagan Empire reached its zenith in the twelfth and early thirteenth centuries. The glory days weren't to last, though. The rulers of Pagan were an extravagant lot and emptied the coffers by constructing at least 10,000 Buddhist temples. Bankruptcy led to a rapid fall in military strength which allowed Mongol armies to overwhelm Pagan in 1287. The plains here are dotted with around 2,000 surviving temples, linked to one another by dusty paths allowing for several days' enjoyable walking.

LEFT Temple building bankrupted the Pagan Empire but left a beautiful legacy.

Battle of Stirling Bridge
STIRLING, SCOTLAND

English king Edward I's campaign, in 1297, to reestablish his authority over Scotland suffered a severe setback at Stirling Bridge. Half of an English army had filed across a wooden bridge (replaced by a stone one in the fifteenth century) when the Scottish army pounced, cutting the English force in two and slaughtering those trapped on the north side of the river Forth. From here it's a 45-minute walk to the summit of Abbey Craig Hill where William Wallace, the Scottish leader, watched the English advance. Climb the 246 steps of the National Wallace Monument for stunning views over Stirling.

Pointe des Espagnols

ROSCANVEL, BRITTANY, FRANCE

Feel the force of the Atlantic as you walk breezy cliff paths linking a string of ancient fortifications.

◆ **DISTANCE**
9 miles

◆ **START**
Roscanvel church

◆ **TYPE OF WALK**
Half-day
family-friendly walk

◆ **WHEN TO GO**
April–October

BELOW Brittany's craggy coastline makes a spectacular route for walking.

As you loiter in the algae-stained walls of ancient fortifications, with gulls and gannets circling above you screaming to the howling winds, it's easy to feel the dread that soldiers based on this bleak Breton headland must have felt.

This is a real time-machine walk which, over the course of about four hours, will take you past battlements (or the former sites of them), forts, and other military structures that cover every century from the fourteenth to the twentieth.

However, perhaps more than the history, it's the wild North Atlantic seascapes, and the cliffs pounded by mighty winter storms, that leave the more lasting impression.

This family-friendly walk begins in the small town of Roscanvel and, following red and white trail markers, heads north along the footpaths to the village of Le Gouerest and then up to the storm-lashed headland of the Pointe des Espagnols, which, as the name indicates, is where Spanish soldiers set up base in the late sixteenth century. From here the GR34 footpath works down the peninsula's dramatic west coast past a number of battlements—some of which date back to the fourteenth century—before swinging east back to Roscanvel.

Larressingle Fortified Village

LARRESSINGLE, GERS, SOUTHERN FRANCE

This tiny village, which is considered one of the most beautiful in France, is surrounded by huge fortifications that make Larressingle not just a stunning example of a fortified medieval village, but also the smallest such fortified village in France. The village gained its defensive walls during the Hundred Years' War (1337–1453) between France and England but the defenses were never actually needed in that war. The surrounding vine-striped countryside is a delight for gentle hiking.

Hundred Years' War

CHÂTEAU DE CASTELNAUD, DORDOGNE, FRANCE

The Château de Castelnaud, which changed hands several times during the Hundred Years' War, is straight out of a fairy tale. A beautiful half-day walk links the castle with the equally impressive cliffside village of La Roque-Gageac.

LEFT The Spanish made their base on the Pointe des Espagnols.

Great Schism
AVIGNON, FRANCE

For a large part of the fourteenth century, Avignon replaced Rome as the seat of the Papacy. But in 1378, the Great Schism pitted a pope in Avignon against a rival pope in Rome. The town contains some of the most glorious religious architecture in France, which can be visited during a stroll around the old parts of the city. Walk along the ramparts and admire the legendary 900-year-old Saint Bénézet Bridge. From Barthelasse Island there are views up to the Pope's Palace.

Medieval Defenses
LES BAUX-DE-PROVENCE, FRANCE

The castle at Les Baux-de-Provence crowns a near-impregnable rocky outcrop with views out across fertile plains. The site has always been of military importance but reached its epoch in the thirteenth and fourteenth centuries when the castle and the tiny village around it were at the sharp end of many sieges and battles. Considered one of the most beautiful villages in Provence, it is best experienced by walking the Crêtes de Baumayrane, a four-hour trail that takes in the old village, as well as a series of lightly wooded ridges and quiet farmland.

RIGHT Considered one of Provence's most beautiful villages, Les Baux-de-Provence was once also an important military stronghold.

Battle of Bannockburn

STIRLING, STIRLINGSHIRE, SCOTLAND

Though the Battle of Bannockburn didn't bring Scotland's independence, it is still celebrated as a major landmark in its history.

◆ **DISTANCE**
1.5 miles

◆ **START**
Visitors' center

◆ **TYPE OF WALK**
Easy

◆ **WHEN TO GO**
All year

RIGHT The equestrian statue of Robert the Bruce stands guard over the former battlefield.

BELOW An aerial view of where the Battle of Bannockburn took place.

Though this battle was a decisive victory for Scottish King Robert the Bruce and his men over the army of England's King Edward II, it did not end the First War of Scottish Independence (that would take another fourteen years). But it did help to establish Scotland as a nation separate from England.

In 1313, Bruce, who had replaced William Wallace as the leader of the independence movement fifteen years beforehand, demanded the surrender of the English garrison at Stirling Castle. Edward could not ignore such a challenge, and the following year the English advanced northward. Bruce deployed his forces in a woodland, three miles southwest of Stirling Castle, and soundly defeated the English, who counted up to 25,000 troops against a third of that number under Bruce.

The exact site of the battle has been debated for years. The visitors' center run by the National Trust of Scotland stands in the most likely spot. It uses interactive technology to bring the battle to life, including a digital projection of troop movements on a 3-D landscape. The battlefield is now a well-maintained lawn, crowned with a circular monument. But walk across the field to the nineteenth-century equestrian statue of Bruce; for some it will outdo what the technology offers indoors.

137

Crow Creek Massacre
CHAMBERLAIN, SOUTH DAKOTA

On the banks of Crow Creek, nearly 500 skeletons were found in a mass burial site that shows evidence of slaughter. A gruesome find, it showed men, women, and children who had limbs removed and who had been scalped. Aspects of the site remain a mystery, as little is known of the attackers. The skeletons were dated to approximately 1325. The site today is easy to miss, just a small grassy hill on a peaceful bank of the Missouri River. You can walk around the mowed area, soaking up the atmosphere and wondering at why such brutality was committed.

138

Rise of the Aztec Empire
MEXICO CITY, MEXICO

Originally nomads from the north who settled in the Valle de México (the site of today's Mexico City) in 1325, the Aztecs formed a "Triple Alliance" with two other valley states, which brought most of central Mexico under their control. By the fifteenth century, the Aztecs (or Mexica) became the dominant group, with their capital at Tenochtitlán—mostly unstoppable until the arrival of the conquistadors in the sixteenth ccentury. Mexico City's central square, the Zócalo, was built over the main square of Aztec Tenochtitlán. Walk to the northern end of the Zócalo, where you'll find the excavated remains of the Templo Mayor, a key Aztec ceremonial structure until the Spanish demolished it.

ABOVE The excavated remains of Templo Mayor in Mexico City's central square.

139

Battle of Minatogawa

KOBE, JAPAN

Go-Daigo, emperor of Japan from 1318 to
1339, made several attempts to overthrow
the Shoguns (military dictators) and restore
monarchy in Japan, which led to civil war.
At this ultimate battle in 1336, the emperor's
leading, and most loyal, samurai, Kusunoki
Masashige, and his brother couldn't face the
shame of defeat and killed themselves in
service to the emperor. To remember the
samurais' show of loyalty, walk the grounds of
the somber but peaceful Minatogawa Shrine in
Kobe, built on the grounds where the battle
was supposedly fought.

140

Battle of Poyang Lake

NANCHANG, JIANGXI, CHINA

China's largest freshwater lake was the site of
one of the largest naval conflicts in China. The
rebel forces of the Red Turban Rebellion, led
by Zhu Yuanzhang, took on the Yuan dynasty
fleet in 1363. After weeks of exchanging
attacks, Zhu decided to end it once and for all
by sending fire ships to sink the enemy fleet.
His victory facilitated the collapse of the Yuan
dynasty and the rise of the Ming dynasty five
years later. Walk in the Poyang Lake National
Nature Reserve to enjoy this beautiful lake.

ABOVE Lake Poyang floods in the summer, leaving the
temple stranded in water.

Battle of Chioggia

CHIOGGIA, VENETO, ITALY

Walk along the ramparts of Chioggia's star-shaped fort, built after Venice was nearly lost to the Genoese.

◆ **DISTANCE**
Less than a mile

◆ **START**
Via San Marco, at the beginning of the ancient Murazzi dam

◆ **TYPE OF WALK**
Paved paths

◆ **WHEN TO GO**
All year

ABOVE RIGHT The star-shaped fort of San Felice offers 360-degree protection to the entrance to the lagoon.

RIGHT The city of Chioggia is Venice's quieter but equally charming neighbor.

The sleepy seaside town of Chioggia, south of Venice, was the site of the final war between the Venetians and the Genoese—leading commercial powers and longstanding rivals.

The two maritime powers came head-to-head in the War of Chioggia, which began in 1378. Venice had dispatched a large fleet to fight the Genoese (who were backed by the Paduans and Hungarians) in the eastern Mediterranean, leaving the city of Venice extremely vulnerable on all sides.

The Genoese took advantage and captured the port of Chioggia. However, on December 22, 1379, in the thick of night, the Venetians managed to close all the passages and fairways leading out of Chioggia, thereby encircling the Genoese.

The following month, the Venetians' Mediterranean fleet returned to Venice and the balance of forces turned again, culminating in the Genoese fleet—who were near starvation— eventually surrendering in June 1380.

You can walk along the ancient Murazzi dam and the ramparts of Forte San Felice, a fourteenth-century fortress strategically built jutting out into the sea to secure the entrance to the lagoon following the war. It was constructed in the shape of a five-pointed star to ensure 360-degree control over the waters. On the third weekend of June, the Palio della Marciliana sees a historical reenactment of the war, with regattas, medieval music, and archery contests.

Battle of Aljubarrota

NEAR BATALHA, PORTUGAL

When King Ferdinand I of Portugal died with no heir, and his daughter Princess Beatrice married King Juan I of Castile, it left Portugal in danger of being integrated into the Castilian empire. In 1385, John of Aviz, with the assistance of longbowmen from England, repelled the Castilians. The victory affirmed Portugal as an independent country, and John of Aviz became King John I of Portugal. Walk around Batalha and visit the monastery of Santa Maria da Vitória na Batalha to celebrate this victory.

Battle of Otterburn
OTTERBURN, NORTHUMBERLAND, ENGLAND

Scotland and England were politically unstable in the late fourteenth century; rulers on both sides were eyeing up each other's territory and border raids increased. In 1388, the Scots ventured 15 miles into English territory at Otterburn in Northumberland. Despite having an advantage of three to one, the English forces were defeated, and the decisive victory kept the two sides apart for some time. You can easily walk to the battle site, which is less than a mile northwest of town, within Northumberland National Park. It is marked with the Percy Cross, erected before 1400 and restored several times since then.

Battle of the Terek River
GEORGIA/NORTH CAUCASUS, RUSSIA

Tokhtamysh, Mongol leader of the Golden Horde, and Timur (or Tamerlane), Turkic-Mongol empire-builder, had been fighting for years before this final clash, in 1395. It ended in victory for Timur, following the defection of Golden Horde emirs. The battle was fought along the Terek River, but the exact location is unknown; some suggest it was near Grozny in the present-day Chechen Republic. There is beautiful walking in the Daryal Gorge in the Kazbegi National Park, which the Terek River passes through.

Battle of Ankara
ANKARA, ANKARA PROVINCE, TURKEY

The Battle of Ankara, in 1402, had more to do with a personal grudge than empire-building. Despite tensions between the Ottomans and Mongols, nothing warranted a war until Ottoman sultan Bayezid I demanded tribute from an emir loyal to the empire-builder Timur. With the Timurid army twice the size of the Ottoman one, the outcome was swift and the sultan was taken prisoner—a first. The fighting was on the Çubuk plain, now an Ankara suburb. Without any visible reminders of the battle, walk around the capital's Museum of Anatolian Civilizations, which has lots on Timur.

Capture of Delhi

DELHI, INDIA

In 1398, Turkic-Mongol empire-builder Timur invaded Delhi, one of the world's richest cities, on the pretext that the sultanate was too tolerant of its Hindu subjects. Legend tells us that the defenders had armed their elephants with chain mail and put poison on their tusks. Timur allegedly routed them by setting hay on fire at the feet of his camel army, provoking them to charge the pachyderms, which panic easily. Timur then executed tens of thousands of the "infidels." Closely associated with the sultanate is the UNESCO World Heritage Site Qutab Minar, a complex you can walk around in the original Old Delhi, studded with ruined tombs and monuments, including the 240-foot-tall twelfth-century Qutab Minar tower.

Battle of Shrewsbury

SHROPSHIRE, ENGLAND

Walk through Shropshire fields which, 600 years ago, were the site of bloody fighting.

◆ **DISTANCE**
2 miles

◆ **START**
Battlefield 1403
farm shop

◆ **TYPE OF WALK**
Green countryside

◆ **WHEN TO GO**
All year

ABOVE RIGHT A church was built on the site of the battle to commemorate those killed.

RIGHT The local farm shop doubles up as an exhibition center and guardian of history.

In 1403, the Earl of Northumberland rebelled against King Henry IV, and Northumberland's son, Sir Henry "Hotspur" Percy, led an army south. He planned to join forces with Owain Glyndŵr, a Welsh prince who was also in rebellion, but before he could do so the royal army intercepted him outside Shrewsbury.

The ensuing battle was the first in which Englishmen used longbows against one another in any numbers and the king's son, the future Henry V, was dangerously wounded in the face by an arrow. Nevertheless, he refused to leave the field and won the day for the king when his troops drove back the rebels in front of them and then turned to strike Hotspur's main force in the flank. Attacked from two directions, Hotspur was defeated and killed.

As well as housing an exhibition about the battle, Battlefield 1403 farm shop also holds the key to the handsome fifteenth-century church, built on the battlefield to commemorate those killed in the fighting. After visiting it, take the trail clockwise around the battlefield. As you head north up a gentle slope through the fields to the crest of the hill, you'll be following in the footsteps of Prince Henry's triumphant advance.

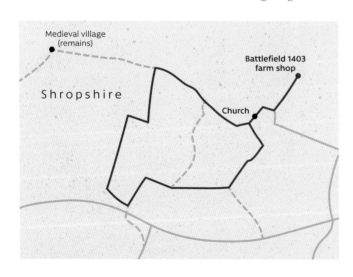

Medieval village
(remains)

Battlefield 1403
farm shop

Shropshire

Church

Glyndŵr Rising
MACHYNLLETH, WALES

Owain Glyndŵr was a Welsh leader who fought fiercely against the rule of Henry IV of England. His revolts from 1400 to 1409 were initially successful, and for a short time Glyndŵr's supporters prolaimed him Prince of Wales. Eventually the uprising was put down. Nevertheless, Glyndŵr became a legend in Wales. Walk around Machynlleth, from Glyndŵr's supposed parliament house to the grounds of Plas Machynlleth, to find his memorial stone.

149

Teutonic Knights
GRUNWALD, POLAND

Walk around the striking monument at the site of the Battle of Grunwald where the Teutonic Knights met defeat at the hands of the alliance of the Kingdom of Poland and the Grand Duchy of Lithuania in 1410. The victory paved the way for the Polish–Lithuanian union to dominate central and eastern Europe.

Battle of Agincourt

AZINCOURT, PAS-DE-CALAIS, FRANCE

Walk around this medieval battlefield, the site of a great victory for the English in the Hundred Years' War.

◆ **DISTANCE**
2 miles

◆ **START**
Azincourt battlefield car park

◆ **TYPE OF WALK**
Leisurely half-day walk

◆ **WHEN TO GO**
July, when the battle is reenacted for a day

Immortalized by Shakespeare in his play *Henry V*, the Battle of Agincourt (Azincourt in modern French) is one of England's most celebrated victories against the French in the Hundred Years' War.

It was assumed that France had the superior army, but Henry V surprised the French with his strategy of using the English longbow in large numbers; 80 percent of the army was made up of English and Welsh archers. It is from this battle that we get the unconfirmed story about the French cutting off any captured archer's two fingers so that they would never be able to draw a bow again.

While there are debates about the exact site of the fighting, a field believed to resemble the rough location of the battle in the commune of Azincourt has been dedicated as the official battlefield of Agincourt, complete with an information board and a memorial stone. Take a walk around the ground, notice the "funnel" formed by the flanking woods in which the French cavalry are said to have become trapped, before walking to the Medieval History Center of Azincourt for more information.

151

Siege of Orléans
ORLÉANS, FRANCE

Joan of Arc was just sixteen when she came to believe that God had chosen her to save France from the English, and persuaded the king to let her lead the troops in taking back the city of Orléans in 1429. Her leadership boosted the city's morale, and the English were driven back. Celebrate the saint with a walk around Orléans.

152

Siege of Compiègne
COMPIÈGNE, FRANCE

Joan of Arc went on to lead a small army to confront the Duke of Burgundy when he besieged the town of Compiègne in 1430. Her troops were severely outnumbered and their escape blocked, when an archer pulled Joan off her horse and captured her. France lost its iconic commander on this day (May 23, 1430). The gate Joan marched through is now a landmark in Compiègne and her statue is a short walk away.

LEFT The memorial stone to the Battle of Agincourt.

Siege of Thessalonica

THESSALONIKI, GREECE

Previously part of the Ottoman Empire, Thessalonica had been under Byzantine rule since 1403. However, in 1422, it angered the Ottoman Empire's Sultan Murad II, when it chose to support one of his rivals. The sultan attacked the town which, unable to defend itself, handed control over to Venice. Sultan Murad refused to recognize Venice's authority and blockaded the city, leading to horrendous conditions within, and many fled. The blockade lasted for seven years until eventually Murad summoned enough forces to overpower the Venetians and claim Thessalonica for the Ottoman Empire. It is possible to walk around some remaining walls of the original city of Thessalonica.

BELOW Walk around the ancient walls of Thessaloniki.

Battle of Varna
VARNA, BULGARIA

A final attempt by the Crusaders to defeat the Ottomans, in 1444, was disastrous. The Battle of Varna pitted 60,000 Ottomans under Sultan Murad II against half as many Crusaders led by Ladislaus III, king of Poland and Hungary (who ignored the warning "The sultan's hunting party is greater than all of your army"). Some 20,000 Crusaders were killed, including Ladislaus, whose decapitated head was put into a pot of honey and carried to the Ottoman capital at Bursa for public display. You can walk around an open-air park museum north of the harbor at Varna which incorporates a cenotaph of Ladislaus and a battle memorial carved into an ancient Thracian tumulus.

Siege of Rhodes
RHODES, GREECE

Rhodes had been the headquarters of the Knights Hospitalers—a Catholic military order—since 1310 and had frequently come under attack from the Ottoman Empire seeking to claim the island for its own. In 1444, Ottoman forces again landed on the island and for several months battles played out in different ports and the citadel in Rhodes was besieged. After one vicious battle, where the Ottomans suffered extensive losses, they abandoned the siege without awaiting orders from the sultan. The old city's moat is now a series of parklands with walking paths, surrounded by the city walls whose towers serve as museums.

Battle of Five Forts
KAKAHI, NORTH ISLAND, NEW ZEALAND

The Ngāti Hotu were a Maori tribe that lived on the North Island of New Zealand. Originally based on the coast at Hawkes Bay, it's thought they moved inland to escape from cannibalistic tribes arriving from Polynesia and Melanesia. They settled around the Lake Taupō area and some at the nearby village of Kakahi which they defended with five forts. Around 1450, the Whanganui Māori tribe came across this settlement and sent for reinforcements to launch an attack. The Ngāti Hotu established a ring of five forts around Kakahi, but it wasn't enough. One by one the forts fell to the attackers and victors hung legs of their victims on the trees along the river, which spurred all survivors to flee and the tribe to vanish from history. Take a walk along the dirt track from the village that roughly follows the river around the site of the battle and enjoy the natural surroundings.

Fall of Constantinople

EDIRNEKAPI, ISTANBUL, TURKEY

Walk along the walls of what was Constantinople,
jewel and bastion of Christendom.

◆ **DISTANCE**
2 miles

◆ **START**
Chora Church
(Kariye Mosque)

◆ **TYPE OF WALK**
Easy

◆ **WHEN TO GO**
All year

BELOW In places, the triple row of
walls in Istanbul were built more
than 1,500 years ago.

In 1453, Constantinople—the capital of all that remained of the
European and Christian Roman Empire of Byzantium—was
captured and occupied by the Asian and Muslim Ottomans.

Though the troops of Sultan Mehmet II (later Mehmet the
Conqueror) vastly outnumbered Constantinople's defenders, the
Byzantines held out for fifty-three days until May 29, a Tuesday.
Mehmet made Constantinople his new capital, replacing
Adrianople (now Edirne) in Thrace. It is said that the conquered
Byzantines deemed Tuesday forevermore a day of ill omen, an
inauspicious day on which to launch a business or start a journey.

Constantinople's triple row of city walls, more than four miles
in length and built a millennium before under Theodosius II,
helped prolong, but not prevent, the city's capture. Large parts of
the so-called Theodosian Walls, including many towers, can still
be seen today. The ambitious could walk along the entire length
from the Golden Horn to the Sea of Marmara. But one of the
best areas to see the walls up close is in the Edirnekapı (Edirne
Gate) district in the shadow of the celebrated Chora Church
(now Kariye Mosque).

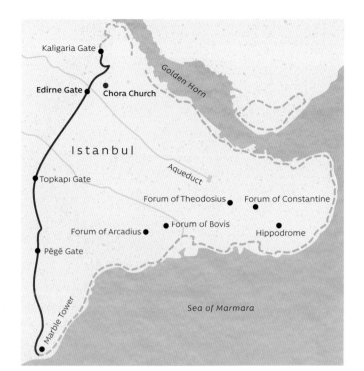

Siege of Berat

BERAT, ALBANIA

In 1455, the Ottomans came to Berat, scaled the poorly guarded walls, and took possession of Berat Castle, which sits strategically on top of a steep hill overlooking the valley. The Albanians, led by Skanderbeg, besieged the city in an attempt to take it back. Although they managed to defeat the relief army sent by the Ottoman sultan, the Albanians ended up retreating due to their own losses and exhaustion. Take a walk from the old town up the steep path to the castle in Berat to understand why this location was so worth fighting over.

159

Siege of Belgrade

BELGRADE, SERBIA

After conquering Constantinople, Mehmet II set his eyes northward, in 1456, to the Kingdom of Hungary with Vienna on its doorstep. His immediate tactic was to seize the border fortress in Belgrade. But a Hungarian counterattack forced a retreat, delaying the Ottoman advance in Europe by decades. Climb up to the battle site at Kalemegdan Citadel in Belgrade.

LEFT Chora Church in Istanbul stands near the ancient walls of Constantinople.

Battle of St. Albans

HERTFORDSHIRE, ENGLAND

The first battle of the Wars of the Roses, in 1455, was fought in the streets of St. Albans and was a victory for the Yorkists. The bell in the city's clocktower (open on summer weekends) sounded the alarm in 1455 and still rings the hour today.

Battle of Northampton

NORTHAMPTONSHIRE, ENGLAND

The Lancastrians were defeated here in 1460 after Lord Grey changed sides and helped the Earl of Warwick's Yorkists into their fortified camp. Although part of the site is now a golf course, there's an exhibition about the battle in nearby Delapré Abbey and a public footpath leads to the heart of the action.

RIGHT The walking route passes Dacre's Cross, a monument to the Battle of Towton.

Battle of Towton

NORTH YORKSHIRE, ENGLAND

Walk around farmers' fields near Towton, the site of
one of the bloodiest battles on English soil.

- **DISTANCE**
  5 miles
- **START**
  Towton village
- **TYPE OF WALK**
  Marked walk
  around fields
- **WHEN TO GO**
  All year

Towton, in 1461, saw the destruction of Henry VI's Lancastrian army and the establishment of the Yorkist Edward IV as King of England.

The battle began in a blinding blizzard with an exchange of archery. With the wind behind them, the Yorkists came off better, prompting the Lancastrians to move forward and attack. The Lancastrians had more men but, with Edward leading by example in the thick of the action, the Yorkist line held until the arrival of reinforcements finally tipped the balance in their favor. As the defeated Lancastrians fled, thousands were slaughtered in the merciless pursuit that followed; others drowned as they struggled to escape across the Cock Beck, which is said to have run red with blood. Contemporary claims that 28,000 died that day were undoubtedly an exaggeration, but Towton was almost certainly one of the bloodiest battles on English soil.

There's a clearly marked trail around much of the battlefield, with boards displaying information about the battle and those involved in it. Finish by walking down the Old London Road, a track in Towton village that leads down to a gloomy crossing of the Cock Beck. It was said that the dead were piled so high here that they formed a bridge across the water.

BELOW Lead Church stands near the battlefield of Towton.

The Ōnin War

KYOTO, JAPAN

A dispute between a high official and a regional lord over who would succeed the heirless shōgun Ashikaga Yoshimasa escalated to become the biggest war in ancient Japan. Around 270,000 samurai soldiers congregated in Kyoto in 1467 to battle for the opposing sides. It is often referred to as "the wasteful war" as it ended with no clear victor, extensive destruction to Kyoto, and thousands of deaths. Walk around Kamigamo Shrine and find the stone which marks the outbreak of the war, then on to Sokoku-ji Temple, which was built on the site of the main battle.

BELOW Kamigamo Shrine in Kyoto holds a stone marking the outbreak of war.

164

Battle of Barnet
GREATER LONDON, ENGLAND

Walk up Barnet's busy high street to the hamlet of Monken Hadley, and you'll be following in the footsteps of Edward IV's Yorkist army as it trudged north in 1471 to confront the Lancastrian forces of Edward's former ally, Warwick the Kingmaker. Fought in thick fog, the ensuing battle was a confused affair. The turning point came when part of Warwick's army returned to the fight after pursuing some fleeing Yorkists, only to be attacked by their own side who thought they were enemies. The Lancastrians were routed and Warwick himself was among the slain, making Barnet a significant turning point in the Wars of the Roses.

165

Battle of Tewkesbury
GLOUCESTERSHIRE, ENGLAND

King Edward IV followed up his victory at Barnet by destroying a second Lancastrian army at the riverside town of Tewkesbury. Much of the area where the heaviest fighting took place has survived, and a marked 45-minute walking route takes you around the key locations. Be sure to visit Tewkesbury Abbey, where some defeated Lancastrians tried to seek sanctuary only to be dragged out and beheaded. The town becomes a riot of color in the summer when its shops fly banners painted with the arms of those who fought in the battle.

ABOVE The Bloody Meadow in Tewkesbury was once the site of heavy fighting.

Burgundian Wars: Battle of Grandson

LAKE NEUCHÂTEL, SWITZERLAND

With the power and wealth to pursue his great ambitions, Charles the Bold, Duke of Burgundy, launched a campaign to expand his empire. In 1476, he turned his sights on the Swiss Confederacy, and took the castle of Grandson after a siege. The Swiss soon came with reinforcements and confronted Charles's forces in a forest near Concise. This caused panic in the Burgundians, who retreated in chaos, leaving much of their treasures to the Swiss. Relive history by walking from the town of Grandson, along the lake toward Concise.

Burgundian Wars: Battle of Nancy

NANCY, LORRAINE, FRANCE

Charles the Bold did not give up his conquest after losing at the Battle of Grandson. In 1477, having regrouped his forces, he marched to Nancy in the hope of capturing the city from his rival. His mistake was to march in winter, and he lost men under the harsh conditions along the way. On reaching their destination, the remaining army engaged in a combat with the Duke of Lorraine's troops, where Charles was killed and mutilated. Walk around the old center of this beautiful city and its three eighteenth-century squares and admire the former capital of the Duchy of Lorraine.

Battle of Taximaroa

CIUDAD HIDALGO, MICHOACÁN STATE, MEXICO

From 1469, the Aztecs launched a protracted offensive against their powerful neighbor, the Purépecha (or Tarascan) Empire. This climaxed in 1478, when the Aztec ruler Axayácatl led 32,000 warriors across the border, where they were met by 50,000 Tarascans at the Battle of Taximaroa. The Purépecha scored a resounding victory, killing or capturing 90 percent of the Aztec army. This may have been partly due to the Tarascans' use of copper for spearheads and shields. Walk around the old town of Ciudad Hidalgo and visit San José Church, which contains some Aztec items.

LEFT Nancy's Stanislas Square features a striking fountain of Neptune in a gilded wrought-iron portico.

ABOVE Predjama Castle in Slovenia is built into the mouth of a cavern.

Siege of Predjama Castle

PREDJAMA, NOTRANJSKA PROVINCE, SLOVENIA

Located in the mouth of a cavern halfway up a hillside in southwestern Slovenia, Predjama Castle looks unconquerable. During the fifteenth-century wars between Hungary and Austria, a pro-Magyar brigand called Erazem (Erasmus) Lueger holed himself up inside and came and went through a secret passage. In 1483, the Austrians attacked and Erazem showered them with fresh fruit to prove he was not a prisoner. But then a servant betrayed him and when Erazem went "to where even the sultan must go alone," he was hit by a cannonball while sitting on the toilet. Predjama Castle is open to visitors year-round.

Siege of Pavagadh

PANCHMAHAL DISTRICT, GUJARAT, INDIA

Champaner in Gujarat is a historical city-state, founded by the Rajput king Vanraj Chavda of the Chavda dynasty. Along with the nearby Pavagadh city, the location sits on a strategic trade route across India. Sultan Mahmud Begda, at war with the Rajputs, laid siege to the city for almost two years from 1483 to 1484. He succeeded in capturing the city, later expanding it and turning it into his new capital. Walk around the site to admire the gates, palaces, arches, temples, and mosques of Hindu and Muslim heritage, and walk up Pavagadh Hill for views of the complex from above.

BELOW A walk up Pavagadh Hill gives great views over the site.

Battle of Bosworth Field

MARKET BOSWORTH, LEICESTERSHIRE, ENGLAND

Enjoy a walk in the countryside where one king died
on the battlefield and another was crowned.

DISTANCE
5 miles

START
Bosworth Battlefield
Heritage Centre

TYPE OF WALK
Gentle countryside walk

WHEN TO GO
All year

Richard III's seizure of the throne in 1483 and the disappearance
of the young Edward V alienated many former Yorkists, enabling
the exiled Lancastrian Henry Tudor to present himself as an
alternative candidate for the crown.

With military support from the French, Henry landed in
Wales in 1485 and marched into England, where he faced
Richard III near Market Bosworth. Richard had a larger army,
but on the day of the battle, some of his troops failed to fight at
all and the powerful Stanley contingent threw in their lot with
Henry. After leading a desperate but unsuccessful cavalry charge
against his rival, Richard was cut down, and the victorious Henry
was crowned on the battlefield, becoming King Henry VII.

Start your walk at Ambion Hill where there's a visitors' center,
memorial, and viewing point. The hill was long considered to be
the site of the battle, but it's now accepted that the fighting took
place about two miles away on either side of an old Roman road
now called Fenn Lanes, and that Ambion Hill was where
Richard camped before the battle. Walk through Ambion Wood
and along a stretch of canal
and you'll reach Fenn Lanes,
which leads south through
farmland down to the
battlefield. After about a
mile, a footpath just before
a farm complex leads to
the area where Richard
probably fell.

Battle of Stoke Field

NOTTINGHAMSHIRE, ENGLAND

This high ground above the Trent River saw the last battle of the Wars of the Roses, in 1487, as Henry VII's forces defeated the pretender Lambert Simnel's German mercenaries, Irish levies, and die-hard Yorkists. A walking trail with information boards guides you around the site.

ABOVE The site of Bosworth Battlefield also offers a pleasant walk through countryside.

LEFT A memorial sundial at the Heritage Centre is topped with a crown.

TOWARD THE MODERN ERA
1500–1699

Enter an era of exploration and economic growth spurred by colonialism and the displacement of native people that saw the conquest of poor and weak nations by stronger and richer ones.

The Portuguese Occupation

KILWA KISIWANI, TANZANIA

Throughout much of the Middle Ages the palm-fringed coastline of East Africa was dotted with Swahili city-states. Some of these, such as Mombasa, Lamu, and Zanzibar, still thrive today, but others, such as Tanzania's Kilwa Kisiwani, are now little more than fading memories of coral stone walls. Like many of these, the end for Kilwa Kisiwani came at the hands of the Portuguese, who burned the city down in 1505. Today, a highly enjoyable half-day walk takes you around what remains of these island ruins.

Battle of Flodden

NORTHUMBERLAND, ENGLAND

After invading England in 1513, James IV of Scotland was confronted by an English army under the Earl of Surrey. The Scots enjoyed a strong defensive position on a steep hill, but goaded by Surrey's artillery, they took the offensive. Struggling down the slopes with their unwieldy pikes, they became hopelessly disorganized, and as they floundered in the boggy ground below the hill, the English cut them to pieces. Thousands died, including James himself. There's excellent footpath access across the battlefield; descend the steep slopes of Branxton Hill and you'll quickly understand the difficulties faced by the Scots.

LEFT Piper's Hill Monument at the site of the Battle of Flodden.

RIGHT The Cammino dei Monaci ends near Melegnano where the Battle of Marignano was fought.

◆ 175 ◆

Battle of Novara

NOVARA, PIEDMONT, ITALY

On June 3, 1513, during the War of the League of Cambrai, the French army besieged Novara, one of the Duchy of Milan's most important cities. The siege lasted two days before the French retreated after receiving news that a strong army of Swiss troops, allied to the Duke of Milan, was approaching. The French camped at two farmhouses outside the city. At dawn on June 6, they were attacked by the Swiss and swiftly defeated. The battle left around 9,000 men dead and led France to withdraw from Italy for a while. It is possible to walk a loop around the battlefield, passing the farmhouses where the infantry and cavalry encamped.

◆ 176 ◆

Battle of Marignano

MELEGNANO, LOMBARDY, ITALY

About 20,000 Swiss and 35,000 Frenchmen came head-to-head at the 1515 Battle of Marignano, the last major battle of the War of the League of Cambrai. It was such a brutal encounter (it left 18,000 dead) that it was dubbed the Battle of the Giants. You can walk part of the Cammino dei Monaci, a 40-mile route that begins in Milan and ends near Melegnano (as the town is now called), passing the chapel of the Church of Santa Maria della Neve, home to an ossuary with bones that belonged to Swiss soldiers who fell in battle. Every September, the town hosts a historical reenactment of the battle.

Watchtowers of Corsica

CORSICA, FRANCE

Grab a bird's-eye view of the jagged Corsican coast from the lofty cliffs of Capo Rosso.

◆ **DISTANCE**
6.5 miles

◆ **START**
Parking Capo Rosso

◆ **TYPE OF WALK**
Half-day
family-friendly walk

◆ **WHEN TO GO**
March-June and
September-October

ABOVE The walk to the top of the coastal watchtower is worth it for the views along the coastline.

RIGHT The watchtowers were built to look out for approaching pirate ships.

Corsica's natural beauty has inspired people to venture here for centuries. Some of these visitors were less welcome than others, such as the rampaging pirates who plagued the Corsican coastline throughout the sixteenth century.

The pirates would burn down villages, stealing and raping as they went. So, the Corsicans—who at the time were subjects of the Republic of Genoa—constructed squat stone defensive towers all along the coastline to help warn villagers of any approaching pirates.

Today, many of these watchtowers still stand and this coastal walk in northwest Corsica takes you to one of the most impressive, which is situated atop huge cliffs that jut out into the Mediterranean like an angry clenched fist.

The walk begins from the Parking Capo Rosso, in the northwest of Corsica, and follows a clearly marked path downhill through coastal scrub to the base of the cliffs. From here the climb to the top looks almost impossible, but follow the trail around to the seaward side of the cliff and a steep rising path takes you up onto the cliff summit where a finely preserved Genoese tower offers a panoramic view along the coast.

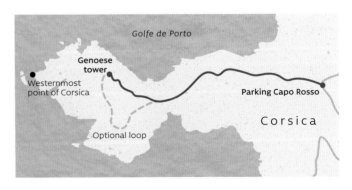

Golfe de Porto

Genoese tower

Westernmost point of Corsica

Parking Capo Rosso

Corsica

Optional loop

Execution of György Dózsa

TIMIȘOARA, TIMIȘ COUNTY, ROMANIA

What was launched as a latter-day crusade in 1514, blessed by the pope and led by the Hungarian Transylvanian man-at-arms György Dózsa, soon disintegrated into revolt, with peasants marching across the Great Plain. The response was brutal. Some 70,000 peasants were tortured and executed; Dózsa was fried alive on an iron throne, crowned with a sizzling metal crown. A walk in the Old Town of Timișoara will lead you past the Virgin Mary Monument, said to mark the site of the martyrdom of Dózsa.

Battle of Ridaniya

RIDANIEH, CAIRO, EGYPT

The Ottomans took a break from their advance through the Balkans when they engaged Mamluk Sultanate forces at Ridaniya (Ridanieh) outside Cairo in 1517. The Egyptians were quickly routed and fled up the Nile. The Ottomans then moved into the capital, taking the citadel and slaying the entire garrison and the sultan, Tuman Bay II, whose body was hung over a city gate. Visit the citadel, where the Ottomans took up residence, staying until 1798. It's on the city's eastern edge and contains museums, mosques, and terraces with breathtaking views.

"La Mala Pelea"

CHAMPOTÓN, CAMPECHE, MEXICO

In 1517, Francisco Hernández de Córdoba embarked on a fateful voyage to the Yucatán peninsula. Looking for water, he and his men went ashore in Champotón, where they saw a promising river that would fill their leaking barrels. First lured into the center of the Maya city, they were then attacked, losing fifty men, and Córdoba himself was mortally wounded. Today, the placid tourist town's *malecón*—seafront promenade—offers shoreline walks for several miles in either direction. The beaches, with white sand as fine as chalk dust, are beautiful, as is the Gulf of Mexico.

LEFT Landing at Champotón on the Yucatán peninsula was a fateful move for Córdoba.

Spanish Conquer the Aztecs

MEXICO CITY, MEXICO

The Spanish conquest of the Aztec empire came after a two-year war in which the Spaniards allied with the Aztecs' Indigenous enemies to defeat the Mexica (the rulers of the empire) at their capital in 1521. During the Battle of Tenochtitlán, the defenders cut the beating hearts from seventy Spanish prisoners-of-war before the altar of Huitzilopochtli, Aztec god of war. In the Zócalo, Mexico City's central square, built on the former site of the Templo Mayor of Tenochtitlán, is a platform dating from about 1400. On its southern half, a sacrificial stone stands in front of a shrine dedicated to that very same god.

◆ 182 ◆

Battle of Mohács

MOHÁCS, BARANYA COUNTY, HUNGARY

Contemplate carved weaponry at the site where the Ottomans conquered Hungary in 1526.

◆ **DISTANCE**
2 miles

◆ **START**
Visitors' center

◆ **TYPE OF WALK**
Easy

◆ **WHEN TO GO**
All year

RIGHT Carved weapons stand guard at the memorial site to this important battle.

The Battle of Mohács is where an independent Hungary died, leading to almost four centuries of partition and foreign domination. It's tempting to blame the ineffectual twenty-one-year-old King Louis II. But rivalries among the nobility, and the violent suppression of the peasant uprising led by György Dózsa a dozen years earlier, had severely weakened Hungary's military might and emptied the treasury. By 1526, Sultan Suleiman the Magnificent, having marched up through the Balkans, was ready to take Buda and then Vienna with his 60,000 troops.

Not able to wait for reinforcements from Transylvania, Louis rushed south from Buda with a ragtag army of 25,000 and was soundly defeated by the Turks in less than two hours. Along with an estimated 20,000 soldiers, the king himself was killed, by drowning in a stream as he shamefully retreated.

The Mohács Historical Memorial Site was opened in 1976 to mark the 450th anniversary of the battle. There's a visitors' center with archaeological finds; outside, more than a hundred carved wooden markers in the shape of bows, arrows, lances, and swords lean this way and that over a mound discovered in the 1970s, which is a common grave from the battle.

Walk around the mound and through a subterranean entrance to a circular courtyard with explanatory panels.

Siege of Vienna
VIENNA, AUSTRIA

After his victory at Mohács, Ottoman sultan Suleiman the Magnificent attacked Vienna in 1529 with an army five times the size of that of the defenders. However, the Austrians had strengthened the walls around their base, St. Stephen's Cathedral, so effectively that they held out and prevailed. Climb the cathedral's south tower, which served as the main command post during the siege.

184

Siege of Eger
EGER, HEVES COUNTY, HUNGARY

When the Ottomans turned their attention to conquering the Hungarian town of Eger in 1552, they expected little resistance. But under the command of István Dobó, 2,000 Hungarian soldiers held out against some 40,000 Turks for a month. The site of the siege, the thirteenth-century Eger Castle, is an easy walk up from the center of town.

Inca Civil War

CUENCA, AZUAY PROVINCE, ECUADOR

Wander the streets of modern-day Cuenca, beneath which lie the ruins of an Inca capital destroyed in a battle between half-brothers.

◆ **DISTANCE**
1.5 miles

◆ **START**
Parque Calderón

◆ **TYPE OF WALK**
Easy stroll along sidewalks

◆ **WHEN TO GO**
All year

ABOVE RIGHT The Catedral Vieja in Cuenca is built from the stones of the ruined Inca city.

RIGHT The archaeological park shows some of the scale of the former city of Tumebamba.

When the great Incan emperor Huayna Capac died in 1527 (possibly from smallpox introduced by Spanish conquistadors), he had intended that his eldest son, Ninan Kuyuchi, become the next ruler of the Incas. However, Kuyuchi died at the same time and instead the title was passed to Capac's legitimate son, Huáscar. This led to a fierce battle with another of Capac's sons (there were allegedly hundreds from many wives and concubines), Atahualpa, a half-brother of Huáscar's, who believed he was more popular and a better fighter and so the throne should be his.

During the conflict, which ran from 1529 to 1532, the city of Tumebamba, whose architecture and design was inspired by Cusco, the great Inca city in what is now Peru, was embroiled by fighting and largely destroyed. The Spanish conquistadors then arrived to hasten the fall of the riven Inca empire.

Today, the city of Cuenca in Ecuador stands on the former site of Tumebumba. Cuenca's oldest church, the Catedral Vieja, was built from the stones of the ruined city and is now a museum. From here, head to the Pumapungo archaeological park for an evocative wander among the remains of Inca foundations and walls, a mausoleum, and a ceremonial bath.

186

Battle of Cajamarca

CAJAMARCA, PERU

In 1532, Pizzarro and his Spanish conquistadors entered the city of Cajamarca and captured the Inca emperor Atahualpa. In the battle that ensued, not a single Spaniard was badly hurt, while thousands of Inca soldiers and attendants were killed. Walk around the Inca Cuarto del Rescate (Ransom Room), which was reportedly filled with a gold ransom in an unsuccessful attempt to save Atahualpa.

Siege of Cusco

CUSCO, PERU

Walk between the town and its citadel to gain a sense of the impressive building skills of the Incas.

◆ **DISTANCE**
0.86 mile

◆ **START**
Qorikancha complex

◆ **TYPE OF WALK**
Uphill

◆ **WHEN TO GO**
All year

ABOVE LEFT The expansive Plaza de Armas in Cusco, where the Inca leader was beheaded.

LEFT Some of the stones in the walls of the Sacsayhuamán citadel are 11 feet tall.

In 1536, the army of Sapa Inca Manco Inca Yupanqui, the emperor of the Inca Empire, violently clashed with the Spanish conquistadors as he sought to restore his empire. On May 6, Inca troops marched toward the heart of Cusco, recapturing the city from the Spanish as they went.

They were close to defeating the Spanish, until Juan Pizarro and his outnumbered—yet better-equipped—forces attacked Sacsayhuamán, a citadel in the northern outskirts of Cusco where the Incas were stationed. The bloody battle left thousands dead; their remains are said to have been feasted on by Andean condors. After months of fighting, the Incas eventually withdrew to the Sacred Valley, leaving the Spanish to revel in their victory in Cusco.

Start your walk at the Qorikancha complex, the Inca temple whose riches were plundered by the conquistadors (its inside walls are thought to have been lined with a cornice of gold). Walk northwest to the Plaza de Armas, where Spanish colonial viceroy Francisco Álvarez de Toledo captured Inca leader Túpac Amaru and had him beheaded in 1571. From the square, it's an uphill walk to the citadel of Sacsayhuamán—its defensive wall is impressive, made of three parallel stone ramparts that zigzag along the plateau. The stones are truly monumental, with many 11 feet tall, and with one block weighing over 300 tons.

Sacsayhuamán

Sapantiana Aqueduct

Iglesia San Cristóbal

Plaza de Armas

Regional Historical Museum of Cusco

C u s c o

Qorikancha complex

188

Castles of the Downs
DEAL, KENT, ENGLAND

Around the time of his divorce from Catherine of Aragon, Henry VIII faced political threats from France and the Catholic Church. He ordered the construction of a series of defenses along the coast of England, one set of which was the Castles of the Downs, built in 1540. The floral-shaped Walmer and Deal castles, and the ruins of Sandown are three of the forty-two artillery fortifications lining the coast. The rounded walls of each castle provided overlapping firepower as defense from attacking ships. A leisurely three-mile walk along the coast connects the three castles.

189

Dacke War
VIRSERUM, SMALÅND, SWEDEN

When Swedish king Gustav Vasa introduced both an unpopular tax system and Lutheranism to his people, the peasants grew dissatisfied. This caused an uprising in Småland in 1542, led by the outlaw Nils Dacke. The king tried to contain Dacke's influence by cutting supplies to the region and spreading propaganda about Dacke. He sent his German mercenaries to attack Småland and, despite large losses, defeated the uprising. Dacke was later killed, and as a warning to others, his head was publicly displayed. Walk around the town of Virserum, where there is a memorial to Dacke.

190

Southsea Castle and the Battle of the Solent
PORTSMOUTH, ENGLAND

With the expansion of Henry VIII's defense system around England, many areas hardly saw any fighting, with the exception of Southsea Castle in Portsmouth. A French fleet invaded from the Solent strait and attacked English ships here in 1545. Henry VIII was at Southsea Castle at the time, and witnessed the sinking of his favorite ship, the *Mary Rose*. Walk between the castle and the Mary Rose Museum to learn more about this historic event.

ABOVE LEFT The floral-shaped Deal castle in Kent.

LEFT Walk from the medieval bridge in Musselburgh to the battlefields of the Battle of Pinkie.

191

Battle of Pinkie
LOTHIAN, SCOTLAND

Scotland's largest ever battle, Pinkie was fought during the "Rough Wooing"—a dispute between England and Scotland over who should marry Mary, Queen of Scots. When the Scots crossed the river Esk near Musselburgh to attack an invading English army in 1547, they walked into deadly fire from archers, artillery, and hand-gunners—even from English ships in the Firth of Forth. The Scots broke and more than 6,000 were killed in the ensuing pursuit. A 1.5-mile walking trail takes you from the medieval bridge in Musselburgh to the large open fields where much of the fighting took place.

Mughal Invasion of India

CHITTORGARH FORT, RAJASTHAN, INDIA

One of India's largest forts, and boasting superb views, Chittorgarh was the scene of three epic sieges: it was sacked by Alauddin Khalji, ruler of the Delhi Sultanate, in 1303; Sultan Bahadur Shah of Gujarat overran it in 1535; and—perhaps most famously—Mughal Emperor Akbar captured the fort in 1568, after which it declined in importance despite remaining an impressive structure. With eight miles of formidable perimeter walls protecting the 700-acre site of palaces, temples, reservoirs, and other structures, exploring the fort—parts of which date back to the eighth century—is a full day's walk.

Battle of Malta
VALLETTA, MALTA

The Knights Hospitalers had ruled Malta for only thirty-five years when the island came under ferocious Ottoman attack from 180 ships and 40,000 soldiers in 1565. Although the knights had been able to strengthen the coastal defense at Fort St. Elmo, the fort fell to the Ottomans and was under siege for another three months. However, against all the odds, the knights emerged victorious. Walk around Fort St. Elmo, which now contains the enormous National War Museum and examines the Great Siege in absorbing detail.

Wars of Religion
SAUVETERRE DE BÉARN, FRANCE

Situated close to the borders of France, Aragon, Navarra, the Basque Country, and the Béarn region, the ancient fortified village of Sauveterre de Béarn was always destined for a life of drama. One of its many dramatic moments came in 1569 when, in a particularly bloody episode, it was attacked and taken over by Catholic Basque armies. Of course today things are far quieter and the village's beautiful riverside setting makes for a great half-day walk taking in the historical highlights of the village and a long riverside amble.

Battle of Lepanto
PATRAS, PELOPONNESE REGION, GREECE

The Battle of Lepanto in 1571 was a naval engagement between a coalition of Catholic states and the Ottomans. Famously, Miguel de Cervantes, the author of *Don Quixote*, was fighting on one of the Spanish ships. It was the largest naval battle in Western history and the first significant victory for a Christian naval force over a Turkish fleet. From the city's waterfront lighthouse, look westward into the Gulf of Patras. The battle took place between the cape in the distance and the island of Oxia to the north. From here, walk up the 200 steps to the Kastro, Patras's castle.

Attack on Sagres
SAGRES, ALGARVE, PORTUGAL

Stand on the high cliffs of Sagres in southern Portugal as waves boom into the rock face and it's easy to understand how this spot once inspired people to wonder what was beyond the horizon. During the Portuguese Age of Exploration, the fortress built on these cliffs was used as a training center for the ship pilots who set out to conquer the world. But Sagres didn't have it all its own way and, in 1587, Sir Francis Drake attacked and destroyed much of Sagres. Privateers such as Drake aren't so common today, but a walk along these cliffs still inspires wonder.

ABOVE LEFT Fort St. Elmo in Malta now contains an impressive military museum.

LEFT The waterfront lighthouse in Patras.

The Battle of Tennō Mountain

KYOTO, JAPAN

Walk between shrines and temples amid lush trees and bamboo forests where this battle took place.

◆ **DISTANCE**
1 mile

◆ **START**
Oyamazaki Gayoseki Park

◆ **TYPE OF WALK**
Well-marked trail, hilly

◆ **WHEN TO GO**
April–June or
September–November

ABOVE RIGHT Hike up the shrines and memorials to this battle.

RIGHT A torii gate, the symbolic gateway between the human and spirt worlds, on the hiking route up Tennō Mountain.

In the mid-fifteenth century, Japan had become mired in civil war as wealthy nobles and rulers enlisted private armies to expand their territories.

The Battle of Tennō Mountain (1582) came after a betrayal: one of Oda Nobunaga's own vassals, Akechi Mitsuhide, forced Nobunaga to commit suicide and took power for himself, amassing an army in what is now the area of Kyoto. While trying to defeat another enemy by allying with a third army, Mitsuhide miscalculated, allowing messages to be read by troops still loyal to Nobunaga.

An army of nearly 40,000 soldiers marched toward Mitsuhide, meeting in the area of Tennō Mountain. The terrain favored Mitsuhide, but the advancing army, led by Toyotomi Hideyoshi, gained control of the mountain. He also sent ninjas into the enemy camp the night before, setting the tone for the battle that would come. Though the battle had steep casualties on both sides, Hideyoshi was the victor.

Today, a trail leads to a large temple, a stone monument, and a painted mural where this important battle is commemorated, with descriptions mostly in Japanese. Lush trees, bamboo forests, and tōrii shrine gates all make it a pleasant place to walk.

Tilbury Fort

TILBURY, ESSEX, ENGLAND

Walk to the spot where Queen Elizabeth I gave her rousing speech after an attempted invasion by the Spanish Armada.

◆ **DISTANCE**
2 miles

◆ **START**
Tilbury Town train station

◆ **TYPE OF WALK**
Easy

◆ **WHEN TO GO**
All year

In August 1588, 130 ships of the Spanish Armada sailed to Flanders with the aim of invading England. In defense, the English sent out ships from Plymouth and a battle took place near the port of Gravelines (now in France).

The lighter and more maneuverable design of the English ships proved a great advantage against the heavier, more cumbersome Spanish galleons. The English emerged the victors, with heavy losses on the Spanish side that would only get worse as the Armada attempted to return home.

After the battle, Queen Elizabeth I sailed to Tilbury Fort to review her troops. Mounted on a gray gelding and wearing ceremonial armor, she gave an impassioned and much quoted speech: "I know I have the body but of a weak, feeble woman; but I have the heart and stomach of a king, and of a king of England too… And should [any] dare to invade the borders of my realm, I myself will take up arms…"

To reach the fort, follow the well-marked path from Tilbury Town train station, past the docks, the customs house, and cruise terminal along the Thames. The fort is managed by English Heritage and is one of the best examples of an artillery fort in England.

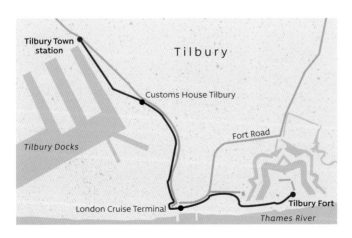

199

Battle of Cádiz

CÁDIZ, ANDALUSIA, SPAIN

This was a series of successful attacks by Francis Drake against the Spanish in 1587. Elizabeth I had executed her Catholic cousin and heir, Mary, Queen of Scots, and feared retaliation. Walk along the shores of the Bay of Cádiz and then south to the Monument to the Heroes of the Armada in San Fernando.

200

Spanish Armada in Ireland

GRANGE, COUNTY SLIGO, IRELAND

After the defeat of the Spanish Armada in 1588, 130 vessels were forced northward by English ships, to return to Spain by sailing around Ireland. More than a third of the ships were wrecked, and thousands of men died. The six-mile De Cuéllar Trail follows in the footsteps of a Spanish captain who survived. Begin the trail at the Armada Visitor Centre in Grange.

ABOVE Old cannons at Tilbury Fort.

LEFT The defensive shape of Tilbury Fort covers attacks from all angles.

Siege of Busan

BUSAN, SOUTH KOREA

Venture from the beach up into forest at the site where
Japanese forces invaded Korea.

◆ **DISTANCE**
2 miles

◆ **START**
Dadaepo Beach

◆ **TYPE OF WALK**
Mix of forested uphill and
flat beach

◆ **WHEN TO GO**
All year

LEFT Walk around the headland
on the vertiginous walkway.

BELOW Dadaepo Beach and the
beautiful mountains behind.

On May 24, 1592, Japanese forces surprised Korea at Busan.
At first, Korean officials didn't believe the warning, mistaking
the Japanese forces for a fishing fleet. Despite having 150 ships
at the ready, the Joseon (Korean) navy did nothing, waiting for
instructions from above that never came.

When nearly 20,000 Japanese warriors came ashore, it was
too late for Busan's commanders to mount much of a defense.
The Japanese sent a request that the Korean forces surrender, but
this was ignored, and thus, the Japanese attacked in full force.
Though an initial push to take Busan Castle wasn't successful, the
Japanese had superior firepower in the form of the arquebus,
which was far superior to the Koreans' spears and arrows. When
the Japanese broke through, they sacked Busan before heading
northward toward Seoul.

Today, Busan is a lovely city. You can start walking at the
Dadaepo Beach area, then go from there up through the forest to
the interesting signal tower, Eung Bong Bong Su Dae, where if
there were an emergency they would light a fire at night or use
smoke during the day to
warn of threats. This signal
system could carry alerts
all the way to Seoul,
200 miles away.

202

Portuguese Campaign Against Kandy

KANDY, SRI LANKA

No one can blame the Portuguese for being attracted to the paradise island of Sri Lanka, but unlike most visitors who come for a sun-filled vacation and then go home, the Portuguese chose to stay—using force—and by the late 1500s they'd conquered much of the island. But one place held out. The powerful highland kingdom of Kandy was attacked by Portuguese forces in 1594, but the invaders were wiped out. Walk around the large lake that stands as the centerpiece of the city and take in the famed Temple of the Tooth.

203

War Against Sigismund

KALMAR TO LINKÖPING, SWEDEN

Sigismund III Vasa, who was king of Poland, also took the throne of Sweden on the death of King John III in 1592. Duke Charles (later King Charles IX), the only living son of the previous Swedish king, Gustav Vasa, made several attempts to negotiate his position, and when these failed he began a revolt. Sigismund raised a foreign army to fight the duke, but unfortunately for him, as a foreign king, the Swedes refused to help him. The duke and his supporters defeated Sigismund and he was deposed in 1599. Follow Sigismund's march to defeat on a 168-mile hike from Kalmar to Linköping along the coast.

204

Linköping Bloodbath

LINKÖPING, SWEDEN

Following his defeat by Duke Charles in 1599 (see above), Sigismund was forced into a conditional truce. He signed a treaty to abdicate the throne, as well as to hand over Swedish noblemen allied to him. Prior to being crowned king, Charles and his court conducted a trial of the remaining prisoners, the Swedish nobles who were senators and advisers to Sigismund. Eight nobles were sentenced, but three were later pardoned. The remaining five were publicly beheaded at the Linköping town square in March 1600. Walk around the city's historical sights and visit the castle museum.

205

Battle of Kinsale

KINSALE, COUNTY CORK, IRELAND

In 1601, King Phillip II of Spain, who wanted revenge for the loss of his Spanish Armada in 1588, sent 4,800 men in support of the Irish cause to drive the English out of Ireland. Unfortunately, a poor choice of landing location meant his fleet was immediately surrounded by English troops at Kinsale harbor. When the Irish arrived, their army was no match for the English. The battle lasted an hour, with the Irish suffering major losses. Follow Gaelic prince O'Sullivan Beare's retreat along the Beara Breifne Way walking trail.

RIGHT The Spanish made a bad choice in landing at Kinsale harbor.

Battle of Sekigahara

SEKIGAHARA, JAPAN

When Toyotomi Hideyoshi died in 1598, leaving a five-year-old heir, feuding clans went into civil war. Two years later there was a decisive battle at Sekigahara, following which the victor Tokugawa Ieyasu's shogunate ruled Japan for two and a half centuries. Walk between the battle camps of opposing armies in Sekigahara in memory of this battle.

Shimabara Rebellion

SHIMABARA, KYUSHU, JAPAN

Wander around the ruins of Hara Castle, where peasants
didn't win their uprising, but their ruler still lost.

◆ **DISTANCE**
1 mile

◆ **START**
Hara Castle ruins

◆ **TYPE OF WALK**
Leisurely walk

◆ **WHEN TO GO**
All year

ABOVE LEFT A statue of the
rebellion's leader, Amakusa Shirō,
at the ruins of Hara Castle.

LEFT Enjoy ocean views from the
Hara Castle grounds.

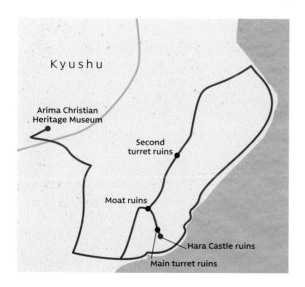

Matsukura Katsuie, a feudal lord under the Tokugawa shogunate
during the Edo period, was notorious for his violent policies of
suppressing Christianity in Japan. In 1637, he drastically raised
taxes to build Shimabara Castle, which further angered peasants
who couldn't meet the financial demands.

As a result, Catholic peasants, led by Amakusa Shirō, began
a rebellion against Katsuie. Armed with weapons plundered
from the Katsuie clan's own storehouses, they assassinated the
local tax official, and besieged various castles of the noble clans
in the area, eventually basing themselves at the previously
abandoned Hara Castle.

The rebellion experienced an early success, being able to
defend Hara Castle against Katsuie's forces. However, as
the assaults continued, they began to run out of supplies. The
shogunate sent a force of more than 125,000 troops which,
with the added support of the Dutch, was too much for the
rebels; after a lengthy siege of
Hara Castle, the rebellion was crushed.
More than 37,000 rebels and supporters
were beheaded, and the shogun
investigated Katsuie, who was
eventually charged and executed for
misruling his domain.

Walk around the Hara Castle ruins,
which offer beautiful ocean views, and
on to the Arima Christian Heritage
Museum to learn more.

Kyushu

Arima Christian
Heritage Museum

Second
turret ruins

Moat ruins

Hara Castle ruins

Main turret ruins

Siege of La Rochelle
LA ROCHELLE, CHARENTE-MARITIME, FRANCE

In the 1620s, La Rochelle was France's third-largest city but it was under the control of the Huguenots, French Protestants. In August 1627, Louis XIII, keen to reinstate Catholicism in France, sent an army of 7,000 soldiers and 600 horses to surround La Rochelle, completely isolating the city with entrenchments and sea walls. La Rochelle held its defense for fourteen months before giving in to an unconditional surrender that paved the way for Huguenots to lose all rights in France. Defense towers and walls from this period can be seen on a walk around the city.

BELOW The pretty French seaside town of La Rochelle, which was besieged for fourteen months.

Mystic Massacre
MYSTIC, NEW LONDON COUNTY, CONNECTICUT

This 1637 raid by Connecticut colonists and their Narragansett and Mohican allies was in response to an earlier Pequot raid on the colonial village of Wethersfield in which nine noncombatants were killed. Led by Captain John Mason, the raiders attacked and burned a fortified Pequot village, killing between 400 and 700 Native Americans. From the Mystic River, walk west to the corner of Pequot Avenue and Clift Street where a grassy circle marks what is thought to be the site of Pequot Fort. It previously included a statue of Mason, but that was removed in 1995 after protests by members of the Pequot tribe.

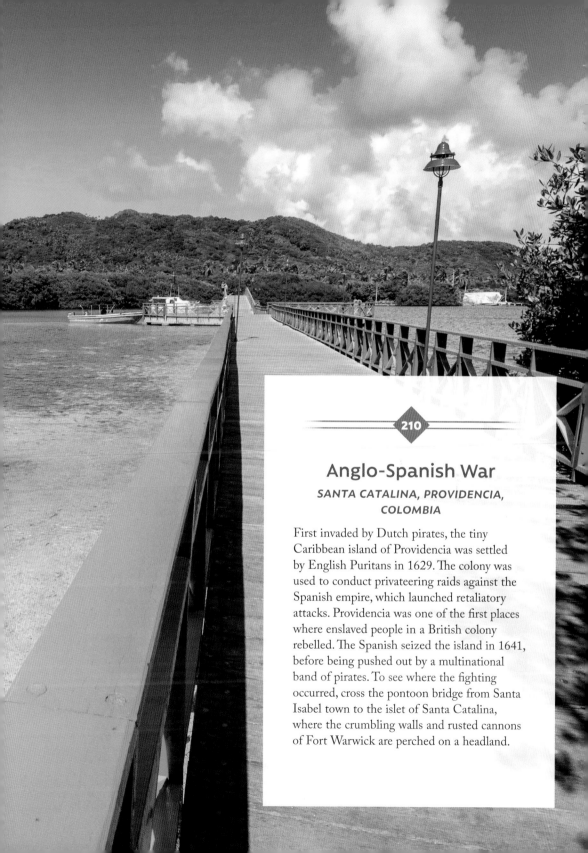

210

Anglo-Spanish War

SANTA CATALINA, PROVIDENCIA, COLOMBIA

First invaded by Dutch pirates, the tiny
Caribbean island of Providencia was settled
by English Puritans in 1629. The colony was
used to conduct privateering raids against the
Spanish empire, which launched retaliatory
attacks. Providencia was one of the first places
where enslaved people in a British colony
rebelled. The Spanish seized the island in 1641,
before being pushed out by a multinational
band of pirates. To see where the fighting
occurred, cross the pontoon bridge from Santa
Isabel town to the islet of Santa Catalina,
where the crumbling walls and rusted cannons
of Fort Warwick are perched on a headland.

Battle of Stratton

CORNWALL, ENGLAND

Retrace the steps of a daring English Civil War attack that secured Cornwall for the king.

♦ **DISTANCE**
3 miles

♦ **START**
Stratton village

♦ **TYPE OF WALK**
Through country lanes
and footpaths

♦ **WHEN TO GO**
All year

BELOW The fields where the
Battle of Stratton took place.

Stratton, in 1643, was one of the English Civil War's most remarkable battles. Despite being heavily outnumbered and dangerously short of ammunition, Sir Ralph Hopton's Cornish Royalists pulled off an extraordinary victory near the coastal town of Bude.

When the Earl of Stamford's Parliamentarian army advanced into Cornwall and occupied the steep hill that now bears his name, Hopton ordered his troops to attack them from the west, south, and north, using the narrow lanes which led up the hill. With their pikemen leading the way, the Royalists battled their way to the summit, fought off a counterattack, and routed Stamford's army.

The best way to understand the significance of this achievement is to follow in the footsteps of Hopton's men and make your way up one of the steep lanes to the top of the hill. The embanked "Cornish hedges" of stone and earth that line these lanes would have provided excellent cover for the Royalist advance. After pausing for breath and enjoying the stunning views from the summit, take the path to the eccentric battle memorial, an arch topped with a recycled church pinnacle. Return to Stratton via the hill's eastern side and you'll see that although the steep slopes protected the Parliamentarians from attack, they also made an orderly retreat virtually impossible when things went wrong.

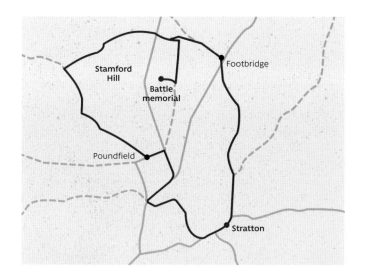

Battle of Adwalton Moor

WEST YORKSHIRE, ENGLAND

The Earl of Newcastle's Royalists were facing defeat in 1643 until a desperate pike charge gave them victory over the Parliamentarians and with it temporary control of Yorkshire. A walk through the rugged moorland here will give you a feel for what the terrain was like at the time.

213

Battle of Roundway Down

WILTSHIRE, ENGLAND

William Waller's Parliamentarians were besieging Devizes in 1643 when a Royalist relief force arrived. Waller redeployed on nearby Roundway Down but his cavalry was routed and his infantry surrendered. Walk to the end of the down to see the steep slopes where many fleeing Parliamentarians tumbled to their deaths.

LEFT The eccentric memorial to the Battle of Stratton incorporates part of a recycled church tower.

214

First Battle of Newbury

BERKSHIRE, ENGLAND

After relieving the siege of Gloucester in 1643, the Earl of Essex's Parliamentarians found their route back to London blocked by Royalist forces at Newbury. A day's hard fighting ended with both armies roughly where they'd started but, short of ammunition, the Royalists withdrew. The Parliamentarians returned safely to London, and Charles I had lost his best chance of winning the war. Round Hill, an area of high ground where heavy fighting took place, is well worth exploring. It's a half-mile walk down the aptly named Essex Street from the imposing monument to Viscount Falkland, a fallen Royalist.

215

Battle of Marston Moor

NORTH YORKSHIRE, ENGLAND

In the English Civil War's largest battle, in 1644 a combined Parliamentarian and Scottish army under the Earl of Leven won northern England for Parliament by decisively defeating Prince Rupert's Royalists. The key action took place on the Parliamentarian left flank where Cromwell and Leslie's Anglo-Scottish cavalry scattered their Royalist opponents before wheeling right to complete the victory. The Long Marston to Tockwith Road passes through the center of the battlefield with the Royalists to the north and the Parliamentarians to the south. Just before Tockwith, walk along Kendall Lane to follow the direction of the decisive Parliamentarian attack.

216

Battle of Montgomery

POWYS, WALES

The Royalists were besieging Montgomery Castle in 1644 when extra Parliamentarian forces arrived in the fields to the north. When some of these new forces rode off to forage, the Royalists sensed an opportunity and attacked. They were initially successful, but were ultimately overpowered by the Parliamentarian infantry. The victory gave Parliamentarians the initiative in North Wales. A footpath from nearby Offa's Dyke leads to the center of the action. The views from the ruins are superb.

LEFT Walk from Offa's Dyke to the ruins of Montgomery Castle, which has excellent views.

Battle of Cheriton

HAMPSHIRE, ENGLAND

The attractive Hampshire countryside was the site of one of Parliament's first major victories of the English Civil War.

◆ **DISTANCE**
5 miles

◆ **START**
Memorial to the Battle of Cheriton

◆ **TYPE OF WALK**
Gentle countryside

◆ **WHEN TO GO**
All year

The start of 1644 saw Sir William Waller's Parliamentarian army pitted against Lord Forth's and Sir Ralph Hopton's Royalist forces in Hampshire. The two armies eventually clashed across a broad valley near the village of Cheriton.

Follow the Wayfarer's Walk trail out of Cheriton and it will lead you up to a circular walk on footpaths and quiet roads that starts on the Parliamentarian side of the battlefield.

The Royalists occupied the high ground to the north. To the east, completely dominating the battlefield, is Cheriton Wood. Realizing the importance of this wood, Waller sent musketeers into it, but the Royalists quickly drove them out. A track on the edge of the wood leads to the Royalist side of the valley.

Although Forth and Hopton were in a strong position, they decided to stand on the defensive and let Waller make the next move. Their plans were scuppered, though, when one of their commanders led his men too far forward and his regiment was attacked and destroyed by Parliamentarian cavalry. The Royalist cavalry joined the battle but found it hard to make any progress among the thick hedgerows and narrow lanes that still cross the battlefield today. With their cavalry exhausted and their outnumbered infantry losing ground, Hopton and Forth were forced to order a general retreat.

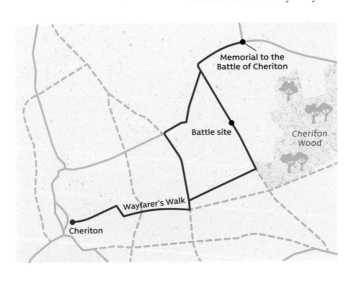

218

Battle of Naseby

NORTHAMPTONSHIRE, ENGLAND

The destruction of the Royalist army at Naseby in 1645 ensured that Parliament would win the English Civil War. From Naseby, walk the Sibbertoft Road to the Cromwell Monument, built on the hill where the Parliamentarians deployed. The Royalists occupied the hill across the valley. An information board explains how the battle unfolded.

219

Battle of Langport

SOMERSET, ENGLAND

Walk along the peaceful Wagg Rhyne watercourse just outside Langport. George Goring posted musketeers here to cover the withdrawal of his Royalist army in 1645, but Thomas Fairfax's Parliamentarian infantry and artillery drove them back, enabling Fairfax's cavalry to ford the Rhyne and rout the main Royalist force.

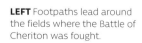

LEFT Footpaths lead around the fields where the Battle of Cheriton was fought.

Battle of Shanhai Pass
SHANHAIGUAN, CHINA

The phrase "Your enemy's enemy is your friend" was put to the test by the Ming dynasty in 1644. It had been fighting the Manchu Prince Dorgon for months when it came under attack from the Shun dynasty, too. Ming General Wu Sangui negotiated with Prince Dorgon to form an alliance against the Shun in exchange for a surrender. The sight of Manchurians charging through the Shanhai Pass surprised the Shun and they were crushed. The victory led to the founding of the Qing dynasty. Follow the victors' footsteps and take a walk through the Shanhai Pass at the east end of the Great Wall.

Battle of Philiphaugh
NEAR SELKIRK, BORDERS, SCOTLAND

The Royalist Marquis of Montrose's Scottish–Irish army had won a series of victories over the Scottish Covenanters (Presbyterians who opposed Charles I), but his winning streak came to an end at Philiphaugh in 1645. Outnumbered by Covenanter cavalrymen, Montrose's ragtag army stood little chance, and after a brief resistance it was routed. A hundred Irish prisoners were shot, and many Royalist camp followers were murdered. Cross the Ettrick Water at Selkirk to walk through the nearby riverside fields where much of the fighting happened.

RIGHT Tracing the Battle of Shanhai Pass will take you into some stunning scenery.

Battle of Torrington

DEVON, ENGLAND

Torrington was under the control of Lord Hopton's Royalists, but they were decisively defeated on a cold February night in 1646 by Thomas Fairfax's Parliamentarians. A plaque on Torrington church explains that it was rebuilt after the gunpowder the Royalists had stored there blew up at the end of the battle. Two hundred Royalist prisoners who were being held inside were killed in the explosion. A walking trail takes you around other key locations, including the site of the main Royalist barricade and the castle mound where a Royalist regiment stubbornly held out.

Battle of Winwick

LANCASHIRE, ENGLAND

After an invading Scottish Royalist army had been defeated by Oliver Cromwell at Preston in 1648, its remaining infantry made a stand behind a stream outside Winwick village. Although they put up a stout resistance, they were eventually outflanked by Cromwell's men and driven back with heavy losses. The survivors soon surrendered. Follow the public right of way which leads north through the fields where the Scots retreated and ends at Hermitage Green Lane, where they initially deployed. The high sandstone bank running along part of the lane would have made this a particularly difficult place to attack.

Battle of Dunbar

EAST LOTHIAN, SCOTLAND

In 1650, with his English army bottled up in Dunbar by the Scots, who were supporting the young Charles II, Oliver Cromwell was in a tricky situation. But when the Scots unwisely left their commanding position on Doon Hill and prepared to attack, Cromwell struck first. Splashing over the Brock Burn stream, his soldiers overwhelmed the Scottish right wing, then routed the rest of their army. Despite the intrusion of a large cement works, Dunbar is a memorable place to visit. Climb to the summit of Doon Hill for magnificent views of both battlefield and coast.

Battle of Worcester

WORCESTERSHIRE, ENGLAND

In 1651, the young King Charles II invaded England at the head of a Scottish army only to be defeated at Worcester by Cromwell's Parliamentarians. Charles watched events unfold from the cathedral tower, which can still be climbed today. Cross the nearby canal bridge where pikes mark the location of a gate through which Charles's cavalry launched a last charge and you'll reach the Commandery, a splendid medieval building that the Royalists used as a headquarters. Just beyond it is Fort Royal Park, the site of a Royalist gun emplacement that was stormed by the Parliamentarians.

LEFT Climb the cathedral tower in Worcester from where King Charles II watched the battle unfold more than 350 years ago.

Battle of Tresco

ISLES OF SCILLY, ENGLAND

Enjoy stunning views as you explore the site of a seventeenth-century amphibious attack.

◆ **DISTANCE**
5 miles

◆ **START**
Old Grimsby

◆ **TYPE OF WALK**
Coastal walk

◆ **WHEN TO GO**
Spring to fall

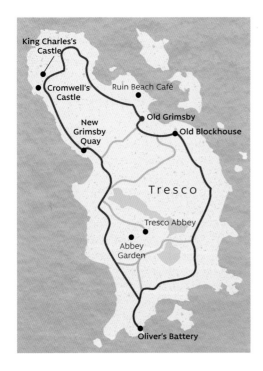

Despite their defeat on the English mainland, some Royalists still held out on the Isles of Scilly, a cluster of small islands thirty miles off Land's End. So in 1651 the English Parliament sent Admiral Blake with a small fleet and 1,000 soldiers to capture them.

Because St. Mary's, the main island, was too strongly fortified to attack directly, Blake decided to capture Tresco first. Start your walk at Old Grimsby on the island's eastern side. Blake sent a flotilla of small boats to land here, but some boats were swept off course by the tide, others landed on the wrong island altogether, and the rest beat a hasty retreat as soon as they came under fire. Undeterred, the Parliamentarians tried again and, after wading ashore, their troops overwhelmed the Royalist defenders. Blake's men could now blockade St. Mary's, which soon surrendered.

A Tudor blockhouse offers grandstand views of the beach where the main action took place. From there take a circular walk around the island. To the south at Carn Near is "Oliver's Battery," a rocky outcrop where the Parliamentarians posted guns to bombard St. Mary's harbor. Further north, an uneven coastal path leads to Cromwell's Castle, built shortly after the battle. Visit the ruins of King Charles's Castle, which the Royalists garrisoned; it's a steep climb but well worth it for the panoramic views.

Battle of Sedgemoor
SOMERSET, ENGLAND

The last major battle on English soil, the Battle of Sedgemoor in 1685 saw the failure of the rebel Duke of Monmouth's surprise night attack against King James II's army. Sedgemoor is an atmospheric place, crisscrossed by paths, tracks, and ditches, and it's easy to see why Monmouth's army lost its way in the dark.

228

Killiekrankie
PERTH AND KINROSS, SCOTLAND

Forces loyal to the deposed King James VII defeated a Scottish government army near the magnificent, wooded gorge of Killiekrankie, in 1689. It's a short walk from the visitors' center to Soldier's Leap, where one fleeing government soldier is said to have escaped after making an improbable 18-foot jump across the fast-flowing river Garry.

ABOVE Cromwell's Castle was built shortly after the Battle of Tresco.

LEFT Climb to the roof of Cromwell's Castle for views along the coastline.

Battle of Warsaw
WARSAW, POLAND

During the Second Northern War, the Polish–Lithuanian Commonwealth was partially occupied by Sweden and Russia, and many towns and cities were seized or destroyed. King John II Casimir of Poland led a combined troop of infantry, winged hussars, and Tartars to confront the Swedish occupiers of Warsaw. Their efforts were repelled and after three days, Casimir admitted defeat and abandoned Warsaw. Take a walk in the Saxon Gardens and visit the Tomb of the Unknown Soldier, which has a dedication to this battle of 1656.

Battle of Santa Cruz de Tenerife
SANTA CRUZ DE TENERIFE, CANARY ISLANDS, SPAIN

In 1657, English Admiral Robert Blake attacked the heavily defended harbor of Santa Cruz de Tenerife in the Canary Islands in an attempt to steal Spanish treasure. Although Blake's attack shattered the Spanish defense and ships, he failed to capture any treasure as it had already been unloaded and was safe on land. Blake claimed a successful attack on the Spanish, but the Spanish also claimed victory for having defended the treasure. Walk along the shoreline of the city where parts of the defense walls still exist.

LEFT Some of the original harbor walls at Santa Cruz de Tenerife still remain.

King Philip's War: Angel of Hadley

HADLEY, MASSACHUSETTS

Explore Hadley Common and learn the true identity of the mysterious uniformed man with the long white beard.

◆ **DISTANCE**
3 miles

◆ **START**
Hadley Common

◆ **TYPE OF WALK**
Easy

◆ **WHEN TO GO**
All year

Plymouth Colony's relations with the Indigenous Wampanoag people remained cordial from its founding in 1620 till the death of Chief Massasoit in 1661. But when the sachem's (chief's) younger son, Metacom, who had been given the English name of Philip by the Pilgrims, became chief, land disputes erupted into violence. What would become known as King Philip's War raged for almost three years in New England.

In 1675, the western Massachusetts town of Hadley came under Wampanoag attack. At the height of battle an old man with a flowing white beard and wearing an antique breastplate emerged from the town rectory and led local residents to victory. This "Angel of Hadley" is now known to have been General William Goffe, one of the fifty-nine regicides—the judges who signed King Charles I's death warrant in 1649. After the restoration of the monarchy in 1660, Goffe escaped to the New World and took refuge for more than a decade in the home of Reverend John Russell at Hadley.

Walk around Hadley Common where the rectory was located and the attack was centered. There's a historical marker identifying Goffe. From here walk down to the Connecticut River and across the Calvin Coolidge Bridge to the Forbes Library in Northampton, three miles to the southeast, where there's a nineteenth-century painting depicting the legend.

Great Swamp Fight

WEST KINGSTON, RHODE ISLAND

In 1675, during King Philip's War, militias from three separate New England colonies attacked the main settlement of the neutral Narragansett tribe in southern Rhode Island, killing 97 warriors and up to 1,000 noncombatants. The Great Swamp Fight Monument is a mile-and-a-half hike from the parking lot in West Kingston.

Pueblo Revolt

SANTA FE, NEW MEXICO

In 1680, Pueblo tribes, led by Popé, a charismatic leader, revolted successfully and brought independence to the region for twelve years. Today, walk outside the Palace of the Governors, which was besieged, in what's now historic Santa Fe.

LEFT View across the Connecticut River from Northampton looking toward Hadley.

234

Battle of Lwów

LVIV, UKRAINE

Ottoman ascendancy in Europe appeared to wane as early as 1675 when the troops of Polish King John III Sobieski, augmented by 1,700 hussars, routed a much larger assembly of Turkish infantry at Lwów (now Lviv), Ukraine. Climb up Castle Hill from the central square to the fourteenth-century ruins of High Castle.

Battle of Vienna

KAHLENBERG, AUSTRIA

Charge into Vienna from the hills as Sobieski did when he liberated the city from the Ottomans.

◆ **DISTANCE**
2 miles

◆ **START**
Kahlenberg Viewing
Terrace

◆ **TYPE OF WALK**
Easy hike

◆ **WHEN TO GO**
March–October, to avoid
slippery conditions

ABOVE LEFT The Kahlenberg
Panoramic Viewing Terrace in
the hills where Sobieski's
troops gathered.

LEFT It's a pleasant walk from the
hills down to the riverfront.

In 1683, the Ottoman Empire laid siege to Vienna. For two
months the city resisted, but with supply lines cut off, it was on
the verge of surrender.

Then, one September morning, in the Kahlenberg hills above
the city, combined Polish and Habsburg troops led by King John
III Sobieski joined forces with the Imperial army of Charles V,
Duke of Lorraine. The battle which followed marked the turning
point of 300 years of Ottoman–Habsburg wars.

Seeing the threat gathering in the hills, the Ottomans
decided to concentrate their efforts on forcing their way into the
city. This gave Sobieski's troops the opportunity to take up bases
in surrounding villages from where the "winged hussars" could
launch an almighty cavalry charge. Joined by other cavalry units,
this is considered the largest cavalry charge in history, and
exhausted and demoralized the Ottoman camp. In less than
three hours, Vienna was liberated from the brink of surrender.

A monument to Sobieski looks over the city from the
Kahlenberg Panoramic Viewing Terrace. From here, it is a
leisurely walk down to the riverfront of Vienna.

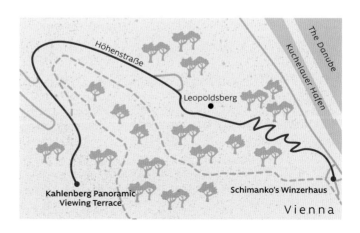

Battle of the Boyne
DROGHEDA, COUNTY LOUTH, IRELAND

The deposed King James II and William of Orange (King William III) both claimed the English throne. William opposed James's sympathies toward a Catholic Ireland and objected to his removal of many high-ranking Protestant officials from positions of power in Ireland. This opposition led to a confrontation and they met on a ford on the river Boyne near Drogheda, in 1690. The ensuing battle was won by William, whereupon James fled to France and never returned. A lovely walk along the loop of the river Boyne takes in this famous battlefield, and more can be discovered at the nearby Battle of the Boyne Visitor Centre.

Battle of Aughrim
AUGHRIM AND BALLINASLOE, COUNTY GALWAY, IRELAND

After James's defeat at the Boyne, his followers, known as Jacobites, continued to fight with French assistance led by Charles Chalmot de Saint-Ruhe. In July 1691, they met William's forces at Aughrim. The Jacobites were on the path to victory when Saint-Ruhe was killed by a cannonball on the battlefield. With the lack of command, Jacobite morale rapidly disintegrated. This was the ultimate end to James's cause in Ireland. The Aughrim Battlefield Trail is a six-mile route around the site of the battle that takes you from the town, through woods and countryside, and past the ruins of Aughrim castle.

Siege of Mombasa
MOMBASA, KENYA

In the sixteenth century, the Portuguese were one of the dominant world powers and, by and large, took whatever bit of land they fancied. Mombasa, the natural deepwater port on the coast of Kenya, was taken by Portuguese forces who established the mighty Fort Jesus (which still stands today). But from 1696 to 1698, the Omani sultans repeatedly laid siege to Mombasa until there were hardly any defenders left. A walk around the old city of Mombasa and Fort Jesus reveals the influence of many cultures on this old trading city.

ABOVE LEFT The impregnable walls of Fort Jesus.

LEFT Omani influence on Fort Jesus.

Battle of Zenta
SENTA, VOJVODINA PROVINCE, SERBIA

After the Turkish attempt to take Vienna was thrashed in 1683, the Ottoman military went into freefall. Buda was liberated from the Turks in 1686 after a seventy-seven-day siege, and an imperial army under Eugene of Savoy wiped out the last Turkish army in Hungary at the Battle of Zenta (now Senta in Serbia) eleven years later. Walk along the banks of the Tisza River, east of Senta, where most of the battle was fought, and head for the city hall. At the top of the tower is a scale model of the battle with detailed maps along the wall and fabulous views.

Last Stand of the Itzá Maya

ISLA DE FLORES, PETÉN DEPARTMENT, GUATEMALA

Discover the strengths—and beauty—of an island city
that repelled invaders for decades.

◆ **DISTANCE**
3 miles

◆ **START**
Malecón

◆ **TYPE OF WALK**
Flat walk around village

◆ **WHEN TO GO**
All year

ABOVE RIGHT The position of Isla Flores in the center of Lake Peten made it almost impregnable.

RIGHT The conquering Spanish made their mark on Flores with their colonial architecture.

As the Maya empire collapsed at the hands of the ever-advancing Spanish, the powerful Itzá Maya retreated to an island fortress in the middle of Guatemala's Lake Petén. There, in a city called Nojpetén, they repelled invaders for decades, often with a cunning strategy of luring the foreigners either to the lake's shallows or to the island's center, pretending to be friendly. Then they would turn on their "visitors" and kill them with spears or volleys of arrows sent from boats hidden in the lake's thick reeds.

Nojpetén succumbed to Spanish conquerors on March 13, 1697. Unlike previous invaders, who had used canoes or small craft in their attacks, Martín de Ursúa y Arizmendi instructed his troops to build a galleon. It was too large and too powerful for the smaller native canoes to withstand. He quickly breached the island's defenses with heavy casualties on the Maya side; the city fell almost immediately.

Today, Flores is a peaceful tourist town with a lovely *malecón*, or walking street, that circles the island. You can shop, eat in cafés, and take in the scenery in a picture-perfect spot that was once a perfect defense against invaders.

THE MODERN ERA
1700–1913

Trek through two centuries known as much for
their enlightenment, invention, and development
as for slavery, violent struggles for independence,
and bloody civil wars.

Slave Route

OUIDAH, BENIN

As you take a half-day stroll from the attractive, pastel-colored town of Ouidah down a well-marked path lined with art, sculptures, and information panels to the tropical beach at the trail's end, it's hard to imagine the sense of horror that must once have hung in the air here. But, back in the eighteenth century, this same trail was walked by tens of thousands of prisoners of war being led to the ships that would carry them far away from Africa to a life of slavery in the Americas.

Raid on Deerfield

DEERFIELD, MASSACHUSETTS

This raid on a colonial settlement in western Massachusetts in 1704 took place during the so-called Queen Anne's War, a conflict among French, Spanish, and English colonists for control of North America. French forces and their Indian allies attacked Deerfield, burning part of the town, killing 56 settlers and taking 112 captives. The original village of Deerfield is now preserved as a living time capsule, with a dozen colonial house museums open. There are marked trails throughout the village tracing the 1704 raid; among its relics is a door bearing tomahawk marks from the attack.

BELOW Hall Tavern houses Deerfield's visitors' center.

Siege of Colonia del Sacramento

COLONIA DEL SACRAMENTO, URUGUAY

In 1704, during the War of the Spanish Succession, the governor of Spanish-held Buenos Aires, Don Alonso Juan de Valdés e Inclán, decided to lay siege to the Portuguese colony of Colonia del Sacramento with a force of 4,000 Indigenous fighters and 650 Spanish soldiers. The defeated Portuguese evacuated all the inhabitants and abandoned the town. The Spanish settled for a decade until the town was returned to Portugal as part of the Treaty of Utrecht. It exchanged hands a few more times before becoming part of an independent Uruguay. Walk around the Portuguese- and Spanish-influenced town center.

BELOW The Spanish and Portuguese colonial powers battled back and forth over the Uruguayan town of Colonia del Sacramento.

Siege of Nice

NICE, FRANCE

Taking place between March 1705 and January 1706, the Siege of Nice was a part of the War of the Spanish Succession, which pitted the victorious besieging forces of Louis XIV against Victor Amadeus II of Savoy. Today Nice is one of the most glamorous towns on the French Riviera. A walk from the harbor up Castle Hill, where the fortress once stood, offers commanding views of the stunning coastal scenery.

Poltava Battlefield

POLTAVA, UKRAINE

Having conquered most of his enemies, the ambitious King Charles XII of Sweden chose to invade Russia in the fall of 1707. Harsh wintry conditions forced a detour toward modern-day Ukraine, where he lost half of his troops en route. After surviving the Great Frost of 1708–1709, he decided to besiege the fortress of Poltava in 1709. A combination of miscommunication between commands, a poorly executed battle plan, and being outnumbered by the superior forces of Tsar Peter the Great led to the defeat of the Swedish army. Various monuments dedicated to the battle for both sides can be visited on a short walk around Poltava.

BELOW The coastline and rooftops of the Old Town from the top of Castle Hill, Nice.

ABOVE RIGHT Glen Shiel in Scotland should have made for an impregnable battle site, but didn't.

246

Battle of Glen Shiel

HIGHLANDS, SCOTLAND

This was the only battle of an abortive Spanish-backed bid to restore the Stuarts to Britain's throne. In 1719, Spanish regulars and rebel highlanders tried to stop an advancing government army by blocking the road through Glen Shiel and stationing troops on the lofty crags above it. It seemed an impregnable position, but when the government troops attacked, the highlanders (including the legendary Rob Roy MacGregor) melted away, leaving the Spanish to surrender. Glen Shiel's steep slopes make this a thrilling battlefield to explore, but to do this properly you'll need good weather and a fair degree of fitness.

247

Battle of Cartagena

CASTILLO SAN FELIPE DE BARAJAS, CARTAGENA, COLOMBIA

During the Battle of Cartagena de Indias (1740–1741), the British Royal Navy repeatedly failed to capture the wealthy Spanish colonial port-city, located on Colombia's Caribbean coast. Driven by commercial and imperial rivalry, Admiral Edward Vernon's men were defeated by a combination of Admiral Blas de Lezo's forces—who were based in an impregnable fortress, the Castillo San Felipe de Barajas— and yellow fever epidemics. Now part of a UNESCO World Heritage Site, the castillo's labyrinthine bunkers, batteries, and parapets make it an evocative place to explore.

Foundation of the Kingdom of Nepal

GORKHA, NEPAL

Clamber up wooded slopes to Gorkha Durbar, the stronghold of Prithvi Narayan Shah.

♦ **DISTANCE**
1.5 miles

♦ **START**
The bazaar, Gorkha

♦ **TYPE OF WALK**
Moderate to steep but
easy to follow

♦ **WHEN TO GO**
Mid-September to
mid-April; the rest of the
year is the monsoon

RIGHT The strategically placed
Gorkha Durbar was instrumental
in the unification of Nepal.

When Prithvi Narayan Shah ascended to the throne of the kingdom of Gorkha in 1743 following the death of his father, there were dozens of different states in what is now the territory of Nepal. Over the following decades he used his hilltop Gorkha Durbar—a heavily fortified palace-temple complex—to launch a series of attacks on these separate factions, defeating them one after another.

Eventually, in 1768, Shah triumphed over his Malla rivals in the Kathmandu Valley and unified the country under his rule, laying the foundations for the modern state of Nepal. His dynasty lasted—on and off—until 2008, when Nepal abolished its monarchy.

This trail starts in Gorkha's bustling bazaar, near the Tallo Durbar, a former palace that has been turned into a museum dedicated to the Shahs—there is an array of eighteenth-century weaponry on display, including a cannon at the entrance. It then climbs a wooded trail to the well-preserved Gorkha Durbar, which occupies a strategic position at the apex of the ridge and is ringed by impressive stone walls. Inside the wood-and-brick palace are the remains of Prithvi Narayan Shah's throne.

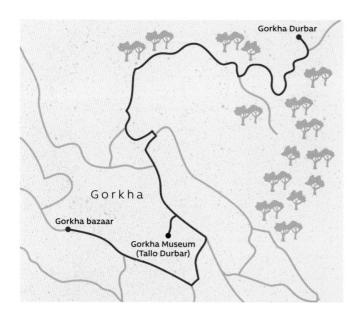

Gorkha Durbar

Gorkha

Gorkha bazaar

Gorkha Museum
(Tallo Durbar)

249

Nuwakot's Hilltop Fortress

NUWAKOT, NEPAL

Prithvi Narayan Shah captured the hilltop fortress of Nuwakot in 1744 and used it as a base for his military victories over the Kathmandu Valley's city-states, as he worked his way toward unifying Nepal. Walk through a sleepy village, once an important trading post, to find the fort's surviving towers and walls.

Battle of Prestonpans
EAST LOTHIAN, SCOTLAND

Charles Edward Stuart's bid to restore his father to the British throne in 1745 received an early boost at Prestonpans when a ferocious charge by his broadsword-wielding Highlanders routed General Cope's government army in less than half an hour. Cope's men fled, leaving the battlefield littered with bodies, severed limbs, and discarded equipment. A former coal mining spoil heap has been landscaped to provide a viewing platform, and with a museum, a choice of walks, three monuments, and an audiovisual display in a converted dovecote, Prestonpans is a fascinating battlefield to visit.

Jacobites in Scotland
OUTER HEBRIDES, SCOTLAND

Bonnie Prince Charlie, son of King James II, fought for his father's claim to the British throne with his army of Jacobites. He first landed in Scotland on July 23, 1745, at the Prince's Beach (Coilleag a' Phrionnsa) on Eriskay. Initially he was successful in his fight southward toward London, until defeat at the Battle of Culloden brought him back to the Outer Hebrides. With the help of Flora MacDonald, who dressed Charles as her maid, he evaded English capture and escaped to France. Walk the Bonnie Prince Charlie Trail, which passes significant Hebridean locations from the Jacobites' plight.

Battle of Falkirk Muir
FALKIRK, SCOTLAND

When Lieutenant General Hawley of the Hanoverians first received warning of a Jacobite attack at Callendar House, he refused to believe it. With the second warning of the attack, he realized the seriousness of the situation and galloped to join his troops. In the rushed chaos, Hawley's men lost some artillery in a boggy area before reaching the battle site. There, confused troops panicked and the battle ended with a victory for the Jacobites, one last significant win of the Jacobite Rising. Take a walk from Callendar House to the Falkirk Muir 1746 Monument.

Battle of Culloden
INVERNESS, SCOTLAND

This brief but bloody battle in 1746 marked the final defeat of Charles Edward Stuart's bid to reclaim the British crown. After their charge across the bleak Culloden Moor failed to break the Duke of Cumberland's government army, Charles's outnumbered troops fled, leaving Cumberland to conduct a brutal pursuit. From the award-winning visitors' center you can walk around the very site of this historic battlefield. Flags mark the positions of the two armies, and you get an excellent sense of how the uneven, boggy ground affected the fighting.

RIGHT You can clearly visualize how the battle unfolded on a walk around Culloden Battlefield.

Battle of the Plains of Abraham (Battle of Quebec)

QUEBEC CITY, QUEBEC, CANADA

Explore Battlefields Park, where the future of Canada was determined.

◆ **DISTANCE**
3 miles

◆ **START**
Battlefields Park

◆ **TYPE OF WALK**
Easy; footpaths

◆ **WHEN TO GO**
All year

ABOVE RIGHT Battlefields Park
has many relics from the war
fought here between the English
and the French.

RIGHT A view over the
St. Lawrence River shows
the strategic importance of
Quebec City.

While English settlements in North America expanded rapidly in the seventeenth and eighteenth centuries, the French population in Canada remained sparse. Britain kept its eye on Quebec, valuable for its timber resources and furs, and launched several unsuccessful campaigns to capture its capital.

In 1759, having taken control of Atlantic Canada, General James Wolfe and his troops began a three-month siege that climaxed with their victory at the Battle of the Plains of Abraham, fought on a plateau owned by a farmer named Abraham Martin just outside the walls of Quebec City. There were fewer than 10,000 combatants and the battle lasted just an hour but proved the decisive moment in the conflict between France and Britain over the fate of New France and led to the creation of Canada. Both Wolfe and French General Louis-Joseph de Montcalm were killed in the battle.

The site of the battle, now Battlefields Park towering above the St. Lawrence River, is a wonderful place to visit year-round and is packed with old cannons, monuments, information boards, and Martello towers. For the complete story, start your walk with a visit to the Musée des Plaines d'Abraham in the park's northeast corner, which thoroughly explores the pivotal battle that shaped Quebec's destiny.

Battle of Plassey

PALASHI, WEST BENGAL, INDIA

On June 23, 1757, the British East India Company under Robert Clive ("Clive of India") defeated the Nawab of Bengal at the village of Palashi. This victory enabled the company to seize control of Bengal and helped to pave the way for the British colonization of much of South Asia. Part of the battlefield has since been washed away by a river, but a patch of open land next to an orchard survives. There are several monuments and shrines here, including a series of obelisks marking the spots where the Nawab's key soldiers were killed.

Fall of Ayutthaya

AYUTTHAYA, THAILAND

For half a millennium, the island city of Ayutthaya was the capital of Siam (now Thailand), home to over a million people and a fabulously rich trading port. In the late eighteenth century, Burma (now Myanmar), seeking to control the coast and its trade, attacked Ayutthaya; the city and kingdom fell in 1767. Buildings were razed, treasures looted or burned, and thousands of citizens were enslaved. Siamese independence was restored within a year and the capital moved to Bangkok; Ayutthaya was left largely abandoned for decades. Spend a good half-day walking through the UNESCO-listed temple ruins strewn across the modern city of Ayutthaya.

Battle of Ponte Novu

CORSICA, FRANCE

Pasquale Paoli liberated Corsica from the Genoese and founded the Corsican Republic in 1755. However, this independence was short-lived. Louis XV of France sent an expeditionary army to the island in May 1769. Troops under the command of the Comte de Vaux fought the local Corsican forces led by Paoli's second-in-command Carlo Salicetti and defeated them at Ponte Novu. Paoli fled to Britain and Corsica was incorporated into France. Time your walk around Ponte Novu with the annual ceremony each May that commemorates this battle.

Battle of Chesma

ÇEŞME, IZMIR PROVINCE, TURKEY

The battle of Chesma, fought off the coast of the Turkish city of Çeşme in 1770, was a decisive engagement of the six-year-long Russo-Turkish War. In a bid to draw the Ottomans' attention away from their Black Sea fleet, Russia sent several squadrons from the Baltic Sea to the Aegean Sea. The plan worked, the Turks moved sixty vessels up to Çeşme Bay and the Russians opened fire, wiping out the Ottoman fleet. From the city center, walk to Çeşme Castle, a majestic Genoese-built fortress bombarded during the attack.

ABOVE RIGHT AND RIGHT The majestic Çeşme Castle with views over the Aegean Sea.

Battles of Lexington and Concord

LEXINGTON AND CONCORD, MASSACHUSETTS

Walk the Battle Road Trail from Lexington to Concord where the American Revolutionary War began.

◆ **DISTANCE**
6 miles

◆ **START**
Lexington or Concord
Visitor Center

◆ **TYPE OF WALK**
Easy; park trail

◆ **WHEN TO GO**
All year

ABOVE RIGHT North Bridge, in Minute Man National Historical Park.

RIGHT A memorial to the British soldiers along Battle Road.

Discontent raged in the Massachusetts Bay Colony during the 1770s as Britain increased both taxes and control over its most rebellious colony.

On April 19, 1775, this discontent flared into fighting. Along a stretch of country road west of Boston, 1,500 British troops and 4,000 colonial militia, known as "minutemen," engaged in the first battles of the American Revolutionary War.

The British opened fire first, just after dawn on Lexington Green, killing eight colonists. At North Bridge in the nearby town of Concord, in what would become known as "the shot heard round the world," minutemen returned fire after British soldiers shot and killed two of them. By early afternoon, the British began to retreat to Boston, arriving in the early evening after several skirmishes. The British counted 73 dead and 227 injured or missing. Colonial casualties numbered 93.

Must-see sites include Lexington's Battle Green, a peaceful triangle of grass with its famous minuteman statue, and North Bridge in Concord, where colonial America first fought back. Linking the two is the five-mile Battle Road Trail running though Minute Man National Historical Park. British soldiers used part of it to march from Boston to Concord, and it's packed with monuments, sites, and buildings related to the battles.

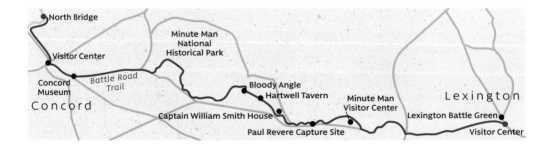

Near Here Are Buried
British Soldiers

April 19, 1775

Battle of Bunker Hill

BOSTON, MASSACHUSETTS

The Battle of Bunker Hill took place on June 17, 1775, during the Siege of Boston in the American Revolutionary War. The colonists were defeated at a great loss to the British—one-third of their deployed forces were killed. The battle proved that the colonists could hold their own against the superior British Army and that any reconciliation between the two was no longer possible. Climb the 294 steps to the top of the Bunker Hill Monument, a 220-foot granite obelisk. Opposite is the Bunker Hill Museum, with a 360-degree mural depicting the battle.

Battle of Trenton

TRENTON, NEW JERSEY

By the end of 1776, after a string of defeats, morale among the Continental Army had sunk to its lowest ebb. In an attempt to lift his men's spirits, George Washington led them across the icy Delaware River and on to Trenton, New Jersey, where they caught a garrison of 1,500 Hessian mercenaries off guard, capturing two-thirds of them. The Trenton Battle Monument is a 150-foot-tall granite column topped with a statue of George Washington. From here, head 10 miles northwest to Washington Crossing State Park, which has lovely marked trails through the woods.

Siege of Ticonderoga

TICONDEROGA, NEW YORK

In 1775, a small revolutionary force of Green Mountain Boys under Ethan Allen and Benedict Arnold, the colonel who would turn traitor at the end of American Revolution, captured a small British garrison at this fort. The British turned the tables two years later when an 8,000-strong army occupied the high ground above the fort, and the Continental Army's force of 3,000 withdrew without a pitched battle. Visit Fort Ticonderoga and its gardens then follow the two-mile Carillon Battlefield Hiking Trail into the nearby woods.

Battle of Saratoga

STILLWATER, NEW YORK

This battle consisted of two engagements: one at Freeman's Farm in September 1777 ending with a British victory under General John Burgoyne, and a second eighteen days later at Bemis Heights with a decisive win for the Americans led by Benedict Arnold. Saratoga was Britain's first major defeat in the American War of Independence and encouraged France to join the conflict. The NPS Saratoga National Historical Park counts four hiking trails, including the four-mile Wilkinson Trail, which passes many of the sites associated with the battle.

LEFT The view from Fort Ticonderoga is the same as it was in the eighteenth century.

Battle of Germantown

PHILADELPHIA, PENNSYLVANIA

Learn about George Washington's battle tactics in the Valley Forge National Historical Park.

◆ **DISTANCE**
8.7 miles

◆ **START**
Park Visitor Center

◆ **TYPE OF WALK**
Easy to moderate

◆ **WHEN TO GO**
All year

ABOVE RIGHT The National Memorial Arch at Valley Forge National Historical Park.

RIGHT The house at Valley Forge where Washington overwintered and retrained his troops.

After British commander-in-chief William Howe captured Philadelphia—then the American capital—he moved the bulk of his force of 9,000 troops to Germantown, a village to the west.

George Washington, head of the Continental Army, sensed an opportunity. He divided his army of 11,000 men so as to attack the British on October 4, 1777, from multiple directions at dawn, as he had done at Trenton the year before. But a heavy fog delayed the advance and cost him the element of surprise. The British took advantage of the confusion and quickly gained the upper hand. The Americans retreated under cover of darkness, having lost 700 men. The British suffered some 500 casualties of their own.

Despite the defeat, many Europeans, especially the French, were impressed by the determination of Washington's army and increased their support. Washington, his army intact, withdrew to Valley Forge, 20 miles to the west, where he wintered and retrained his forces.

Valley Forge National Historical Park is a symbol of Washington's endurance and leadership. It has more than 35 miles of designated hiking trails. The paved 8.7-mile Joseph Plumb Martin Trail connects many of the key historic and interpretive sites in the park, including historical buildings, re-created encampment structures, memorials, and museums.

Battle of Kings Mountain
BLACKSBURG, SOUTH CAROLINA

Most of the Revolutionary War was fought in the north. In 1780, the British turned south, expecting to meet up with loyalist militias. They did just that at Kings Head but were defeated in one hour by the patriots. A two-mile trail at the NPS Kings Mountain National Military Park encircles the battlefield.

Siege of Yorktown
YORKTOWN, VIRGINIA

The Continental Army's victory at Yorktown in 1781 was the last major battle of the American Revolution. The surrender of General Charles Cornwallis led Britain to sue for peace. At the NPS Yorktown Battlefield site, there are self-guided driving tour routes totaling 16 miles, some of which can be explored on foot.

Invasion of Menorca
MAHÓN (MAÓ), MENORCA, BALEARIC ISLANDS, SPAIN

In the eighteenth century, the Mediterranean island of Menorca was ruled by the British, but naturally, the Spanish crown wasn't happy about this. Teaming up with the French in 1781, the Spanish launched an invasion of the island and kicked the Brits out. Following the coastline from the port town of Maó to the fortress of St. Philip, this three-mile walk retraces the Franco-Spanish invasion of Menorca and, alongside history, it offers some beautiful coastal views.

Battle of Focșani
FOCȘANI, VRANCEA COUNTY, ROMANIA

In 1789, the combined forces of the Russian Empire and the Habsburg Monarchy were able to accomplish in Moldavia what Eugene of Savoy had done in Zenta (then in Hungary) almost a century before: drive the Turks out. The Battle of Focșani lasted but seven hours; the allies stormed the Ottomans' entrenched camp with a huge army and drove them out, killing 1,500 men. The exact location of the battle is unclear. Walk around what's left of Focșani's old town and head for the Union Museum, which has exhibits with details of the battle.

BELOW The Corsican town of Calvi, which was under siege for several weeks.

St. Clair's Defeat
FORT RECOVERY, OHIO

Arthur St. Clair, governor of the Northwest Territories, suffered a defeat in 1791 that was possibly the worst loss of U.S. forces to Native Americans in history. Caught napping by a surprise morning attack by an alliance of Miami, Shawnee, and Delaware, St. Clair retreated under heavy arrow fire, abandoning the wounded and leaving arms and other equipment behind. Just twenty-four men got away without injury. Two years later, the same spot would become a U.S. victory. A replica stockade and museum are at the site, and you can walk through Fort Park to the river, where the original battle began.

Siege of Calvi
CORSICA, FRANCE

Using the French Revolution to renew his ambitions for an independent Corsica, the exiled Pasquale Paoli appealed to the British for help. A joint British-Corsican force, which included a small squadron led by Captain Horatio Nelson, arrived in Corsica in 1794, landed at Saint-Florent, and captured the remote harbor town. This was followed by a successful siege and capture of Bastia and then on to the final French stronghold, the heavily fortified town of Calvi. The town was under siege for several weeks, with steady fire from both sides—it was during this battle that Nelson was blinded in one eye, but after being treated he returned to action. Walk around the towns' preserved fortifications and the beaches.

Battle of Arklow

ARKLOW, COUNTY WICKLOW, IRELAND

Wander around the seaside town where the
Irish Rebellion met too great a resistance.

◆ **DISTANCE**
7.5 miles

◆ **START**
Seaview Avenue

◆ **TYPE OF WALK**
Half-day walk

◆ **WHEN TO GO**
All year

ABOVE RIGHT There's a breezy walking path behind South Beach in Arklow.

RIGHT Explore the jetty protecting the harbor's entrance by South Beach.

In 1798, a secular, underground organization known as the Society of United Irishmen launched a rebellion with the aim of cutting Ireland's connection with Great Britain and establishing an Irish republic.

In most areas of the country, the uprisings were unsuccessful, but in Wexford, the United Irishmen took control of the town. They followed this with an assault on Arklow to the north, sending 10,000 men to attack the British-held town, which was garrisoned with only around 1,700 men. The rebels' plan was to approach from all directions. The government troops, however, with vastly superior firepower to the pikes of the rebels, slaughtered hundreds, including one of the rebel leaders, Father Michael Murphy.

Lacking ammunition and leadership and with morale dented by the large number of casualties, the remaining rebels retreated over the Avoca River under the cover of nightfall. The government forces were then able to take back control of Wexford and effectively quash the Irish Rebellion.

A circular walk takes you around the town and to the South Beach areas, along roads used by the rebels, past locations where British soldiers were treated for injuries, and to the site of the battle at King's Hill.

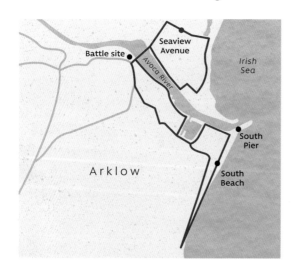

Battle of Vinegar Hill

ENNISCORTHY,
COUNTY WEXFORD,
IRELAND

The Battle of Vinegar Hill on June 21, 1798, effectively broke up the United Irishmen's forces. British soldiers bombarded the Irish camp with new shelling technology, forcing the troops to scatter. Those who could not escape were killed. Take a walk around the hill before visiting the museum in town.

Battle of Collooney

COLLOONEY,
COUNTY SLIGO, IRELAND

During the 1798 rebellion a combined French-Irish army marching toward Sligo was confronted by British troops north of Collooney. Lieutenant Bartholomew Teeling single-handedly disabled the British gunnery by shooting the marksman with a pistol, forcing a British retreat. Walk from the center of town, across the river, and up to the monument dedicated to Teeling.

Siege of Seringapatam

SRIRANGAPATNA, KARNATAKA, INDIA

Walk through the ruins of Tipu Sultan's fort where the "Tiger of Mysore" was slain, a victim of the ruthless commercialism of the East India Company.

♦ **DISTANCE**
0.4 mile

♦ **START**
Tipu Sultan's fort

♦ **TYPE OF WALK**
Easy stroll, mostly along paths

♦ **WHEN TO GO**
The dry, slightly cooler January–March period

ABOVE RIGHT The ruins of Tipu Sultan's fort are an evocative site, with a monument where the Mysore ruler was slain.

RIGHT The obelisk erected at Seringapatam in memory of the British soldiers who fought against Tipu Sultan.

Located on an island in the Kaveri River in the southern state of Karnataka, the fortified city of Seringapatam (or Srirangapatna) was the site of the last battle in the fourth, and final, Anglo-Mysore War between the British East India Company and the Kingdom of Mysore, led by Tipu Sultan.

Dating back to the late 1760s, the conflicts were driven by the company's ruthless commercial and colonial expansion. Seringapatam was the capital of Mysore's ruler, Tipu Sultan, a renowned political and military leader who became known as the "Tiger of Mysore." But after being besieged for a month, the island stronghold finally fell. On May 4, 1799, East India Company soldiers breached the walls, reportedly with the help of a traitor in the Tiger's camp. Tipu Sultan was killed and Seringapatam was captured and looted.

Today, it's easy to bring the siege to life by exploring the ruins of Tipu Sultan's fort and palace, particularly the ramparts, batteries, and the water gate, a secret entrance to the complex. The site where the Mysore ruler was slain is now marked with a monument. You can also visit the riverside bases of the East India Company forces.

Battle of the Pyramids

IMBABA, GIZA, EGYPT

The Battle of the Pyramids of 1798 is so called because it took place at a village within sight of the ancient monuments 10 miles to the southwest. Here, French forces under Napoleon Bonaparte wiped out almost the entire Ottoman army with its base at Cairo's citadel. Climb up to the citadel, on a limestone spur on the city's eastern edge; from there you'll get a not-dissimilar view of the Pyramids to the one the combatants had. As Napoleon himself admonished: "Forward! Remember that from those monuments yonder forty centuries look down upon you."

BELOW When a battle was fought within sight of the Pyramids, Napoleon reminded his troops that they were watched by forty centuries of history.

Second Anglo-Maratha War

CHIKHALDARA, MAHARASHTRA, INDIA

Against the wishes of confederacy leaders in the Maratha Empire, the British signed a treaty to support and restore Baji Rao II, son of a previous fugitive of the empire, as peshwa (prime minister). Prompted by disgust at the influence of the East India Company over India, a second Anglo-Maratha War erupted in 1803. Sir Arthur Wellesley (later Duke of Wellington) defeated the combined Maratha army at the Battle of Assaye, then went on to capture the Gawilghur Fort near Chikhaldara, previously considered unassailable. Walk up to the fort for beautiful views of the mountains and valleys.

Battle of Trafalgar

LONDON, ENGLAND

The Battle of Trafalgar was a naval engagement off southwest Spain in 1805 between the French and Spanish navies, and the British fleet under Admiral Nelson. When he realized his fleet was outnumbered, Nelson rammed his opponents, proclaiming: "England expects that every man will do his duty." Two hours later, he was mortally wounded. In London, visit Trafalgar Square dominated by Nelson's Column; at the top, the admiral looks down the Mall surveying his "fleet"—lampposts topped with little ships. From here walk east to St. Paul's Cathedral; his tomb is in the crypt.

Battle of Santo Domingo

SANTO DOMINGO, DOMINICAN REPUBLIC

Three years into what would become known as the Napoleonic Wars, squadrons of French and British warships clashed at close range off the coast of French-occupied Santo Domingo. The outcome was decisive: the French lost all of their ships and 1,500 men, while the British lost no ships and fewer than 100 sailors died. In Santo Domingo, walk to the UNESCO-listed Ozama Fortress, completed in 1508 and the oldest European military construction in the New World. Just past the entrance is the impressive Torre del Homenaje (Tower of Homage); townspeople would have watched the 1806 battle from its rooftop lookout.

BELOW Townspeople watched the naval battle of Santo Domingo from the Torre del Homenaje.

British Invasions of Buenos Aires

BUENOS AIRES, ARGENTINA

In 1806 and 1807, British forces twice invaded the city of Buenos Aires—then under Spanish colonial rule—during the Napoleonic Wars, but were repelled by local militias on both occasions. During the second invasion there was fierce fighting in the streets of the neighborhoods of Monserrat, San Telmo, and Balvanera in the city center. Walk through them to Plaza Miserere, a leafy square built on the site where the British troops were ultimately defeated in what became known as the Battle of Plaza del Mercado.

Battle of Corunna

A CORUÑA, GALICIA, SPAIN

British troops under the command of General Sir John Moore were forced into a swift retreat when their attempts to help the Spanish in their fight against Napoleon's invading French forces failed. But as the British waited for evacuation ships at Corunna in January 1809, their camp came under attack from the French. In the final moments of the ensuing battle, Moore was mortally wounded and died. Walk along the harbor front where the British ships eventually arrived, to the San Carlos Gardens in the old town, where you'll find Moore's tomb and a lookout over the sea engraved with the Charles Wolfe poem about his death and burial.

BELOW This bustling market street in Buenos Aires was once the site of fierce fighting.

Battle of Wagram
DEUTSCH-WAGRAM, AUSTRIA

The French victory against the Austrians at the Battle of Wagram in 1809 during the Napoleonic Wars was decisive but costly. With almost 25 percent of all soldiers on both sides killed or wounded, the battle was particularly bloody. But it did succeed in breaking up the Austrian- and British-led alliance against France. The battle was fought on the Marchfeld, a large and fertile plain on the north bank of the Danube opposite Vienna, and today Austria's vegetable patch. Little battle evidence remains, but a walk from the village of Aderklaa to the village of Deutsch-Wagram crosses sites where fighting took place. Here, there's now a museum in the building which was the Austrian headquarters.

Battle of Grand Port
MAHÉBOURG, MAURITIUS

The Battle of Grand Port in 1810 was a naval engagement between the French and British on the southeast coast of today's Mauritius (then called Île de France). It was the first and only French naval victory over the British Royal Navy during the Napoleonic Wars. Stroll along the waterfront of Mahébourg, a small town south of Vieux Grand Port; the waters here are littered with shipwrecks from the battle, and there's a Battle of Grand Port Memorial nearby. Then walk to the Historical Naval Museum, housed in the building where injured commanders of both sides were taken.

BELOW The British Royal Navy was roundly defeated at the Battle of Grand Port in Mauritius.

Battle of Buçaco

BUÇACO NATIONAL FOREST, PORTUGAL

Visit the mountainous terrain where this battle was fought and relive Wellington's victory over the French.

◆ **DISTANCE**
10 miles

◆ **START**
Palace Hotel of Buçaco

◆ **TYPE OF WALK**
Full-day hike

◆ **WHEN TO GO**
April–October

BELOW Stones from the convent where Wellington stayed after this battle were used to build the Palace Hotel.

The Peninsular War had been going on for three years, and the British were getting more involved in Portugal and Spain. In 1810, Napoleon ordered Marshal André Masséna to drive the British from Portugal for him, so he could make further advances in Spain.

The French army met Lord Wellington's Anglo-Portuguese troops in the mountain range of Serra do Buçaco. Masséna originally thought he would be able to easily overpower Wellington's troops and ordered a direct attack rather than attempting to go around the main army.

However, Wellington's troops were already occupying the heights of the hills with officers and their charges stationed on the flanks, giving Wellington the advantage over Masséna's men. After a day of fierce battle, large losses in the ranks forced the French to retreat.

A walk in the steep hills of Buçaco National Forest gives you an idea of the terrain on which this battle would have been

fought, and you can clearly see why Wellington would have had the advantage with the ridge. Start and end at the hotel built from the stones of the convent where Wellington spent the night after the battle.

Skirmish at Barba del Puerco

PUERTO SEGURO, SALAMANCA, SPAIN

Being on one of the crossings on the Agueda River, Barba del Puerco (now Puerto Seguro) became a place of many battles during the Peninsular War. A skirmish in 1810 saw the British drive back a nocturnal French assault. Experience the drama with a walk around the Agueda River gorge.

Battle of Albuera

LA ALBUERA, EXTREMADURA, SPAIN

This took place in 1811 during the Peninsular War, which pitted Britain, Spain, and Portugal against France for domination of Iberia. The result was indecisive. The battle was fought in the open plain between Badajoz and La Albuera; walk to the center of the latter, where a memorial was unveiled in 2001.

LEFT The Buçaco National Forest has beautiful walking trails around the site of the nineteenth-century battle.

Battle of Tippecanoe
BATTLE GROUND, INDIANA

The Battle of Tippecanoe in 1811 erupted when Indiana governor William Henry Harrison—later the ninth American president—and his men attacked the headquarters of a confederacy of Indians associated with the Shawnee leader Tecumseh. It was an American victory though Tecumseh continued to play a key role in military operations on the frontier until his death two years later. The Tippecanoe Battlefield and Museum is a National Historic Landmark located in a 96-acre park. Hiking trails link sites associated with the battle, including an 85-foot obelisk marking the battle site.

Battle of Salamanca
ARAPILES, SALAMANCA, SPAIN

In 1812, having already forced the troops of French Marshal Auguste de Marmont out of Portugal, Lieutenant-General Arthur Wellesley—by this time Earl of Wellington—marched to confront them at Salamanca, an important supply center for the French troops. After several weeks of cat and mouse maneuvers, the two sides met south of the city at Arapiles, where Wellington successfully used the valleys and ridges to his advantage, waiting to see Marmont's tactics before committing his men. Wellington won the battle and was able to march on to liberate Madrid. There are many walking trails around the plains near Arapiles where the battle took place.

Battle of Borodino
BORODINO, MOSCOW OBLAST, RUSSIA

Wanting to force Russia back into the continental blockade, Napoleon ordered an invasion of Russia in 1812 with the multinational Grande Armée. After a fierce engagement at Borodino, Russian General Kutuzov saw the declining condition of his troops and decided to withdraw from the battlefield. This gave the Grande Armée the victory they needed to then occupy Moscow. A walk around the woods of Borodino with its military monuments reveals the many battles this small village endured.

LEFT The countryside around Borodino is full of battle memorials from across the ages.

Battle of the Thames
BOTHWELL, ONTARIO, CANADA

The War of 1812 between the United States and Britain is seldom remembered in the UK but is considered a "second war of independence" in America. In 1813, the British occupied Detroit; the U.S. Navy on Lake Erie cut them off and they fled up the Thames River into Ontario with their Indian allies under Tecumseh. General William Henry Harrison pursued them and attacked, killing Tecumseh. Fairfield on the Thames National Historic Site marks the village destroyed by the American forces. Monuments linked to the battle can be found along a two-mile walk of the area.

Battle of the Pyrenees

SAN SEBASTIÁN, GIPUZKOA, SPAIN

The Battle of the Pyrenees (1813) was launched in the unsuccessful hope of relieving the French garrisons who were under siege at Pamplona and San Sebastián. There were a number of different battle sites throughout the western Pyrenees and the luminous green Basque Country. As the focus of the action was the gorgeous beach city and culinary wonder of San Sebastián, start there at Zurriola Beach, from where you can head up onto the cliffs and follow a coastal path past a secret bay or two, before descending down into the natural harbor of Pasaia, a classic half-day experience.

Battle of Leipzig
LEIPZIG, SAXONY, GERMANY

Also called the Battle of the Nations due to the large coalition of countries involved, this engagement in 1813 during the Napoleonic Wars involved 560,000 soldiers and 2,200 artillery pieces, making it the largest battle in Europe before World War I. On the very spot of some of the bloodiest fighting and from where Napoleon ordered his army to retreat stands the awesome Monument to the Battle of the Nations, completed in 1913 for the battle's centenary. Walk around the base of the 300-foot-tall monument and up its 500 steps to a platform and breathtaking views at the top.

Battle of Bayonne
BAYONNE, BASQUE COUNTRY, FRANCE

The last major battle of the Peninsular War, the Battle of Bayonne in 1814 pitched French troops against a besieging army of British, Portuguese, and Spanish soldiers. As with many battles, there wasn't much justification for this fight. Days earlier, Napoleon had abdicated and the French had little to gain by launching the attack against the besieging forces. After initial success, the French were pushed back into Bayonne with heavy loss of life. This walk takes in the sturdy ramparts surrounding the gorgeous old town of Bayonne. Allow yourself half a day to truly appreciate this small city.

BELOW The awe-inspiring Monument to the Battle of the Nations in Leipzig, Germany.

Battle of Horseshoe Bend

NEAR DADEVILLE, DAVISTON, ALABAMA

Take a walk around the horseshoe-shaped bend of the Tallapoosa River which was so fatal to the Red Sticks.

◆ **DISTANCE**
2.5 miles

◆ **START**
Horseshoe Bend
visitors' center

◆ **TYPE OF WALK**
Mostly flat walk
on pavement

◆ **WHEN TO GO**
All year

RIGHT Fort Jackson, from where Andrew Jackson and his men planned their attack.

Andrew Jackson would go on to become the seventh president of the United States, but the test of his mettle was in the Creek War, a battle between two warring factions of Creek tribes.

The Red Sticks fought against the Lower Creek nation, which allied itself with Jackson to help defeat its foe. However, when Jackson's alliance was victorious, he forced both Creek factions to sign a contract that ceded control of much of modern-day Alabama and parts of Georgia.

The decisive battle was that of Horseshoe Bend in 1814, where Jackson defeated the Red Stick forces in a multi-pronged attack that included Lower Creek tribes. The Red Sticks were camped in a bend of thc Tallapoosa River, and Jackson had one brigade cross the river while others attacked with cannons and bayonets. Around 80 percent of the Red Sticks were slaughtered, while Jackson lost only about fifty men.

Today, the site is a national park. From the visitors' center, a 2.5-mile walk crosses a field, skirts the river where the brigade crossed, and circles back up through some forest, before connecting again with the field.

Tallapoosa River

Visitors' Center

Horseshoe Bend National Military Park

Alabama

294

Battle of Baltimore

BALTIMORE, MARYLAND

This 1814 battle during the War of 1812 is celebrated in the United States not because it was an American victory over the British but because the resistance of the city's Fort McHenry inspired Francis Scott Key to compose the words to what would eventually become the national anthem. The dramatic seawall trail loops around the National Park Service's McHenry National Monument.

295

Battle of New Orleans

CHALMETTE, LOUISIANA

This 1815 battle lives on not because it was an American victory over the British eighteen days after the War of 1812 ended, but because the song "The Battle of New Orleans" from 1959 is still playing in many minds. The NPS Chalmette Battlefield, south of New Orleans, has a reconstructed rampart and outdoor exhibits for self-guided tours.

Battle of Waterloo

HAMEAU DU LION, BRAINE-L'ALLEUD, BELGIUM

Climb up the Butte du Lion for a bird's-eye view of the field that foxed Napoleon at the Battle of Waterloo.

◆ **DISTANCE**
2.5 miles

◆ **START**
Memorial 1815

◆ **TYPE OF WALK**
Easy; multiple steps

◆ **WHEN TO GO**
All year

ABOVE RIGHT Steps lead to the top of the Butte du Lion monument for views over the battlefield of Waterloo.

RIGHT The perfect symmetry of the Butte du Lion monument.

On June 18, 1815, the French army under Napoleon was defeated by a British-led coalition led by the Duke of Wellington and Field Marshal Gebhard von Blücher's Prussian army. The battle result was hardly a foregone conclusion; "the nearest-run thing you ever saw in your life" was how Wellington assessed it later. It began at around 11:00 a.m. with roughly 70,000 troops on each side desperately fighting for territory. Historians believe that without the arrival of Blücher at the eleventh hour—4:30 p.m. to be precise—the Battle of Waterloo might have gone the other way. But when it was over, Napoleon's dreams of conquering Europe had been shattered.

The main battlefield site is known as Hameau du Lion (Lion Hamlet), three miles south of central Waterloo town. It contains a number of sights and museums, notably the Memorial 1815, an underground museum and visitors' center at the battlefield built to mark the bicentenary. However, the best way to appreciate the lie of the land is to climb the 225 steps up the Butte du Lion (Lion Mound), a grassy cone topped by a bronze lion. From here you can survey the battlefield's deceptively minor undulations that flummoxed Napoleon's infantry.

Peterloo Massacre

ST. PETER'S SQUARE, MANCHESTER, ENGLAND

In August 1819, about 50,000 people gathered in St. Peter's Fields, Manchester, demanding the reform of Parliament. Cavalry charged them with sabers, killing eighteen and wounding 400. The event became known as Peterloo, in ironic reference to the Battle of Waterloo. Walk around St. Peter's Square, the site of the massacre, where the striking Peterloo Memorial by Jeremy Deller was unveiled to mark the bicentenary in 2019.

Battle of Boyacá
NEAR TUNJA, COLOMBIA

On August 7, 1819, the forces of "El Libertador" Simón Bolívar won a decisive victory over Spanish troops, opening up the route to Bogotá and securing the independence of Nueva Granada (modern-day Colombia and Venezuela). Walk along the Teatinos River, where the battle took place, where there is now a collection of monuments. They include the reconstructed Boyacá bridge, built to replace the eighteenth-century original, which was nearly destroyed in the battle, plus a triumphal arch, a sculpture of Bolívar, and a chapel.

299

The Black War
HOBART, TASMANIA, AUSTRALIA

Relations between European colonizers and Australian Aborigines were hostile from the moment the Europeans arrived and made claims on land that didn't belong to them. Between the mid-1820s and 1832, violent conflict erupted between the Aborigines and the colonizers in Tasmania (then called Van Diemen's Land). Martial law was declared, which almost annihilated the Indigenous population. Walk the Hobart waterfront, then up the main street to Old Government House to follow the route taken in 1832 by the small number of Aboriginal clans on their way to negotiate an end to the Black War.

RIGHT The Hobart waterfront in Tasmania, where Aboriginal clans passed on their way to end the war.

Anglo-Ashanti Wars

PRINCES TOWN, GHANA

Take in the contrast between a tropical beach paradise and a grim slave fort along Ghana's stunning coastline.

◆ **DISTANCE**
3 miles

◆ **START**
Princes Town

◆ **TYPE OF WALK**
Half-day beach walk

◆ **WHEN TO GO**
October–March

ABOVE RIGHT The imposing entrance to Fort Groot Fredericksborg overlooks a grassy courtyard.

RIGHT The beach by Princes Town offers soft sand for a walk.

The coastline of the West African nation of Ghana is one long sweep of idyllic yellow sands backed by tens of thousands of palms that bend and bow in the sea breeze like seductive dancers. It should be a vision of paradise, but if it is then it's a scarred paradise, because all along this coastline stands a string of imposing forts, used as both defensive positions and to store slaves.

Several major battles took place along this coast between the British, who had colonial expansion in mind, and the Ashanti Empire, who were the most powerful kingdom in the region at the time. Together they were known as the Anglo-Ashanti Wars. The first of these, in 1824, was an especially brutal affair in which almost the entire British force was wiped out and one of the few survivors was imprisoned in a room containing the decapitated heads of his former military commanders.

Although there are no walking routes focused exclusively on these battle sites, it is possible to walk around some of the forts. One of the best focuses on Fort Groot Fredericksborg, on a luxuriantly green headland just outside the small town of Princes Town. Start your walk from the beach lagoon a few minutes west of Princes Town and walk barefoot across the sands to the headland on which the fort is sited, climb up to this and poke about its mildewed corners before descending off the headland to the east. You can then walk as far as you like along the near-deserted beach to the east of Princes Town, which is backed by a lagoon.

Battle of Pichincha

QUITO, ECUADOR

This trail brings to life a short, sharp confrontation on the side of a volcano that secured Ecuador's freedom from Spain.

◆ **DISTANCE**
8 miles

◆ **START**
Plaza Grande

◆ **TYPE OF WALK**
Moderate to hard, mostly uphill and at altitude—make sure you are acclimatized before setting off

◆ **WHEN TO GO**
All year, though June–September is the driest period

Fought at altitude on the slopes of the eponymous volcano in May 1822, the Battle of Pichincha freed the city and administrative region of Quito from Spanish colonial rule, paving the way for the creation of the independent nation of Ecuador.

After an arduous march from the coast, the rebel forces of General Antonio José de Sucre climbed to a breathless 11,500 feet above sea level before royalist soldiers spotted them, pursued them up the Pichincha volcano, and opened fire. An intense three-hour battle ensued, with heavy losses for both sides, until General Sucre's men forced their opponents to retreat. They then advanced to the outskirts of Quito, which swiftly surrendered.

Today, it is possible to walk in the footsteps of General Sucre's forces. Start in Quito's Plaza Grande (Plaza de la Independencia), a large square home to a towering column celebrating Ecuador's hard-won independence, before walking northwest up the lower slopes of Pichincha to the Cima de la Libertad, a monument marking the site of the fighting. Continue up to the cable-car station, which provides a panoramic vantage point for surveying the battlefield below.

ABOVE RIGHT Hikers near the summit of Pichincha, the volcano on the outskirts of Quito, Ecuador.

RIGHT It was after a battle at 11,500 feet that Sucre's rebels won Ecuador's freedom.

Chile's War of Independence

FUERTE SAN ANTONIO, ANCUD, CHILE

This eighteenth-century fort in the Chiloé archipelago was the last refuge of Spanish colonial forces in Chile until they were finally turfed out on January 19, 1826. A short, windswept walk takes you along the fort's sturdy, reconstructed walls to see several vintage cannons.

French Conquest of Algeria

ALGIERS, ALGERIA

The conquest of Algeria by the French took over seven decades and cost hundreds of thousands of lives. The origins of the dispute date back to 1827, when the regent of Algeria and the French consulate had an argument. The former struck the latter with his flyswatter, precipitating a three-year naval blockade, which hurt the French more than the Algerians. In 1830, French forces invaded and took Algiers after a three-week campaign. Walk along the marina in the port of Sidi Fredj (then Sidi Ferruch) where the French had their beachhead and the invasion began.

Battle of Konya

KONYA, KONYA PROVINCE, TURKEY

This battle in 1832 pitted Egypt and Turkey against each other, hastening the decline of the Ottoman Empire. Egypt had set out the year before to seize Syria, mopping up Jerusalem and coastal Palestine and Lebanon too. The final battle came at Konya where, though outnumbered two to one, the Egyptians were victorious. The battle took place alongside the Konya-Constantinople Road, just north of the ancient walled town. The battlefield is a plateau lying between hills to the west and marshes and swamps to the east. It's an effortless walk, although there's little to recall the battle site.

Waterloo Creek Massacre

MOREE, NEW SOUTH WALES, AUSTRALIA

During the frontier wars, as retaliation for five stockmen killed by the Namoi, Weraerai, and Kamilaroi people, a troop of mounted police officers tracked down and killed up to fifty Kamilaroi people between December 1837 and January 1838. The inquiry into the incident was dropped due to a lack of solid eyewitness accounts. The actual site of the massacre is vague, but take a walk around Moree and visit the Dhiiyaan Aboriginal Centre to learn more about the culture.

Dogra-Tibetan War

LADAKH, INDIA

This high-altitude battle, which raged from 1841 to 1842, was between a Sikh army and a Tibetan army over control of the trans-Himalayan region of Ladakh and its lucrative trade routes. Although the Sikhs initiated the battle, they were quickly defeated. However, Sikh reinforcements were sent and the tide swung the other way. In the end, a treaty was signed that maintained the status quo. Ladakh offers many world-class trekking routes that take in soaring Himalayan scenery, shimmering lakes, and ancient monasteries.

RIGHT Walk across Devil's Bridge at the site of the Battle of Konya.

Battle of the Alamo

SAN ANTONIO, TEXAS

Stroll around the battle sites that have taken on almost mythological proportions in the Lone Star State.

◆ **DISTANCE**
1.5 miles

◆ **START**
Visitors' center

◆ **TYPE OF WALK**
Easy; footpaths

◆ **WHEN TO GO**
All year

ABOVE RIGHT The Alamo Cenotaph at the Alamo Mission.

RIGHT The Alamo Church has been standing since 1755.

In February 1836, anywhere from 1,800 to 6,000 Mexican troops under General Antonio López de Santa Anna attacked the Alamo Mission at San Antonio de Béxar. After thirteen days' pounding, it was taken and all 189 defenders—including such legendary figures as Jim Bowie and Davy Crockett—were brutally killed.

Santa Anna's cruelty prompted many republican Texians and Tejanos to join the Texian Army. Just a month later, they defeated the Mexican Army at the Battle of San Jacinto. The newly formed Republic of Texas would last almost a decade, until it joined the Union as the twenty-eighth state in 1845.

Built as a mission in 1755, today's complex contains only two buildings—the Alamo Chapel and Long Barrack—which featured in the battle of 1836. Efforts are being made to reclaim the footprint of the battlefield beneath the concrete of the plaza. In the meantime, a stroll around the grounds will take you past the historical buildings and exhibition halls. Just half a mile to the west over the San Antonio River is San Fernando Cathedral. A sarcophagus inside is said to contain the ashes of the Alamo defenders.

Battle of Okeechobee

LAKE OKEECHOBEE, FLORIDA

In 1837, Seminole Indians resisting forced relocation to an Oklahoma reservation were attacked at Lake Okeechobee by a militia led by Colonel Zachary Taylor, the future twelfth president of the United States. Both sides claimed victory. The Okeechobee Battlefield Historic State Park has several trails that follow sections of the battle site along the lake.

Battle of Blood River, Boer-Zulu War

NCOME-BLOOD RIVER HERITAGE SITE, KWAZULU-NATAL, SOUTH AFRICA

On December 16, 1838, 464 Voortrekkers (Boers) and their servants commanded by Andries Pretorius defeated King Dingane's 10,000-strong Zulu *impi* (army) led by Ndlela kaSompisi. The Voortrekkers formed a defensive *laager* (encampment) by lashing ox-wagons together in a ring, from which they shot mercilessly at the Zulus, killing 3,000 as they fled across the Ncome River that ran red with blood. No Voortrekkers died and only three were injured. Today visitors can walk around a replica laager of bronze wagons and the Ncome Monument and Museum which commemorates the Zulus who fell in the battle.

Flagstaff War

RUSSELL, NORTHLAND, NEW ZEALAND

Discover how a flagstaff intended for friendship became the symbol of Māori rebellion on a walk amid beautiful scenery.

◆ **DISTANCE**
3.8 miles

◆ **START**
Russell Museum

◆ **TYPE OF WALK**
Half-day walk

◆ **WHEN TO GO**
All year

LEFT The walk up Flagstaff Hill offers great views over the Bay of Islands.

The Treaty of Waitangi of 1840 gave Māoris the right to undisturbed possession of their lands, forests, fisheries, and treasures in return for becoming British subjects. However, what has been described as a translation misunderstanding in the Māori language version of the treaty caused great disagreement over the intention of the treaty, which hindered pre-treaty land sales from going ahead.

Conflict in parts of the affected areas between government troops and Māori fighters turned into a series of battles and wars throughout New Zealand from 1845 to 1846.

Hōne Heke, an influential chief, incited war by cutting down the flagstaff on Flagstaff Hill at Kororāreka numerous times as a challenge to the British authorities; the flagstaff had been the chief's own gift of friendship to New Zealand's first British resident, and government representative, James Busby. After cutting it for the fourth time, Hōne Heke led fighters into the town to attack British defenses, starting the war. Various battles broke out in many areas, including a direct attack at Hōne Heke's settlement.

From the town of Russell (formerly Kororáreka), walk up trails surrounding Flagstaff Hill and northward along the Tapeka Point Track for great views of the Bay of Islands.

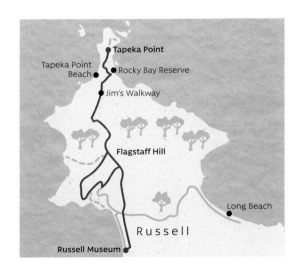

Tapeka Point

Tapeka Point Beach

Rocky Bay Reserve

Jim's Walkway

Flagstaff Hill

Long Beach

Russell

Russell Museum

Fort de l'Îlette de Kermorvan

BRITTANY, FRANCE

Guarding the entrance to Le Conquet, a small beach and fishing town in western Brittany, l'Îlette de Kermorvan has been inhabited since prehistoric times but the scant remains of the fort date only to the 1800s. Today, a fabulous, marked three-hour walk takes in the windblown Plage des Blancs Sablons, the river bordering Le Conquet and the islet and fort itself (though this can only be reached at low tide).

Battle of Buena Vista

SALTILLO, COAHUILA STATE, MEXICO

The Battle of Buena Vista (or La Angostura) in 1847 was an inconclusive skirmish during the two-year Mexican-American War. It pitted 4,500 American troops under General Zachary Taylor against a Mexican army three times that size led by Alamo veteran General Antonio López de Santa Anna. The battle took place at La Angostura (the narrow pass) near the village of Buena Vista, but the battle site is not accessible. Instead explore Saltillo, eight miles north, where the Battle of La Angostura Museum recalls what it portrays as the triumph of Mexico over the United States.

Battle of Cerro Gordo

XALAPA, VERACRUZ STATE, MEXICO

Two months after the stalemate at Buena Vista, General Santa Anna led more than 12,000 soldiers against American forces of the same size at Cerro Gordo in Veracruz. The Mexicans were outflanked and suffered high casualties; the Americans went on to occupy Mexico City. The battle took place at an inaccessible mountain pass called La Atalaya, 30 miles east of Xalapa. Walk through the latter's old town; an obelisk located between the Church of San José and Alcalde y García Market commemorates Ambrosio Alcalde and Antonio García, two Xalapeños who were executed here after the battle.

Battle of Mestre

MESTRE, VENETO, ITALY

In 1848, Italian volunteers attacked and looted the Fort of Marghera in Mestre on the Venetian mainland, which had been occupied by Austrian troops since June that year. Serving as an important link between the Venetian lagoon and the mainland, the fort later became an integral part of the city's extensive defensive system, known as the Campo Trincerato di Mestre. Built on marshy land on the edge of the lagoon, the fort is in the shape of a six-pointed star. You can walk along its outer walls, soaking up views of Mestre and beyond.

RIGHT The stunning cathedral in Saltillo, Mexico, where there is also a Battle of La Angostura Museum.

Battle of Bicocca

NOVARA, PIEDMONT, ITALY

The Battle of Bicocca (also known as the Battle of Novara) was fought during the First Italian War of Independence in 1849, between the Austrian Empire and the Kingdom of Piedmont-Sardinia, resulting in the defeat of the Piedmontese. Start your walk at Novara's Chiesa della Bicocca, where you can see a cannonball lodged in the facade, then head south to visit the Ossuary housing the remains of the fallen. Stop at Villa Monrepos, whose gated entrance damaged by cannonballs has become a symbol of the battle, and continue your walk south to various farmhouses that still show the marks of bullets on their walls.

Battle of Temesvár

TIMIȘOARA, TIMIȘ COUNTY, ROMANIA

Hungary's 1848–1849 attempt to free itself from the Habsburg Empire gained momentum in its first year, and the country even declared itself free. But the new Habsburg emperor, Franz Joseph, grew impatient and sought the assistance of Tsar Nicholas I, who obliged with tens of thousands of troops. The Hungarians were defeated at the Battle of Temesvár in August 1849, with much fighting around the castle. Explore what's left of Timișoara's fortress on foot, including Huniade Castle, which now houses a local museum, the Theresia Bastion, with wine bars and restaurants, a casemate, and a small part of the curtain wall.

Taiping Rebellion

NANJING, JIANGSU, CHINA

Hong Xiuquan, a Hakka-Chinese revolutionary and self-proclaimed brother of Jesus, had a vision to convert the Han Chinese to Christianity as a way to overthrow the Manchu-led Qing dynasty. Between 1850 and 1864, his army, known as the Taipings, fought and occupied much of the Yangtze valley, massacring Manchurians along the way, believing them to be demons. Eventually, Hong's armies were defeated by groups of decentralized Qing troops, and the rebellion ended after the death of Hong. This rebellion weakened the status of the Qing dynasty, which collapsed less than fifty years later. Walk around Nanjing, where the Taiping rebels had established their short-lived Heavenly Kingdom.

Battle of Sinop

SINOP, SINOP PROVINCE, TURKEY

On November 30, 1853, a Russian armada attacked a squadron of Ottoman ships anchored in Sinop harbor on the Black Sea. The ambush left some 3,000 Turks dead against three dozen Russian casualties. The battle sparked the Crimean War, in which the Ottomans allied themselves with the British and French to prevent Russian expansion. Walk around the heavy stone walls of Sinop Fortress, which was not strong enough to stop the Russians. Several towers still stand, some 82 feet tall; walk to the easternmost one and climb to the top. It offers stunning views of the harbor where the battle took place.

Battle of Balaclava

BALAKLAVA, CRIMEA, UKRAINE

Walk through the valley immortalized in Tennyson's poem "The Charge of the Light Brigade," and climb Cathcart's Hill.

◆ **DISTANCE**
5 miles

◆ **START**
Travnia Square

◆ **TYPE OF WALK**
Easy to moderate

◆ **WHEN TO GO**
Avoid winter

ABOVE RIGHT A Russian gun battery from the Battle of Balaclava.

RIGHT Today there are few signs that this was the site of a historic battlefield.

The Battle of Balaclava in October 1854 was the second major battle of the Siege of Sevastopol, a year-long attempt by allied British, French, and Ottoman forces to capture the Black Sea port of Sevastopol during the Crimean War.

During the Victorian era, this and other battles of the Siege of Sevastopol were memorialized in song, story, and verse while the nurses who treated the allied wounded during these battles, most famously Florence Nightingale and Mary Seacole, were much celebrated.

A heart-wrenching walk is to Cathcart's Hill—a gentle rise about five miles north of Balaklava on the way to Sevastopol—which was the first battlefield cemetery for British soldiers who died in the Crimean War. On a hilltop close to what is called the Valley of the Shadow of Death stands a damaged memorial obelisk; the plaques that carried the names of the 23,000 dead buried here are missing. Tsar Alexander II gifted the land, and early lithographs show a verdant slope covered in mismatched Victorian-style gravestones. Sadly, it became a casualty of the fighting of World War II and tensions during the Cold War.

Battle of Malakoff

SEVASTOPOL, CRIMEA, UKRAINE

The Battle of Malakoff took place on September 8, 1855, when the French army attacked a redoubt in Sevastopol harbor during the eleven-month siege. Stroll along the seafront on Primorsky Boulevard to the column commemorating Russian ships scuppered at the mouth of the harbor the year before, making it impossible for enemy ships to pass.

Battle of Magenta

MAGENTA, LOMBARDY, ITALY

Explore the town of Magenta and its park—both full of memories of this battle.

◆ **DISTANCE**
3.7 miles

◆ **START**
Piazza Liberazione

◆ **TYPE OF WALK**
On paths

◆ **WHEN TO GO**
All year

ABOVE RIGHT The facade of Casa Giacobbe, the Austrian headquarters, is peppered with bullet and cannonball holes.

RIGHT The Obelisk-Ossuary in the Parco Unità d'Italia is a memorial and tomb to 4,200 soldiers.

The Battle of Magenta was fought in 1859 between France and Austria during the Second Italian War of Independence. Supported by the Kingdom of Piedmont, French emperor Napoleon III was intent on driving the Austrians out of northern Italy. More than 130,000 men were transported by rail—the first mass movement of troops by train—to Austrian-occupied northern Italy, confronting the Austrians at Magenta.

The French had a narrow victory, and Napoleon III and Piedmontese king Victor Emmanuel triumphantly marched into Milan four days later. Their victory would incite cities to rise against their Austrian oppressors, paving the path for the unification of Italy.

A walking trail traces major historical sights related to the battle, with explanatory panels shedding light on the events. The walk starts at Piazza Liberazione, the scene of the last clashes between the French and Austrians, taking in, among other sights, Casa Giacobbe, which served as the Austrians' headquarters and whose facade is peppered with bullet and cannonball holes. The trail takes you to leafy Parco Unità d'Italia, home to a monument to French general and politician Patrice de MacMahon, who was made Duke of Magenta for his role in the victory, and the Obelisk-Ossuary, a pyramidal building housing the remains of 4,200 soldiers. There's a reenactment of the battle every year in June.

Battle of the Volturno

CAPUA AND CASERTA, CAMPANIA, ITALY

In 1860, 30,000 supporters of the revolutionary Giuseppe Garibaldi clashed with 25,000 Bourbon troops along the river Volturno. Start at Capua's Ponte Romano, head south over the river to reach the beautiful amphitheater and, from there, continue to Caserta; you will be rewarded with incredible views of the Royal Palace of Caserta, the former residence of the House of Bourbon-Two Sicilies.

India's First War of Independence

MEERUT, UTTAR PRADESH, INDIA

India's First War of Independence (also known as the Indian Rebellion) broke out in Meerut in May 1857. Although it was ultimately unsuccessful, it struck a crucial blow against British colonialism. The city was home to the East India Company's second-largest garrison, whose Indian soldiers rose up as anger against British rule grew and amid rumors that gun cartridges—which soldiers were expected to open with their teeth—were greased with animal fat, which was unacceptable to Hindus and Muslims alike. Today you can stroll through Meerut's Sadar Bazaar, the bustling market where the uprising began.

Destruction of the Summer Palace

BEIJING, CHINA

Joint British-French troops marched into Beijing in 1860 to force China to give in to Western trade and influence during the Opium War. The troops began to loot the Imperial Summer Palace, and when it became known that trade delegates—including the celebrated journalist Thomas Bowlby—had been tortured to death by the Chinese, British commander Lord Elgin ordered the destruction of the palace. Stroll around the ruins of the palace in Yuanmingyuan Park, a bitter reminder of the relationship between China and the West.

BELOW The ruins of the Old Summer Palace in Beijing.

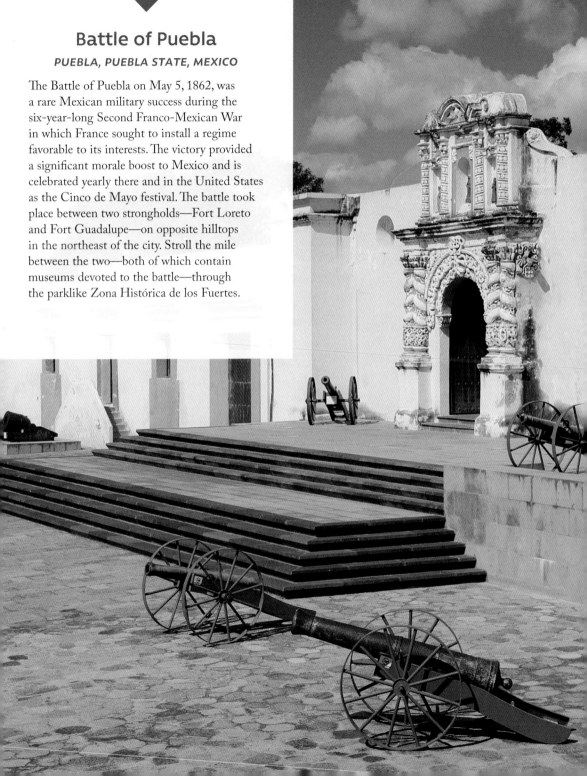

Battle of Puebla

PUEBLA, PUEBLA STATE, MEXICO

The Battle of Puebla on May 5, 1862, was a rare Mexican military success during the six-year-long Second Franco-Mexican War in which France sought to install a regime favorable to its interests. The victory provided a significant morale boost to Mexico and is celebrated yearly there and in the United States as the Cinco de Mayo festival. The battle took place between two strongholds—Fort Loreto and Fort Guadalupe—on opposite hilltops in the northeast of the city. Stroll the mile between the two—both of which contain museums devoted to the battle—through the parklike Zona Histórica de los Fuertes.

Battle of Fort Sumter

CHARLESTON, SOUTH CAROLINA

In December 1860, South Carolina seceded from the Union. The U.S. Army moved its small command from Fort Moultrie on Sullivan's Island to Fort Sumter, a more secure island fortress at the entrance to Charleston Harbor. In April 1861, the South Carolina militia—the Confederate Army did not yet exist—began bombarding Fort Sumter. A day later the U.S. Army surrendered, and the American Civil War had begun. Fort Sumter is part of the National Park Service and accessible by ferry. Visit the fort and its exhibits first, then explore the grounds with their views across the harbor.

First Battle of Bull Run

MANASSAS, VIRGINIA

The American Civil War officially began when rebel troops attacked Fort Sumter in April 1861. But real combat did not come until three months later at the First Battle of Bull Run at Manassas, Virginia, just 25 miles southwest of Washington. Although the two sides were equally matched, with about 18,000 troops each, the Confederates won handily, and the Union retreated. At the Manassas National Battlefield Park, a 5.4-mile trail explores the battlefield in detail.

ABOVE The first fighting of the American Civil War happened in what is now Manassas National Battlefield Park.

Battle of Fort Donelson

DOVER, TENNESSEE

Control of the rivers would be key to success in the Civil War. The Union's seizure of this Confederate fort near the Tennessee–Kentucky border in 1862 opened up the Cumberland River, an important avenue for the invasion of the South. The victory elevated Ulysses S. Grant from an unproven leader to the rank of major-general; he deprived the Confederates of a key resource by capturing more than 12,000 soldiers. Fort Donelson National Battlefield offers four trails to explore the battle site. They vary in length, with moderate to strenuous sections, and take between 45 and 90 minutes.

Battle of Shiloh

SHILOH, TENNESSEE

This battle took place over two days in April 1862 when the Confederate Army of Mississippi attacked General Ulysses S. Grant's army from its base in Corinth, Mississippi. The Union forces' counterattack and victory the next morning doomed the Confederate military initiative in the region. The carnage was unprecedented, with the highest number of casualties (24,000, of whom 3,500 were killed) of any battle on American soil up to that date; Confederate morale plummeted. The Shiloh National Military Park has many paths that lead visitors to monuments, tablets, and other sites away from the roads.

ABOVE Gravestones in Shiloh National Cemetery.

Battle of Antietam
SHARPSBURG, MARYLAND

Walk through the battle lines and cemetery of Antietam to feel the full scale of America's bloodiest day of fighting ever.

◆ **DISTANCE**
2 miles

◆ **START**
Visitors' center

◆ **TYPE OF WALK**
Easy

◆ **WHEN TO GO**
All year

ABOVE RIGHT A huge statue of a soldier, known as "Old Simon," stands guard at the Antietam cemetery.

RIGHT The battlefield at Antietam is one of the best preserved in the United States.

Wednesday, September 17, 1862, was—and remains—the bloodiest single day in American history. For it was then, at the Battle of Antietam in northern Maryland, that 23,000 soldiers were killed, wounded, or went missing after twelve hours of savage combat.

The battle began after Major General George B. McClellan of the Union Army pursued Confederate General Robert E. Lee into Maryland and then launched attacks against Lee's army behind Antietam Creek. The result was inconclusive, and it is generally believed that had the ever-cautious McClellan sent all his Union forces in, as Lee had done, instead of just three-fourths of his men, the outcome would have been more definitive.

President Abraham Lincoln would relieve McClellan of his command two months later. But the Battle of Antietam proved that the Union Army could stand against the Confederates in their first incursion into the North. Equally important, it gave Lincoln the confidence to issue the preliminary Emancipation Proclamation at a moment of strength rather than desperation just four days after the battle.

Visit and explore Antietam National Battlefield, one of the best-preserved war sites in the United States. There are ten short trails (all under two miles) traversing the battlefield to choose from. The trails are gently rolling, but the surface can be slightly uneven, so good walking shoes are recommended. Don't miss Antietam National Cemetery, where 4,776 Union dead are buried. Some 1,836 (or 38 percent of them) are unknown.

Battle of Chancellorsville

FREDERICKSBURG, VIRGINIA

This was actually a series of four battles over a week in April and May 1863. Despite facing a Union Army twice the size of his own, General Robert E. Lee scored a Confederate victory. Each of the battlefields at Fredericksburg and Spotsylvania National Military Park offers trails of between one and seven miles.

332

Siege of Vicksburg

VICKSBURG, MISSISSIPPI

The Confederate surrender to General Ulysses S. Grant after a forty-seven-day siege in July 1863 gave the Union full control of the Mississippi River, splitting the South in two. The Tour Road at Vicksburg National Military Park offers pedestrians up to 16 miles of access past the battlefield and related sites.

Battle of Gettysburg

GETTYSBURG, PENNSYLVANIA

Join the two million people each year who visit the site of one
of the bloodiest battles of the American Civil War.

◆ **DISTANCE**
2.5 miles

◆ **START**
Cemetery Ridge

◆ **TYPE OF WALK**
Easy to moderate

◆ **WHEN TO GO**
All year

RIGHT Wooden fencing marks
the sites of the battle lines.

BELOW Gettysburg National
Cemetery, where Abraham
Lincoln delivered his rousing
Gettysburg Address.

The battle, fought over three days at the beginning of July 1863,
was a victory for the Union Army and forced General Robert
E. Lee's Confederates into retreat. The battle involved the
largest number of casualties of the entire war (more than 50,000)
and, combined with the Union victory at Vicksburg the next day,
is often described as the war's turning point.

Today the site is managed by the National Park Service and is
designated as a National Military Park. Trails of between one
and ten miles guide visitors around the battlefield from Little
Round Top—the site of the 20th Maine's legendary stand—
to the High Water Mark, where fighting climaxed during
Pickett's Charge.

Start at Cemetery Ridge, near the visitors' center, where the
battle lines of the Union Army were situated. The Confederate
Army launched repeated attacks on this line during the battle,
and it is possible to walk along the route of one such attack,
Pickett's Charge, by following a line of wooden fencing and a
path of mown grass. A mile north is Gettysburg National
Cemetery, where 3,500 casualties of the battle were laid to rest
and where President
Abraham Lincoln delivered
his stirring Gettysburg
Address four months later.

334

Battle of Atlanta
KENNESAW, GEORGIA

Part of the Atlanta Campaign, this Union victory in July 1864 occurred two months before the city fell. With no preserved battlefield, visit Kennesaw Mountain National Battlefield Park 25 miles southeast, where the Confederates were victorious just a month before. Here there are over 22 miles of interpretive trails to explore.

335

Battle of Appomattox Court House
APPOMATTOX, VIRGINIA

This is where it all ended—five years of brothers killing brothers—on April 9, 1865. Here Confederate General Robert E. Lee surrendered to Union General Ulysses S. Grant, ending the Civil War. Appomattox Court House National Historical Park has almost eight miles of walks through history.

Battle of Corrientes

CORRIENTES, CORRIENTES PROVINCE, ARGENTINA

On April 13, 1865, Paraguayan naval forces attacked the city of Corrientes, which lies on the banks of the Paraná River. This drew previously neutral Argentina into the War of the Triple Alliance (1864–1870) alongside Brazil and Uruguay. Driven by territorial disputes and regional tensions, the conflict ended with Paraguay defeated and devastated. Take a walk along the *costanera*—a breezy riverside path popular at sunset—to see where the Paraguayan navy fired on its Argentine counterpart before capturing the city.

BELOW Walk along the riverside *costanera* for views of sunset over the Paraná River, Argentina.

Wagon Box Fight

BANNER, JOHNSON COUNTY, WYOMING

The Wagon Box Fight was an ambush in August 1867 by up to 800 Lakota Sioux warriors on a party of twenty-six U.S. Army soldiers and six civilians gathering wood near Fort Phil Kearny in northern Wyoming. The soldiers defended the group with state-of-the-art lever-action rifles fired from behind a defensive wall made of wagons removed from their chassis, and were able to hold off the attackers for several hours with few casualties, after which a detachment from the fort arrived and drove the attackers away. There are three short trails to follow at the fort, one of which leads to the site of Wagon Box.

Battle of Hakodate
HAKODATE, HOKKAIDO, JAPAN

The Boshin War between the Imperial Army and the Tokugawa shogunate was coming to an end when government forces captured the shogun's capital, Edo. The shogunate fleet had already been reduced by a combination of enemy action and bad weather, and they refused to give up the ships they had left. Instead, they sailed them to Hokkaido. Government forces caught up in May 1869 and a six-day battle broke out around Hakodate Bay, resulting in the Ezo Republic surrendering to the Imperial government. Visit the memorials of the war on a walk around the Hakodate Dock.

BELOW Hakodate Dock has memorials to the nineteenth-century battle.

Paris Commune
PARIS, FRANCE

In 1871, civil war broke out between radical Parisians and the national government when the new Third Republic's national assembly agreed to Prussia's harsh terms in the Treaty of Frankfurt. The insurgents established the Paris Commune and took control of the city, but the French army regained the capital only nine weeks later, leading to mass executions, exiles, and rampant destruction. Explore Père Lachaise Cemetery, where you'll find the moving Communards' Wall. Here the last of the insurgents fought a hopeless, all-night battle among the tombstones; in the morning the survivors were lined up against a brick wall, shot, and buried in a mass grave.

Battle of the Little Bighorn

BIG HORN COUNTY, MONTANA

Famous as the site where General Custer breathed his last, this peaceful trail tells a wealth of history.

◆ **DISTANCE**
1.5 miles

◆ **START**
Visitors' center

◆ **TYPE OF WALK**
Marked path

◆ **WHEN TO GO**
All year

ABOVE RIGHT A memorial to the fallen Indian warriors at Little Bighorn.

RIGHT A path leads from the cemetery to the river bluffs where the battle was fought.

Cutting through the sweeping grass prairies of Montana is a deep ravine carved by the Little Bighorn River. It is where the Battle of the Little Bighorn—also known as Custer's Last Stand and the Battle of the Greasy Grass—was fought as part of the Great Sioux War of 1876, in which the U.S. Army attempted to round up nomadic tribes and have them live in reservations.

The army attempted to use the element of surprise to surround a gathering of Lakota, North Cheyenne, and Arapaho tribes on the floor of the river valley. However, the tribes' warriors, led by Crazy Horse, got wind of the attack and forced the U.S. Seventh Cavalry into a retreat, chasing them up the steep ravines of the river gulley, dragging soldiers from their horses as they fled, until finally Lieutenant General George Armstrong Custer and around fifty of his men were driven back to the top of Calhoun Hill, surrounded by warriors, and killed.

Take a walk back through time from the National Cemetery where the army's fallen were buried, up to Calhoun Hill, and along a dusty path back to the river bluffs where stone cairns mark the sites where warriors fell. It's an evocative site.

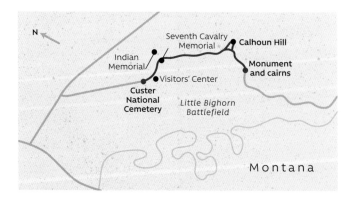

Cochise Stronghold

COCHISE, ARIZONA

The remote Dragoon Mountains of southern Arizona were home to Chief Cochise and his band of 1,000 Chiricahua Apaches from 1861 to 1872. Though he was captured and escaped several times, he was never defeated. The main Cochise Indian Trail, named after him, is a challenging five-mile walk beginning in the East Cochise Stronghold Campground.

Battle of Shiroyama

KAGOSHIMA, KYUSHU, JAPAN

Follow a winding path to a statue dedicated to the great samurai Saigō Takamori, and views over Kinkō Bay.

◆ **DISTANCE**
1 mile

◆ **START**
Tsurumaru Castle

◆ **TYPE OF WALK**
Mixed, with flat pavement and stepped inclines

◆ **WHEN TO GO**
All year

ABOVE RIGHT The statue of Saigō Takamori.

RIGHT Views across the bay to Sakurajima volcano.

Saigō Takamori is one of the most influential samurai in Japanese history, credited with helping to bring about the beginning of modern Japan. However, despite his hero status, he was a rebel in his time and died fighting against the Japanese Imperial Army in the Satsuma Rebellion. After a push into neighboring Kumamoto, he was forced to retreat back to his hometown, Kagoshima, taking refuge on Mount Shiroyama in Kagoshima city. Surrounded by Imperial forces who were determined not to let him escape, he finally accepted defeat and took his own life on September 24, 1877. His loyal retainers charged down from the mountain to their own deaths shortly afterward.

Despite his grisly end, Takamori is celebrated not only in his native Kagoshima but throughout Japan. Ueno Park in Tokyo even has a statue of him.

This walk is in Kagoshima. Start at the remains of Tsurumaru Castle's wall, which has bullet holes in it. From there, walk past a statue in Takamori's honor. Then, behind nearby Terukuni shrine, a moss-covered, sometimes slippery path leads up to Shiroyama Observatory, which looks out over the city and across Kinkō Bay to Sakurajima volcano on the other side. It's a lovely view and bears little witness to the tragic end of one of Japan's last great samurai.

Isandlwana

KWAZULU-NATAL, SOUTH AFRICA

Lord Chelmsford's British 24th Regiment was defeated here by 20,000 of King Cetchwayo's Zulu foot soldiers on January 22, 1879, in the first engagement of the Anglo-Zulu War. After watching silently from a valley, the Zulu *impi* stormed over Isandlwana Hill and encircled the British camp in their traditional "horns and chest of the buffalo" formation. In the ensuing battle, 1,329 of the 1,700 British soldiers were slain. Today, walking trails go to the white-painted cairns marking British graves, while memorials include one to the Zulus: a giant bronze replica of an *isiqu*, or necklace of valor.

Rorke's Drift

KWAZULU-NATAL, SOUTH AFRICA

The British commandeered this Swedish mission as a hospital and supply depot in the Anglo-Zulu War. On January 23, 1879, two survivors of Isandlwana arrived, warning of imminent attack, and ninety minutes later 4,000 Zulu *impis* launched their assault. The 110 British soldiers refused to surrender and defended from behind barricades of grain bags and biscuit boxes. The impis withdrew, losing around 500 men, while seventeen British officers were killed. The mission is now a museum and there are a number of British and Zulu graves and memorials to wander around on the battlefield.

RIGHT White cairns mark the graves of British soldiers at Isandlwana, South Africa.

Battle of Tacna

TACNA, TACNA PROVINCE, PERU

On May 26, 1880, Chile recorded a crucial victory on the Intiorko plateau—just north of the city of Tacna in the Atacama Desert—fighting a Bolivian–Peruvian alliance during the War of the Pacific. Walk across the plateau, visiting a museum and monument—the Alto de Alianza—dedicated to the battle, then follow the route of the allies' retreat to Tacna, where they surrendered. As a result, Bolivia was forced out of the war and its entire coastline—a region rich in valuable nitrates—was taken by Chile, which remains a bone of contention, and has left Bolivia a landlocked country.

Battle of Arica

ARICA, ARICA PROVINCE, CHILE

As well as Bolivia's coastline, the War of the Pacific allowed Chile to seize a chunk of southern Peru, including the port of Arica. Following a naval blockade and bombardment, Chilean soldiers landed and, on June 7, 1880, captured the Morro de Arica, a steep hill overlooking the "city of everlasting spring" and the last holdout of the Peruvian army. Today you can hike up from the seafront to the 456-foot summit, where a history museum, a statue of Christ to symbolize peace between the two nations, and glorious views of the Pacific await.

Samoan Civil Wars

APIA, UPOLU, SAMOA

On Malietoa Laupepa's exile and death, conflicts broke out between supporters of rival contenders Mata'afa Iosefo and Laupepa's son Malietoa Tanumafili. Germany, the United States, and the United Kingdom all wanted to protect their individual interests in the Pacific and became involved with their own preference for a leader in Samoa. Battles were fought from 1886 to 1899, spanning two civil wars, and resulting in the partition of the islands into American Samoa and German Samoa. A walk around the capital of Apia from one memorial to another shows just how many foreign interests were here in Samoa.

Battle of Wounded Knee

PINE RIDGE INDIAN RESERVATION, SOUTH DAKOTA

What is also more accurately known as the Wounded Knee Massacre occurred in December 1890 after a botched attempt by U.S. soldiers to disarm Lakota Indians on a reservation created just a year before. When the soldiers opened fire, the Lakota fought back as well as they could, but many had already been disarmed. Up to 300 Indians died, two-thirds of them women and children; twenty-five soldiers were killed. You can visit this National Historic Site and its monument, then walk up the hill to where the Lakota victims were buried in a common grave.

TOP Chilean soldiers captured the strategically important hill of Morro de Arica.

ABOVE Christ of Peace looks over the town of Arica.

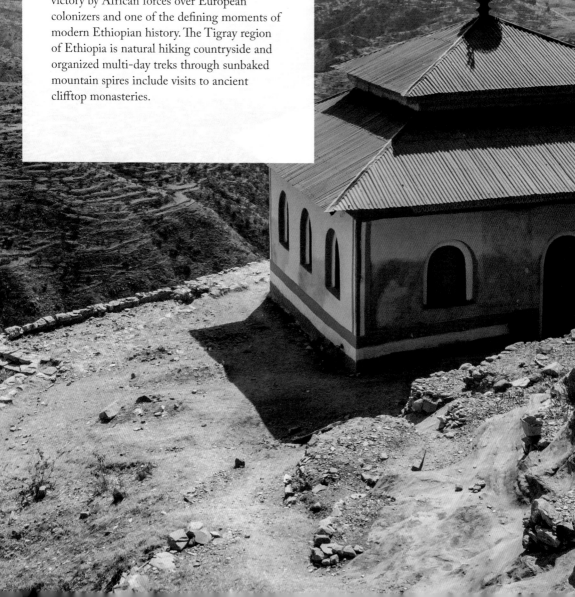

First Italian-Ethiopian War

TIGRAY, ETHIOPIA

When Italian forces invaded Ethiopia in 1895, it's likely that they expected an easy victory. But, just outside the town of Adwa (in Tigray province) the Ethiopian forces, under the command of Emperor Menelik II, decimated the Italian forces in what became the first victory by African forces over European colonizers and one of the defining moments of modern Ethiopian history. The Tigray region of Ethiopia is natural hiking countryside and organized multi-day treks through sunbaked mountain spires include visits to ancient clifftop monasteries.

Anglo-Zanzibar War

STONE TOWN, ZANZIBAR, TANZANIA

Zanzibar (now part of Tanzania) was made a British protectorate in 1890. After the death of the sultan in 1896, the British worried that the new sultan, Khalid bin Barghash, would not be as favorable. Facing an ultimatum to leave his palace (Beit al-Hukum), Barghash barricaded himself in, and at 9:00 a.m. on August 27, 1896, just two days after he'd come to power, the British bombarded the palace from naval ships. The building quickly collapsed with 3,000 defenders inside, the sultan fled, and the entire war lasted thirty-eight minutes—the shortest recorded war in history. Stone Town's historical narrow alleyways are delightful for a wander, then visit the Beit al-Ajaib (the Palace Museum) on the seafront; the adjacent site of Barghash's Beit al-Hukum is now a garden.

Battle of Talana Hill

TALANA MUSEUM AND HERITAGE PARK, KWAZULU-NATAL, SOUTH AFRICA

At the outbreak of the Anglo-Boer War on October 11, 1899, some 4,000–5,000 British troops were dispatched to Dundee under Major-General Sir William Penn Symons to protect the coalfields. The advancing Boers took Talana Hill on October 20, 1899, and bombarded the British. The successful counterattack forced the Boers off the hill but only at great cost and 255 British soldiers fell, including Major-General Symons. Today's historical hiking trail goes from the museum across the battlefield passing Symons's cairn, to the remains of two British forts and Boer gun emplacements on top of the hill.

BELOW Zanzibar's Palace Museum holds more stories from the world's shortest war.

352

Battle of Dagu Forts

HAI RIVER, NEAR TIANJIN, CHINA

In 1900, thousands of Boxers—an Indigenous peasant movement that aimed to end foreign influence in China—rose up in the Boxer Rebellion. Foreign forces, missionaries, and civilians came under attack. Mounting an attack from the sea, an alliance of foreign armies managed to take control of the Dagu (or Taku) forts on the Hai River, which can be walked around today.

Truku War

TAROKO GORGE, TAIWAN

Traverse marble tunnels and pass turquoise waters on this walk where the Truku people fought against Japanese troops.

♦ **DISTANCE**
2 miles out and back

♦ **START**
Tunnel of Nine Turns
bus stop

♦ **TYPE OF WALK**
Leisurely half-day walk

♦ **WHEN TO GO**
All year

ABOVE LEFT The territory is full of natural wonders on the Tunnel of Nine Turns trail.

LEFT The Taroko Gorge makes unbelievable fighting terrain.

During the Japanese occupation of Taiwan (1895–1945), the Japanese drove much of the Indigenous population from their coastal settlements into the mountains. The Truku, also called the Taroko, from Taiwan's east coast around Hualien and Taroko Gorge, were the most active in resisting Japanese rule, waging guerrilla warfare against the occupiers by ambushing and killing Japanese soldiers and merchants. Keen to overpower the Truku warriors and to take control of the mountains for their natural resources, in May 1914 Sakuma Samata, governor-general of Taiwan, mobilized 20,000 soldiers to fight against the 2,000 Indigenous combatants around Taroko.

The Truku resisted for three months but were inevitably defeated. The Japanese pacified the community, confiscated all weaponry, dispersed the Truku away from their traditional lands, and enforced rules that discouraged the practice of traditional Truku social structure, culture, and beliefs. This was the last attempt at a Truku uprising.

There are plenty of walking and hiking trails in Taroko Gorge. For a good introduction to the geography and the landscape, walk the Tunnel of Nine Turns trail with a number of viewpoints that include glass floors, and experience the deep marble gorges and river rapids among which this war was fought.

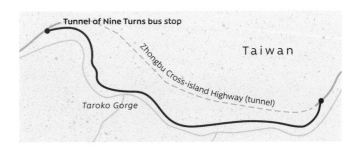

⬦ 354 ⬦

Battle of Ciudad Juárez

CIUDAD JUÁREZ,
CHIHUAHUA STATE, MEXICO

The first major battle of the protracted Mexican Revolution, which ran from 1911 to 1920, was a victory by 2,500 rebels under Pancho Villa and others against 700 federal forces. The outcome led to the resignation of President Porfirio Díaz, ending the revolution's first phase. The battle was fought hand-to-hand throughout the city just over the border from El Paso, Texas; there is no single battle site. Walk instead from the historic center to the Museo de la Revolución en la Frontera (Museum of the Revolution in the Borderland), which leaves no stone unturned on the Mexican Revolution, with special emphasis on Ciudad Juárez.

⬦ 355 ⬦

Battle of Cuautla

CUAUTLA, MORELOS STATE, MEXICO

This victory of rebel forces under Emiliano Zapata against the federal army came just a day after Pancho Villa's win at Ciudad Juárez. Both triumphs forced Porfirio Díaz to agree to sue for peace and resign as president. Losses were high; the battle has been described as "six of the most terrible days of battle in the whole [Mexican] Revolution." Head for the Plaza Revolución del Sur, where you'll find Zapata's grave and a monument to the revolutionary leader. In Anenecuilco, four miles southwest of Cuautla, what's left of the adobe cottage where he was born is now a small museum.

ABOVE The iconic figure of Emiliano Zapata at his grave in Cuautla.

Battle of Veracruz
VERACRUZ, VERACRUZ STATE, MEXICO

This occurred in 1914 during the long-running Mexican Revolution when companies from the U.S. Atlantic Fleet supported by U.S. Marines seized the Veracruz waterfront. The battle involved much street fighting—something neither side was used to—and resulted in both a seven-month occupation of the port and blockade of a delivery of German arms to the deposed dictator Victoriano Huerta. Take an atmospheric walk along the gritty waterfront and then head inland to the town center and the Museo Histórico Naval (Historic Naval Museum), which offers a complete lesson in Mexico's maritime heritage, including the attacks by U.S. forces.

Battle of Columbus
COLUMBUS, NEW MEXICO

In March 1916, Pancho Villa and his troops crossed the U.S. border to raid the town of Columbus, New Mexico, for supplies. Villa was defeated in less than two hours, but the United States then sent 10,000 troops into Mexico in retaliation. This was the first time the United States used airplanes for reconnaissance and the last time it was attacked by a foreign power marching into its land. From the Columbus Historical Museum in a disused railway depot, walk a half-mile south to Pancho Villa State Park, which includes Coote's Hill. Here, Villa observed the raid and sharpshooters fired upon the town.

BELOW The last foreign invasion of the United States was into the town of Columbus, New Mexico.

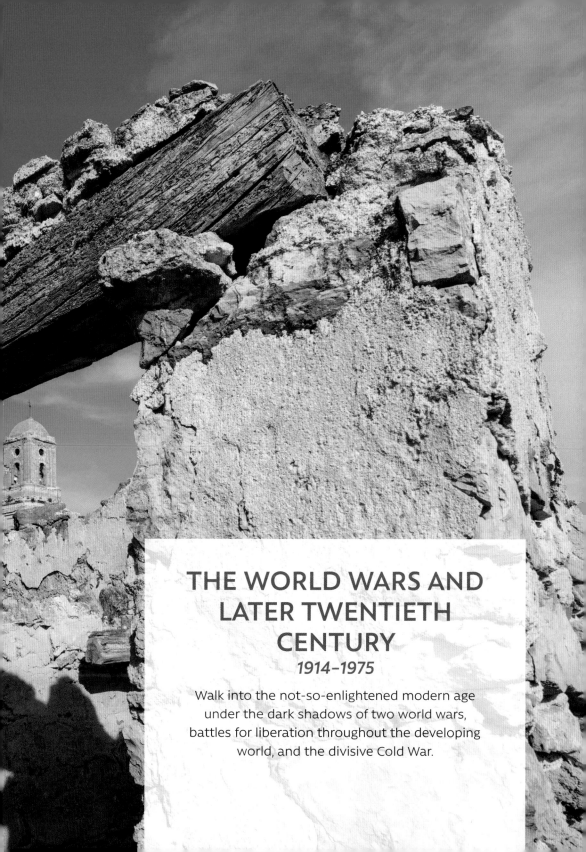

THE WORLD WARS AND LATER TWENTIETH CENTURY
1914–1975

Walk into the not-so-enlightened modern age under the dark shadows of two world wars, battles for liberation throughout the developing world, and the divisive Cold War.

Battle of Mons
HAINAUT, BELGIUM

A small Belgian coal-mining town witnessed the opening shots of the British Army as it entered World War I in 1914. In the suburb of Nimy, original buildings still stand where men of the Royal Fusiliers assembled for battle. Walking along the Condé canal, you pass the railway bridge where they were positioned. After climbing the grass bank, you can stand by the track where the Fusiliers' machine guns held the Germans back. Below, a memorial plaque commemorates those who fought and died here.

First Ypres
FLANDERS, BELGIUM

In the biggest British battle of 1914, Belgian, British, and French soldiers dug in along the low ridges of flat Flanders to stop the German army's "Race to the Sea." Walking the edge of Polygon Wood, the 1914 landscape of open fields is almost the same. Here Brigadier-General FitzClarence led a charge of the Irish Guards. The impressive bronze Black Watch soldier stands defiant in his kilt on the spot where they halted the charge of the elite Prussian Guard, although FitzClarence and many of his men lost their lives in the battle.

BELOW The railway bridge in Hainaut where the British Army first fired shots in World War I.

RIGHT The defiant Black Watch soldier stands on the spot where the Allies stopped the German advance.

 360

 361

Battle of Morhange

LORRAINE, FRANCE

As the German army marched on Paris as part of the Schlieffen Plan, there were huge battles along the Franco-German border. Morhange (Mörchingen) was then in Germany, and you can see German graves in the woods, and an original German railway station built to bring men to the front. Walk the ridge west of the town to the battle's memorial column. Walking in the fields here, it's sobering to think that 27,000 Frenchmen died in a single day along this frontier in August 1914, many of whom are in graves in the French Cemetery at Riche.

Battle of Le Cateau

NORD, FRANCE

During the Retreat from Mons, with the Germans on his heels, General Sir Horace Smith-Dorrien decided to make a stand along the old Roman roads near Le Cateau-Cambrésis. Walking out of the town, which has changed little since 1914, you find British and German soldiers buried side by side in the cemetery on the high ground. Continue to a British Memorial across the valley, where the Second Suffolks made their last stand and were all but wiped out; its white panels are inscribed with the long list of men and regiments engaged in a battle that cost 7,000 lives.

The Christmas Truce

FLANDERS, BELGIUM

Take a moment to reflect as you explore the battlefield
that fell quiet for Christmas Day.

◆ **DISTANCE**
1.5 miles

◆ **START**
Prowse Point
Military Cemetery

◆ **TYPE OF WALK**
Mainly flat, can be muddy

◆ **WHEN TO GO**
All year, but December
for commemorations

ABOVE RIGHT A cross in St. Yvon
overlooks the field where the
Christmas truce took place.

RIGHT A rudimentary bunker
dates back to 1914.

Across Flanders Fields, British and German soldiers came
together for a Christmas truce in December 1914.

Prowse Point cemetery, named after British officer Bertie
Prowse, is a small cemetery where men were buried behind the
trenches. More recent burials have been added as battlefield
archaeologists retrieved the remains of soldiers who fell in 1914.

A FIFA memorial nearby talks of Christmas Day soccer
during the truce, but there is very little historical evidence for
this. Behind it, reconstructed trenches with barbed wire and an
original bunker are used for reenactments of the truce each
December. Walking farther along, an older wooden cross up
a bank in the hamlet of St. Yvon overlooks the ground where
cartoonist Bruce Bairnsfather met the Germans during the truce,
and scribbled his Old Bill cartoons in the cellar of a nearby
cottage, now marked with a plaque.

Continue on to a copse in the fields, where there are signs of
Messines mine craters from later in the war, but on a bend is the
site of the Birdcage, scene of a pre-Christmas battle where
Prowse and his men fought. The bodies left unburied afterward
were what led to a truce taking place here in front of the dark
mass of Ploegsteert (Plugstreet) Wood.

Battle of the Marne

MARNE RIVER, NEAR BRASLES, FRANCE

Walking a ridge outside Paris overlooking the fields where 2.5 million British, French, and German soldiers clashed in September 1914, you come to Mondemont-Montgivrou. The buildings show signs of battle damage and the impressive red totem memorial depicts French General "Papa" Joffre in his moment of victory.

Terragnolo Valley Fortifications

TRENTINO, ITALY

Hike this spectacular mountain trail carved into the rock that takes you through a deep gorge with trenches and shelters, before ending at the ruins of a military fortress.

◆ **DISTANCE**
4.5 miles

◆ **START**
Serrada

◆ **TYPE OF WALK**
Steep in places

◆ **WHEN TO GO**
April–October

ABOVE RIGHT It's possible to explore the shelters carved into the rocks.

RIGHT The ruins of the impressive Forte Dosso delle Somme.

The Forra del Lupo walking route in the jagged mountains of the Dolomites is one of the area's most striking trails, snaking its way through a gorge flanked by high rock walls where, in World War I, the Austro-Hungarians carved trenches and shelters into the rock face.

Starting at Serrada, the path gradually climbs up the Terragnolo Valley to reach the Forte Dosso delle Somme. You'll initially walk through a steep wooded area to reach a frontline trench that develops along high rock walls, where you can see defensive positions looking out over the valley. Small observation posts and artillery positions dot the route, and you can descend a set of stairs carved into the rock to reach the troops' shelters.

The path ends at the ruins of the Forte Dosso delle Somme, built between 1911 and 1914, and connected to the valley by a military road. From the fort, you can soak up panoramic views of the Pasubio mountain massif, which saw fierce fighting throughout the war, while along the road you can see the ruins of the barracks that housed the soldiers.

Serrada

Forte Dosso
delle Somme

Piazza

Trentino

Mountain Warfare

TRENTINO, ITALY

On March 13, 1918, the Austrians lit 55 tons of TNT at the foot of the Dente Italiano (Pasubio mountain massif), changing the topography of the mountains forever. From Passo Pian delle Fugazze, hike the awe-inspiring Road of the Heroes as it snakes its way up the mountainside, displaying plaques honoring fifteen soldiers who were awarded the Gold Medal of Military Valor.

Forte Pozzacchio

NEAR ROVERETO, TRENTINO, ITALY

Carved into the mountainside, Forte Pozzacchio was the last of the Austro-Hungarian fortresses built between the nineteenth and early twentieth centuries. Between June 1915 and May 1916, it was occupied by Italian soldiers. Walk to the fort from Pozzacchio or Valmorbia—you can see the troops' lodgings as well as lookout points and firing stations.

Battle of Tanga
TANGA, TANZANIA

One of the greatest World War I victories for Germany's Schutztruppe (its colonial troops in Africa) came in November 1914, after the British unsuccessfully attempted to take Tanga from German East Africa. The British were defeated, and fled leaving arms and supplies to the Germans. Today visitors can walk around old German architecture such as Old Tanga School and the residence of the German district commissioner (now the Palm Court Hotel). Raskazone Beach is where the British disembarked, and the German Cemetery contains graves of sixteen Germans and forty-eight *askaris* (local troops) killed in action.

Eastern Alps
COGOLO, TRENTO, ITALY

When hostilities between the Empire of Austria-Hungary and the Kingdom of Italy began in 1915, the Viozhütte (Rifugio Vioz), the highest refuge in the Eastern Alps, was immediately placed under Austrian military command. To provide better coordination for high-altitude operations, the Austrians built a cable car from Cogolo (3,800 feet) to Punta Linke (12,000 feet), with a transit station built inside an ice tunnel. You can hike from Doss dei Cembri to the Punta Linke site, where you can still see a German-made diesel engine and rye straw shoes worn by soldiers on sentry duty.

Italian Front
ALTO ADIGE, ITALY

During World War I, the front ran close to the Tre Cime di Lavaredo (Three Peaks of Lavaredo), the Italians' most advanced outpost that served as the border between Austria-Hungary and Italy. The area saw heavy fighting between the Alpini (Italian mountain troops) and the Austrian Kaiserjäger. One hotly contested peak was the Paternkofel. A circular loop from Rifugio Auronzo takes you around this mountain, with trenches, fortifications, tunnels, and iron ladders leading to high positions still visible today.

Second Ypres
FLANDERS, BELGIUM

Although it was later prohibited by the Geneva Protocol of 1925, in April 1915 Germany decided to employ poison gas, and chemical warfare began, with a chlorine gas cloud enveloping British, Canadian, and French trenches near Ypres. Start at the Brooding Soldier memorial at Vancouver Corner—a tall stone figure with its head bowed. Here, more than 2,000 Canadians died in two days. Walk to St. Julien, to the memorial near Kitchener's Wood where the shattered Canadians held on despite having only improvised gas masks to protect themselves.

LEFT As the border between Austria-Hungary and Italy, the Dolomites saw fierce fighting.

Battle of Loos

NORD, FRANCE

Wander from the lone tree of the battlefield to the cemetery where so many fallen soldiers lie.

◆ **DISTANCE**
3.5 miles

◆ **START**
Le Rutoire Farm, Vermelles

◆ **TYPE OF WALK**
Some uphill

◆ **WHEN TO GO**
All year

RIGHT The Lone Tree was a clearly visible landmark on the battlefield at Loos; this new one has replaced the original.

BELOW Dud Corner Cemetery contains 2,000 graves and a memorial to 20,000 more.

The Battle of Loos in September 1915 was the largest battle of World War I to date. Walking to Le Rutoire Farm, an isolated farm complex in the fields near Vermelles, you can see some of the original shell-pocked walls of the farm, and a British concrete observation bunker. This was an advanced brigade headquarters in 1915.

Walk onto the tracks taking you to a single tree out in the fields, the Lone Tree. The original was cut down for a souvenir by veterans, but it was a significant feature on this otherwise open landscape, devoid of cover. Ahead is the rising ground where the German trenches were, and after this you'll find Loos-en-Gohelle village, where you can look back and see the battleground from the German perspective.

On September 27, 1915, the Irish Guards went into battle here, and a young officer, John Kipling, was posted missing. His father was writer and poet Rudyard Kipling. Continue on to the Dud Corner Cemetery and Loos Memorial; this is one of the larger battlefield cemeteries with nearly 2,000 graves and over 20,000 soldiers named on the memorial to the missing, including John Kipling. Rudyard came here in 1930 for the cemetery's opening to remember "my boy Jack," as he called his son.

Battle of Neuve Chapelle

ARTOIS, FRANCE

This battle in March 1915 marked the first time British soldiers actively attacked the Germans. English and Indian troops advanced successfully. Walking through the village seeing the small battlefield cemeteries, continue to bunkers in nearby Bois de Biez and walk to the Indian Memorial: the Star of India guarded by two tigers.

Battle of Navarin Farm

CHAMPAGNE, FRANCE

A pyramid-like monument covered in memorial plaques with the figures of soldiers marks the spot where French Foreign Legionnaires fought in September 1915, including British and American volunteers. Walk around the crumbling trenches among old barbed wire. Nearby are German bunkers and extensive French cemeteries.

Gallipoli Campaign

GALLIPOLI PENINSULA, ÇANAKKALE PROVINCE, TURKEY

On this beautiful coastline, walk in the trenches where so many Australian and New Zealander servicemen died.

◆ **DISTANCE**
7.5 miles

◆ **START**
Chunuk Bair (New Zealand Memorial)

◆ **TYPE OF WALK**
Easy to moderate

◆ **WHEN TO GO**
All year; avoid weekends

When the Ottoman Empire joined the Central Powers in 1914, it closed the Dardanelles strait, blocking one of the Allies' major supply routes. First Lord of the British Admiralty, Winston Churchill, decided that it was vital the Allies take control of both the Dardanelles and the Bosporus straits and capture Istanbul, but the first attempt to force the Dardanelles, in February 1915, failed.

Undaunted, two months later British, Australian, New Zealander, and Indian troops landed on the Gallipoli Peninsula (Gelibolu in modern Turkish). It was a disaster from the start. Allied troops were hemmed in by the Turks, forced to dig trenches for protection, and staged bloody assaults to try and gain footing. After nine months of ferocious combat, with approximately 250,000 casualties on each side but little headway, the Allied forces withdrew in January 1916.

The best way to explore the various battlefields is to follow in the footsteps of the original combatants. A 7.5-mile walk along the trails of the Northern Gallipoli Peninsula starting at Chunuk Bair and heading south will take you past monuments, battle sites, trenches, and cemeteries, including Lone Pine. It ends at the landing site at Anzac Cove.

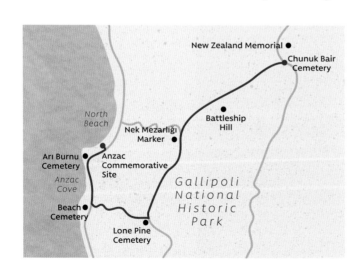

Suvla Bay Landings
GALLIPOLI, TURKEY

The Suvla landings in August 1915 were meant to end the Allies' campaign in Turkey, but instead ended in stalemate. Walking from the beach past Hill 10 British Cemetery, you find the remains of a farm and gully where the Sandringham Company of the Norfolk Regiment disappeared; their bodies were found here after the war.

376

Lone Pine
GALLIPOLI PENINSULA, ÇANAKKALE PROVINCE, TURKEY

This battle between the Australian and New Zealand Army Corps (ANZAC) and the Ottomans in August 1915 was a diversionary attack to draw the latter's attention away from the main Allied assaults on the peninsula and ended in an ANZAC victory. The moving Anzac cemetery is a two-mile walk southwest of Chunuk Bair.

ABOVE Start your walk in the trenches at Chunuk Bair.

LEFT The Commonwealth War Graves Beach Cemetery at Anzac Cove on the Gallipoli Peninsula.

Battle of the Somme

BEAUMONT-HAMEL, SOMME, FRANCE

Walk through distinctive zigzagging trenches and bomb craters on this perfectly preserved battlefield.

◆ **DISTANCE**
2 miles

◆ **START**
Newfoundland Park, Beaumont-Hamel

◆ **TYPE OF WALK**
Good tracks, slight climb

◆ **WHEN TO GO**
All year

RIGHT A statue of a bellowing caribou cries out for the loss of the Canadian soliders.

The Battle of the Somme began at 7:30 a.m. on July 1, 1916, when British and Commonwealth soldiers went into battle on an eighteen-mile front. The battle raged until November 18, 1916, but on that first day alone, nearly 20,000 British soldiers died.

At Beaumont-Hamel a whole section of the battlefield was uniquely preserved in memory of the Canadian soldiers from Newfoundland who died there. At the entrance, there are native trees and rocks from Newfoundland before grass-covered trenches snake off in every direction. A complete battlefield is here: the reserve line, the support line, and the front line, with No Man's Land and the German trenches beyond. The trenches zigzag on purpose, to minimize the effect of shell fire. Shell craters can be seen everywhere, hinting at the power of artillery.

You can walk through trenches and get a sense of how claustrophobic they were. Overlooking where the Newfoundlanders attacked, a bronze caribou with its mouth open cries out in loss; of around 800 men who went into battle, more than 700 became casualties. You can walk the ground they advanced over, down to the "Danger Tree" where so many fell. There are small battlefield cemeteries, with many unidentified graves, and beyond, the German trenches seem permanent still, even a century later.

Grass has covered the scars, but this unique part of the Somme is still full of grief.

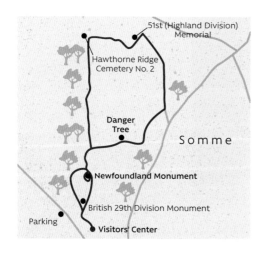

TOP A bunker at Fort Douaumont.　　　　**ABOVE** The powerful Thiepval Memorial.

Battle of Verdun

MEUSE, FRANCE

Fought over 300 days, the Battle of Verdun was the longest battle of the war, beginning in February 1916 with a bombardment of 2.5 million shells in nine hours. Walking along the rows of French crosses at Douaumont Cemetery, you come to the imposing ossuary, beneath which are the bones of more than 120,000 soldiers. There's a memorial to French Muslim soldiers, preserved trenches and bunkers, and inside Fort Douaumont you can see working gun turrets and half-lit corridors where men fought and died. On top of the fort, massive shell craters show just how shattered this landscape was.

Battle of Fromelles

NORD, FRANCE

To support the British on the Somme in 1916, Lieutenant-General Richard Haking led a joint British and Australian division to attack a strongly fortified German position near the Aubers Ridge. However, the troops found themselves unprepared, outnumbered, and approaching on open ground. They came under direct fire from the German line, resulting in more than 7,000 casualties within twenty-four hours. Take a walk between the villages of Fromelles and Neuve-Chapelle, where you cross the front lines of both sides. Visit the German bunker remains at Fromelles, the war memorials, and cemeteries.

Battle of Thiepval

SOMME, FRANCE

It took two months of fighting and the assistance of tanks for the Allies to take Thiepval in September 1916, the largest village behind the German lines on the Somme. Walking from a small quarry south of the village, you can see chalk marks of old trenches in the fields. In the grounds of the mighty Thiepval Memorial, opened in 1932, the Missing of the Somme—more than 73,000 soldiers—are commemorated. In the visitors' center, movies explain the history of the battle, and at a small memorial on the ridge you can see just what a killing ground the Somme was.

Battle of the Ancre

ANCRE RIVER, PICARDY, FRANCE

The river Ancre runs through the northern Somme battlefield. In November 1916 Britain's sea-soldiers, infantry of the Royal Naval Division, took the river valley and village of Beaucourt. Graves of those who lost their lives are in the Ancre British Cemetery at Beaumont-Hamel, including the son of press baron Lord Rothermere. From here, walk up a track where German trench lines once ran to a concrete bunker. In Beaucourt, a Portland stone memorial shows the badges of the many naval units, all named after famous admirals such as Nelson, a unique formation that came from an idea of Winston Churchill's.

Easter Rising

DUBLIN, IRELAND

Although Britain had agreed to home rule for Ireland in 1914, World War I delayed its enactment. In April 1916, impatient republicans marched into Dublin and occupied key positions. After less than a week of fighting, the rebels surrendered to the British forces. The insurrection would have had less impact in Ireland had the British not made martyrs of the rebel leaders by executing sixteen of them. Support for the republicans rose dramatically. View key Rising sites by walking for a half-hour north of St. Stephen's Green and over the Liffey to the General Post Office, then west to the Four Courts.

Air War in Britain

LONDON, ENGLAND

In 1915, fifty-two zeppelin raids killed 556 people and injured 1,357. Later in the war, the Germans developed more powerful twin-engine Gotha bombers, killing and injuring even more people. Both Cleopatra's Needle on the Embankment and Lincoln's Inn Chapel off Chancery Lane bear shrapnel marks from zeppelin raids. From the latter, walk to Bartholomew Close, where a device destroyed several houses, killed two men, and exposed medieval half-timbering at St. Bartholomew the Great for the first time in centuries.

RIGHT The area around the Four Courts in Dublin was subjected to heavy fighting in the Easter Rising.

Russian Revolution

ST. PETERSBURG, RUSSIA

Walk with the revolutionaries who brought about the world's first socialist state and the formation of the Soviet Union.

◆ **DISTANCE**
3.4 miles

◆ **START**
State Hermitage Museum

◆ **TYPE OF WALK**
Leisurely half-day walk

◆ **WHEN TO GO**
All year

RIGHT Palace Square in St. Petersburg, the city where the Russian Revolution began.

Protests and riots over food shortages began in February 1917 along St. Petersburg's Nevsky Prospekt. A march by people demanding bread turned into riots and looting of the palaces. The Russian people, already unhappy with their poor living conditions, combined with the mutiny of the Russian army, which suffered major losses in World War I, turned against Czar Nicholas II. Even the troops whom Czar Nicholas ordered to suppress the protesters refused to do so, and joined the protests themselves. The czar abdicated and a provisional government was formed by the Duma, members of the lower house assembly.

The turn of events allowed Bolshevik leader Vladimir Ilyich Lenin to return from exile in April, spreading his ideology and influence. Lenin's anti-war sentiments improved the popularity of the Bolshevik among the working population. Political factions began fighting all over Russia, and a revolutionary military committee, led by Leon Trotsky, began an armed uprising. In a coup known as the October Revolution, the Bolsheviks took control and formed their own government, ultimately leading to the creation of the Soviet Union.

Follow the path of the revolution and take a city walk around St. Petersburg, where the first movements of the Russian Revolution began.

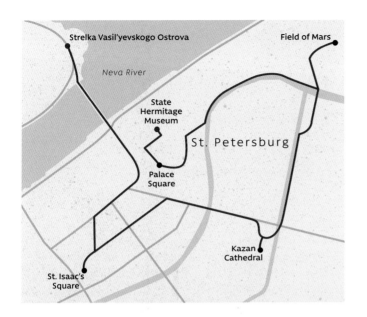

Revolution Spreads
MOSCOW, RUSSIA

The 1917 revolution spread rapidly from St. Petersburg to Moscow. Political speeches were given by both the Duma government and the Bolsheviks in order to gain support. In March 1918 post-revolution Moscow became the capital of Russia. Walk around Red Square, where Lenin's embalmed body is on display inside a mausoleum.

Mines on the Messines Ridge

FLANDERS, BELGIUM

Discover the craters left by mines detonated under the Messines Ridge.

DISTANCE
2 miles

START
Spanbroekmolen
mine crater

TYPE OF WALK
Good tracks

WHEN TO GO
All year

ABOVE RIGHT The bronze figure of a tunneler.

RIGHT This crater in Flanders is now known as the Pool of Peace.

Spanbroekmolen was the site of a windmill that stood on the crest of the Messines Ridge, high ground south of Ypres taken by the Germans in 1914. A German strongpoint, it was one of nineteen targets chosen to be destroyed by huge mines placed underground by British and Commonwealth tunnelers.

Although it is now partially hidden by trees, as soon as you walk through the gate you find yourself on the lip of this enormous crater formed by 45 tons of explosives. The field opposite was the battlefield. From here, walk to the Wytschaete road, which was the boundary between soldiers from the north of Ireland, and those recruited in the south; this was the first time they had fought side by side.

Farther up, another crater, known as Peckham Crater, is free of trees and clearly shows the size of the damage done by 43 tons of ammonal in June 1917. Continue along the road past the Maedelstede Farm Crater, the third of the mines here, and the memorial to the Irish regiments stands outside Wytschaete Military Cemetery, with graves from every year of the war. In the village, outside Wytschaete church, is a bronze figure of a tunneler—one of the Flanders "clay kickers" who had their finest hour here on this ridge.

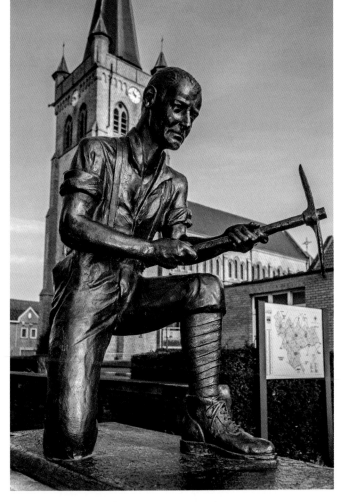

Third Ypres

FLANDERS, BELGIUM

Third Ypres was a battle in the mud. Walking from the Menin Gate Memorial, where the "Last Post" is played each evening, take a route along the Menin Road via Hell Fire Corner, blasted to bits in 1917, on to the former front lines at Bellewaerde Ridge.

Passchendaele

FLANDERS, BELGIUM

As part of the Third Battle of Ypres, the Canadians moved up to Passchendaele in October 1917. In ten days they lost over 16,000 men, but took the village—in a snowstorm. At Tyne Cot Cemetery, the largest British cemetery in the world, walk along the hillside and to the Canadian Memorial in what is now Passendale.

Hindenburg Line

PAS-DE-CALAIS, FRANCE

Wander through battlefields that featured in the film *1917* and on to a museum full of relics from the fighting.

◆ **DISTANCE**
2 miles

◆ **START**
Écoust-Saint-Mein

◆ **TYPE OF WALK**
Easy going, slight climb

◆ **WHEN TO GO**
All year

ABOVE RIGHT Nature is reclaiming parts of the Hindenburg Line.

RIGHT The "Slouch Hat" memorial to Australian soldiers in Bullecourt.

During the winter of 1916–1917, the Germans constructed a new line of defense, the Hindenburg Line, between Arras and Soissons, withdrawing to it in the spring of 1917. British units followed, taking the battle to them there.

The village of Écoust featured in the Sam Mendes movie *1917* when Lance Corporal Schofield runs through the burning town. Taken by the British, it became a route to the front line. A grass mound marks the spot where the rubble of the old village was piled up and left. Walking onto the nearby railroad embankment, a small British cemetery is one of many in the area with dead from the final two years of the war. From here, continue across farmland tracks to a vast open landscape with a high point overlooking Croisilles—a view also seen in the movie.

In those early battles this area was grassland with shallow chalk-cut trenches, captured brilliantly in the motion picture. Fighting took place in April and May 1917 when British, and later Australian, soldiers battled their way through the Hindenburg Line.

You can walk into the village of Bullecourt where that Australian sacrifice is seen in the "Slouch Hat" memorial by the church and the excellent war museum full of the relics of war found in the surrounding fields.

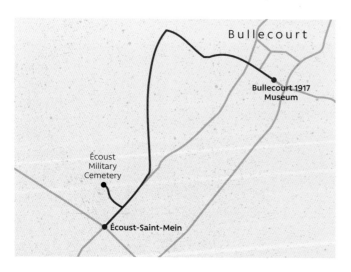

Bullecourt

Bullecourt 1917 Museum

Écoust Military Cemetery

Écoust-Saint-Mein

Vimy Ridge

PAS-DE-CALAIS, FRANCE

Go underground into chalk tunnels, cross battlefields, and finish at the Canadian National Vimy Memorial.

◆ **DISTANCE**
1.5 miles

◆ **START**
Canadian visitors' center

◆ **TYPE OF WALK**
Uneven ground

◆ **WHEN TO GO**
All year

ABOVE RIGHT The impressive white stone memorial to the Canadian soldiers.

RIGHT Well-preserved trenches can still be seen at the battle site.

During the Battle of Arras, the Canadian Corps attacked the high ground of Vimy Ridge on April 9, 1917. For the first time, men from every part of Canada fought side by side as the nation came together on these slopes.

From the visitors' center, guides offer tours into some of the underground chalk tunnels, and on to trenches preserved in concrete and vast mine craters that cover the battlefield. Each tree here was planted for a missing Canadian soldier. Further on are two Canadian battlefield cemeteries: long rows of graves, with some soldiers as young as sixteen. Walking up to the highest point of the ridge at Hill 145, you follow the route of the Canadian attack. Five days of fighting cost 10,000 casualties.

Nearly two decades later, the stunning Vimy Memorial was unveiled before a crowd of thousands of Canadians, many of whom had lost someone in the war. Approaching it, the white stone figures become clear: Mother Canada with head bowed low at the loss, an altar with sword and helmet laid across, and two great columns rising to the heavens. On the walls are more than 11,000 names of the missing. Their legacy was to create the foundations of a new and emerging nation.

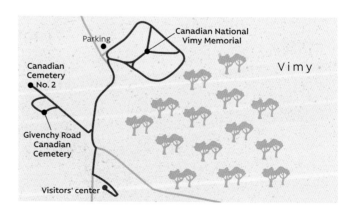

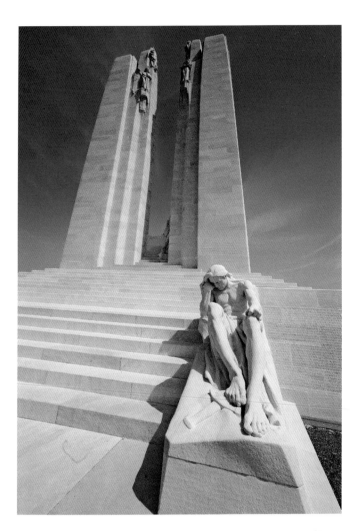

Chemin des Dames
AISNE, FRANCE

A French Tank Memorial on the slopes of this ridge near Reims commemorates the first use of these fighting machines in the war on September 9, 1916. Walk to the crest and go underground into the Caverne du Dragon to explore the chalk tunnels where fighting took place, and learn of the losses that led to the French Mutiny, when demoralized troops continued to defend but refused orders to attack.

Cambrai
NORD, FRANCE

In November 1917, Cambrai was the first mass use of tanks in the war. Walking from the West Riding Division Memorial in Havrincourt, follow the farm tracks used by tanks onto the Flesquières Ridge. Here in a museum you'll find an original British tank excavated from the battlefields in 1998.

Battle of Caporetto

NEAR KOBARID, PRIMORSKA REGION, SLOVENIA

Walk a section of the "Walk of Peace" through Slovenia's stunning Soča valley.

◆ **DISTANCE**
4.7 miles

◆ **START**
Walk of Peace visitors' center, Kobarid

◆ **TYPE OF WALK**
Moderate

◆ **WHEN TO GO**
Avoid winter

ABOVE LEFT Reconstructed trenches near Kobarid.

LEFT The Kobarid Historical Trail leads through the beautiful valley of the Soča River.

The victory of the combined Austro-Hungarian and German forces at the final battle of the Isonzo (or Soča) Front in October 1917 was one of the greatest and bloodiest military campaigns fought on mountainous terrain in history. By the time the fighting had stopped twenty-six days later, hundreds of thousands of soldiers lay dead or wounded, gassed or mutilated beyond recognition. Casualties on the Soča Front for the entire 1915–1917 period, including soldiers and civilians behind the lines, numbered almost a million.

The "miracle of Kobarid" (in Slovenian, Caporetto in Italian) routed the Italian army and pushed the fighting back deep into Italian territory. The Italian retreat is vividly described in the novel *A Farewell to Arms* by Ernest Hemingway, who was wounded during the campaign while driving an Italian ambulance.

The 200-mile-long Walk of Peace connects the most important remains and memorials of the Isonzo Front of Slovenia's Upper Soča region. Along the way, you'll pass cemeteries, commemorative chapels, and outdoor museums. A shorter option is to follow the Kobarid Historical Trail for just under five miles, which will take you past trenches, gun emplacements, and observation posts of the Italian defense line, as well as through the beautiful valley of the Soča River.

Battle of Aqaba

AQABA, JORDAN

This was a key battle in 1917 during the Arab Revolt, a two-year insurrection during World War I aimed at creating a unified and independent Arab state. Though ultimately unsuccessful, Arab forces with the assistance of T.E. Lawrence (Lawrence of Arabia) were able to oust the Ottomans and capture the Red Sea port. Walk around the waterfront's Great Arab Revolt Plaza to take in the 450-foot Arab Revolt Flagpole with its massive banner and the Aqaba Fort with a Hashemite coat of arms at the entrance commemorating the revolt.

BELOW Inside the Aqaba Fort in Jordan.

Battle of Megiddo

NEAR MEGIDDO KIBBUTZ, NORTHERN DISTRICT, ISRAEL

A victory for the Allies in 1918, this was the last of their offensives in Palestine during World War I. It opened the way to Damascus; the Axis powers surrendered the following month. The fighting took place over a very wide area with only some of the action near Tel Megiddo. But Field Marshal Edmund Allenby chose the name for its biblical (and symbolic) resonance: Armageddon. Tel Megiddo National Park, a UNESCO World Heritage Site, has walking trails from more than twenty-five distinct historical periods.

Battle of the Lys

FLANDERS, BELGIUM

The river Lys runs along the Franco-Belgian border. In April 1918, fighting took place there in one of the final German offensives. Walking to the crest of Kemmel Hill (Kemmelberg), the highest point in Flanders, you find the impressive Art Deco memorial that commemorates France's dead; climb the tower of the Belvedere restaurant for spectacular views across the landscape. Down in the village churchyard, there are British graves and nearby a Demarcation Stone on the spot where the Germans were stopped.

BELOW Walk across former battlefields and up to the crest of Kemmel Hill, Belgium.

The Kaiser's Battle

AISNE, FRANCE

With the United States now part of the Allied cause, on March 21, 1918, the Germans launched Operation Michael, often called "the Kaiser's Battle" after their emperor. Outside the city of St. Quentin you can walk from the British Cemetery at Savy, seeing the graves of men who died that day, across to rising ground known as Manchester Hill by a quarry near Francilly-Selency. The Manchester Regiment was surrounded here and defended it that day to the last man; among them was Lieutenant-Colonel Wilfrith Elstob, who was awarded a posthumous Victoria Cross. His body was never found.

398

Third Battle of the Aisne

AISNE, FRANCE

The Chemin des Dames, a ridge of high ground northwest of Reims, witnessed a massive German attack against British troops on May 27, 1918. Among the trees of the Bois des Buttes, you can walk along the trench lines and into the village of La Ville-aux-Bois lès Pontavert to a memorial to the Devonshire Regiment and British gunners who made their last stand in the woods and were awarded the Croix de Guerre by the French for their bravery. Beyond the village, walk to the British graves at La Ville-aux-Bois British Cemetery.

399

Second Battle of the Marne

MARNE, FRANCE

In the summer of 1918, a final German offensive took place on the Marne. American troops played a vital role with the U.S. Marine Corps fighting among the dark trees of Belleau Wood. In the American Cemetery, walk between the rows of white crosses where more than 2,200 "Doughboys"—American infantrymen—are buried; the chapel lists the names of the missing. In the woods, you can see trenches and shell holes, the Marines' Memorial, and German field guns.

400

Riqueval Bridge

BELLICOURT, AISNE, FRANCE

In September 1918, Riqueval Bridge was the only crossing point along this part of the St. Quentin Canal in northern France. If it were destroyed, attackers would have to swim across the canal under fire. However, patrols of Staffordshire troops took the bridge intact from the Germans, enabling a victorious advance. Around the bridge today are remains of German bunkers and a British memorial. You can walk across the original bridge, down onto the canal bank, and north to the Riqueval Tunnel; there are German defenses at the tunnel entrance and up a path is a memorial to American troops.

LEFT Riqueval Bridge was a strategic crossing point captured by the Allies during the war.

401

Liberation of Mons

HAINAUT, BELGIUM

For Britain, the war ended where it had begun in 1914, at Mons. Canadian troops supported by British cavalry entered the city in the final moments of conflict. Among them was George Ellison, a miner from Leeds, who died on horseback close to the city, one of the last British soldiers to die in the war. Walk across the Conde Canal footbridge into Ville-sur-Haine, where there's a memorial to Canadian soldier George Lawrence Price, the last Commonwealth soldier to die in the war, just two minutes before the Armistice came into effect at 11:00 a.m. on November 11, 1918. Both their graves are found in the nearby St. Symphorien Cemetery.

Amiens

SOMME, FRANCE

Trace the path of the beginning of the end, when Allied soldiers broke through the German lines on the Somme.

◆ **DISTANCE**
3 miles

◆ **START**
Villers-Bretonneux

◆ **TYPE OF WALK**
Open countryside

◆ **WHEN TO GO**
All year; ceremonies take place on April 25

ABOVE RIGHT The memorial tower to ANZAC fighters is visible for miles around.

RIGHT The memorial is to more than 10,000 missing ANZAC soldiers.

The Australians fought at Gallipoli in 1915 as part of the Australian and New Zealand Army Corps (ANZAC). By 1918 they had become their own corps, but in the spring of that year ANZAC units helped stop the German advance on the Somme, particularly at Villers-Bretonneux.

Here, there's a Franco-Australian Museum where you can learn of the sacrifice of these troops before walking to Adelaide Cemetery. The grave of an unidentified Australian soldier was exhumed from here in 1993 and taken to Canberra as their Unknown Warrior; a unique headstone on what is now an empty grave records this.

Walk across the fields that saw fighting in the Allied advance on August 8, 1918, when the German lines on the Somme were smashed, signaling the start of the end of the war, you will then reach the huge Villers-Bretonneux Military Cemetery. Australians, British, and Canadians lie side by side on the slopes of the hill and a large tower is part of a memorial to more than 10,000 missing ANZACs. It shows damage suffered during fighting in May 1940. Behind the cemetery is the Monash Centre, a modern visitors' center telling the story of Australia's contribution to the war in France and Flanders, which alone cost them over 45,000 dead.

Second Battle of the Sambre

SAMBRE-OISE CANAL NEAR ORS, NORD, FRANCE

Follow the canal towpath, past where British poet Wilfred Owen was killed just one week before the end of the war.

◆ **DISTANCE**
2.5 miles

◆ **START**
Ors village

◆ **TYPE OF WALK**
Canal path

◆ **WHEN TO GO**
All year

ABOVE LEFT Among the graves of the British soldiers is that of Wilfred Owen, killed just one week before the war ended.

LEFT Walk through Mormal Forest to the house where Wilfred Owen was based.

The last great battle of World War I took place on November 4, 1918, when more than 100,000 men went into battle. Trench warfare was over, and the fighting across open fields reached the Sambre Canal, which the Germans defended. Standing on the canal bridge, you will find the memorial to war poet Wilfred Owen, who died in the battle here. Arguably the greatest single voice of the war, he had recently proved his bravery with the award of the Military Cross.

Walking along the canal towpath you come to a road on the left, and here you are standing close to where Owen was encouraging his men on the canal bank when he was killed just a week before the end of the war.

Following the road and walking around the village toward the station, you find Owen's grave in the French civilian cemetery; a plot of British graves are nearly all from the day he died, including two men awarded the posthumous Victoria Cross. The inscription on his grave is from one of his poems, chosen by his mother. Walking up through the nearby Mormal Forest, you come to the Forester's House, in the cellar of which Owen wrote his final letter home. Now a visitors' center, it tells the story of Owen, his life, and his poetry.

Finnish Civil War

HELSINKI, FINLAND

When the Finnish Civil War came to the streets of Helsinki, life surprisingly went on almost as normal. Shops and cafés stayed open and citizens came out to watch, and would be told by soldiers to back away. The fight for power came just after the declaration of independence in 1917, and was between the "Whites" of the de facto first government of independent Finland (supported by Germany) and the Socialist Workers' Republic "Reds" (supported by Russia). It ended in May 1918 with the Whites victorious, but no official peace treaty was ever signed between the political factions. Take a short walk around the Kamppi neighborhood, where much of the fighting took place, and reflect in the Chapel of Silence.

405

Battle of Sakarya

POLATLI, ANKARA PROVINCE, TURKEY

This 1921 battle near the Sakarya River 50 miles southwest of Ankara was an important Turkish victory against the Greek invaders and marked a turning point in the Turks' war of independence. A national park marking the battle site opened in 2015; stepped trails connect the grandiose hilltop monuments.

Great Smyrna Offensive

IZMIR, IZMIR PROVINCE, TURKEY

Visit Izmir, where a seafront promenade is packed with layers of history.

◆ **DISTANCE**
1 mile

◆ **START**
War of Independence
Monument, Kordon

◆ **TYPE OF WALK**
Easy

◆ **WHEN TO GO**
All year

ABOVE LEFT The distinctive
promenade in Izmir.

LEFT The Republic Tree
monument dedicated to the
War of Independence.

After their defeat in 1922 at the Battle of Dumlupınar—the last engagement of the Greco-Turkish War—the Greeks retreated to Smyrna (today's Izmir) on the coast, 175 miles to the west. Despite lacking most kinds of motorized vehicles—logistic support was based mainly on oxcarts—and being outnumbered two to one, the Turks recaptured Smyrna on September 9 and drove the Greek army completely out of the city in just two weeks. Four days after the fierce fighting abated, a devastating fire destroyed most of the Greek and Armenian neighborhoods in the city, with tens of thousands of civilians dying and many more seeking shelter. The Greek army no longer had offensive capabilities and was unable to organize a controlled retreat, leading to numerous Greek prisoners of war. The last of the Greek army left Anatolia ten days later.

From the War of Independence Monument, walk along Izmir's iconic seafront promenade, called the Kordon, where much of the fighting took place and where as many as 400,000 Greek and Armenian refugees crammed together to escape from the fire. After passing the ubiquitous monument to Kemal Atatürk, the first president of the new Turkish Republic, head southwest for a short distance to the City Museum and Archive with lots of information on the offensive.

Nanchang Uprising

NANCHANG, JIANGXI PROVINCE, CHINA

After overthrowing the Qing dynasty, the nationalist Kuomintang and the Communist Party formed a two-party government alliance, but soon turned on each other. In 1927, Chiang Kai-shek of the Kuomintang ordered a purge of Communist Party members from the alliance, and executed them. Countering the massacre, the Communist Party, led by Mao Zedong, attacked and took the city of Nanchang as the first official engagement of the civil war, which continued until 1949, when the Kuomintang retreated to Taiwan. Walk around the Xihu District in Nanchang, where a memorial was erected to mark the uprising.

Maginot Line

ALSACE, FRANCE

After suffering many of the deadliest battles in World War I, in 1929 the French began to construct a barrier to deter future invasions. A system of bunkers, pillboxes, and casemates named after André Maginot, the French war minister, was to run from Switzerland along France's eastern borders to the coast of the English Channel, but unfortunately it never got that far. The Germans outflanked the line in their 1940 invasion of France, rendering the defense a failure. However, it is still one of history's most intimidating military projects. Follow the trail along the line in Alsace, which takes you close to many of the fortifications.

Indian Independence Movement

SABARMATI ASHRAM, AHMEDABAD, GUJARAT, INDIA

Mahatma Gandhi began his 241-mile Salt March in 1930 from his *ashram* (religious retreat) beside the Sabarmati River. This twenty-four-day trek against the British authorities' unfair salt tax was a legendary act of civil disobedience during India's fight for independence from British colonial rule, and sparked waves of demonstrations and direct action by millions. Today you can retrace the start of the march, heading from the ashram along the river and through Ahmedabad.

Second Italian-Ethiopian War

TIGRAY, ETHIOPIA

In 1935, 200,000 Italian soldiers launched an unprovoked attack on Ethiopia. They quickly overran the defending army and the Ethiopian emperor, Haile Selassie, was forced into exile. One of the initial battle sites was the historic city of Aksum, which is the legendary home of the queen of Sheba and the reputed resting place of the Ark of the Covenant. A day's walk links the city's many historical and religious sites, which span several thousand years.

ABOVE RIGHT A fort on the Maginot Line sits among poppies—the symbol of the war.

RIGHT The entrance to a fort on the Maginot Line.

Brunete Offensive

QUIJORNA, MADRID, SPAIN

A walk in the hills around Quijorna reveals evidence of the Spanish Civil War.

- **DISTANCE**
  6.3 miles
- **START**
  Quijorna Town Hall
- **TYPE OF WALK**
  Half-day hike
- **WHEN TO GO**
  April-October, for
  better weather

ABOVE RIGHT The hills around Quijorna offer tranquil walking routes now.

RIGHT Break up a walk in the hills with the exploration of a bunker.

After the loss of Bilbao and Málaga in the earlier stages of the civil war, the Spanish Republican government needed to convince the French—who were supplying them with arms—that they were still capable of military action. In 1937, when the rebel Nationalists, under General Franco, besieged Madrid, the forces of the Republican government launched a surprise offensive. They selected the location of Brunete on the outskirts of Madrid, as it was on the crossroads that the Nationalists used for resupplies. The easy terrain of the area was also an opportunity to use the new tanks acquired from the Soviets.

For two weeks, a bloody battle was fought under a scorching midsummer sun. Both sides suffered heavy losses. On top of the loss of troops, the Republicans also lost so much equipment that it gave the Nationalists an advantage later in the war. Ultimately the Spanish Civil War was to end with a Nationalist victory and the dictatorship of Franco, which lasted until 1975.

Many of the civil war bunkers and battle structures remain in the region. A scenic circular walk into the hills from Quijorna, a town that saw fierce fighting during the battle, reveals the open grounds and landscape the battles were fought on.

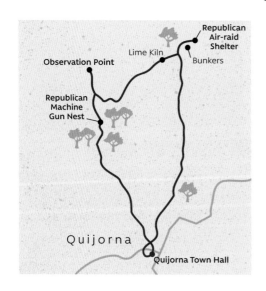

Republican
Air-raid
Shelter

Lime Kiln

Observation Point

Bunkers

Republican
Machine
Gun Nest

Quijorna

Quijorna Town Hall

Battle of Guadarrama

SIERRA DE GUADARRAMA, SPAIN

Determined to end the Republican government in Madrid, General Emilio Mola led his Nationalist troops from the north toward the capital in July 1936. The goal of the operation was to coordinate with General Franco's advance from the south. However, Mola's troops encountered government troops from Madrid in the Guadarrama mountain range. Unable to match their artillery and superior air firepower, the Nationalists surrendered. Ernest Hemingway's novel *For Whom the Bell Tolls* is based on the Spanish Civil War in the Guadarrama mountains. The range is dotted with bunkers and trenches, and is popular with both literary and historic hiking enthusiasts.

Siege of Madrid

MADRID, SPAIN

Nationalist troops under General Franco besieged Republican-held Madrid in order to gain control and topple the government. The Nationalists made the most intense effort to take Madrid in November 1936. Madrid held the invasion to the west of the city on the famous slogan "No pasarán" (They will not pass). The defense was supported by the XI International Brigade, a foreign volunteer troop that included Esmond Romilly, Winston Churchill's nephew, among its ranks. Walk around Parque del Oeste in Madrid for bunkers and forts from the civil war.

Battle of Jarama

ARGANDA DEL REY, MADRID, SPAIN

After failing to take Madrid, General Franco's plan B was to travel southeast to sever the ties between Madrid and the temporary Republican capital of Valencia. To do this, they had to break the line at the Jarama River near Arganda del Rey. In February 1937, Franco's troops attempted to break through the International Brigade units holding the line. Although unprepared and outnumbered, the brigade defended with determination and this line remained unbroken for the rest of the war. Walk across the river from the village to the lookout points with sweeping views of the surroundings.

Battle of the Ebro

CORBERA D'EBRE, CATALONIA, SPAIN

Toward the end of the civil war in July 1938, the Republicans planned a large attack on Nationalist advances across the Ebro River. A sizable army under Lieutenant Colonel Juan Modesto crossed the Ebro and captured Corbera. The goal was to capture nearby Gandesa. The Nationalists intensified their bombing in the area, totally destroying Corbera and forcing the Republicans back on the defensive. For three months, the Republicans suffered severe losses without ever achieving their goal. Walk around the old town of Corbera d'Ebre, which was intentionally left in ruins as a memorial to the war.

ABOVE The town of Corbera d'Ebre has been left in ruins as a memorial to the Spanish Civil War.

LEFT The Guadarrama mountains outside Madrid are popular with hikers for their literary and military links.

◆ 416 ◆

Capture of Barcelona

BARCELONA, CATALONIA, SPAIN

Barcelona defined the beginning and the end of the Spanish Civil War. The opening shots were fired in the city's central street, Las Ramblas, in 1936, starting three years of conflict that would result in the loss of around one million lives. The defining moment leading to the end of the war came when General Franco captured Barcelona in January 1939, at which point the Republicans attempted to negotiate peace. Franco refused, claiming victory, and took up dictatorial power over all of Spain. A walk around Las Ramblas is a walk in the footsteps of the combatants.

ABOVE Las Ramblas in Barcelona is linked with the beginning and the end of the Spanish Civil War.

◆ 417 ◆

Bombing of Guernica

GUERNICA Y LUNO, BISCAY, SPAIN

Still in the midst of the civil war, early signs of World War II came to the Basque Country in 1937 when the Nazi Luftwaffe and the Italian Aviazione Legionaria bombed Guernica, targeting civilians on behalf of Franco, who wanted to instill terror in the surrounding areas. It was an opportunity for the Nazis to test their recently developed Luftwaffe, founded in 1933. Several artists have depicted this brutal attack against unarmed civilians. They include Pablo Picasso, whose *Guernica* anti-war painting became one of his best-known works. Walk around Guernica y Luno and visit the air-raid shelters.

Marco Polo Bridge Incident

WANPING, BEIJING, CHINA

The Japanese had been expanding their presence in China since 1931. By 1937, troops had surrounded Beijing and were stationed on the outskirts just across the Yongding River from the Kuomintang-controlled army. One night, the Japanese requested to cross the river to search for a soldier who had not returned to his camp. The Chinese refused and opened fire across the Marco Polo Bridge. Walk from the bridge to Wanping Fortress, shelled by the Japanese during the conflict, and visit the Anti-Japanese War Sculpture Garden.

BELOW The Japanese invasion of China got as far as the Marco Polo Bridge in Beijing's suburbs.

Nanjing Massacre

NANJING, JIANGSU PROVINCE, CHINA

The Marco Polo Bridge Incident incited the second Sino-Japanese War. Chiang Kai-shek's Kuomintang and Mao Zedong's Communist troops formed a temporary alliance to fight the Japanese invasion. But in December 1937, the Japanese marched into and took over Nanjing, then capital of the newly formed Republic of China. Encouraged by their commanders, the troops are said to have raped and murdered civilians for six weeks. An international tribunal later estimated that there had been at least 200,000 casualties and at least 20,000 cases of rape. A walk around Nanjing Massacre Memorial Hall is a solemn reminder of the war crimes that were committed.

The Winter War

SUOMUSSALMI, FINLAND

Walk through woods past the detritus of war, where Russia tried to invade Finland, but couldn't overpower the Finnish soldiers with their knowledge of the terrain.

◆ **DISTANCE**
25 miles

◆ **START**
Suomussalmi
Tourist Office

◆ **TYPE OF WALK**
Full day, one way along
paved roads

◆ **WHEN TO GO**
Ideally in summer

ABOVE RIGHT The wreckage of war can be seen along this walking route.

RIGHT The Winter War monument outside Suomussalmi with stones to represent the soldiers who died in the fighting.

While fighting Nazi Germany in Word War II, Joseph Stalin was eyeing the resources available across the border in Finland. Spreading rumors that Finland was being used as a base to invade Russia, the Soviet Union launched a mass operation and invaded Finland in November 1939. Throughout the winter, Finnish troops, familiar with the forest environment and skilled skiers, fought several successful battles along the northern border. However, the Soviets had the advantage of numbers.

With no sign of a definitive outcome, a cease-fire was called and the Moscow Peace Treaty was signed with conditions favorable to Russia. At the signing, the Finnish president reportedly said, "May the hand wither that is forced to sign a document such as this." A few months later, he suffered a stroke that paralyzed his right arm.

The main road out of Suomussalmi toward the Russian border is lined with the same forests crisscrossed with trails that Finnish troops used to their advantage during the war. This long walk will take you from one memorial to another, passing open trenches and museums, ending at the Raate Frontier Guard Museum near the border.

Battle of Kuhmo
KUHMO, FINLAND

Soviet troops advanced toward
northern Finland in 1940 to
cut off the country from its
neighbors. As they approached
Kuhmo, the Finnish troops,
operating on skis, employed a
tactic which came to be known
as a *motti*, which involved
surrounding and immobilizing
the Russians. This led to
large-scale victories. See the
history at the Winter War
Museum then walk into the forest
where the fighting happened.

Dunkirk

DUNKERQUE, NORD, FRANCE

Without Dunkirk, there would have been no D-Day.
A walk along the port and beach is full of history.

- **DISTANCE**
  1.5 miles
- **START**
  Dunkirk War Museum
- **TYPE OF WALK**
  Some beach, some paved
- **WHEN TO GO**
  All year

LEFT The Mole in Dunkirk allowed big ships to take more than 200,000 soldiers to safety.

BELOW A German bunker along the coast from Dunkirk.

By 1940, the German Blitzkrieg had pushed the British and French back to the coast, and plans were made to evacuate more than 300,000 soldiers during Operation Dynamo.

In one of the old fortress buildings, used as a headquarters during the fighting, there is now a museum that tells the story of the British contribution through objects and photographs, as well as the sacrifice France made to make evacuation possible.

Walking onto the seafront at Dunkirk (Dunkerque in French), you will find the classic beaches where the Little Ships—a British fleet of yachts, fishing trawlers, and lifeboats—came in to take men off, under artillery fire and attacks from German dive-bombers. But only a third of the men left Dunkirk from the beaches. Walk on from the Dunkirk monument overlooking the beaches, toward the harbor and the Eastern Mole—a stone jetty with a wooden extension at the far end. On the way you'll pass battle damage on many buildings and walls, and German bunkers as you cross a bridge. With deep water on either side, the Mole allowed much larger ships to load soldiers and the wounded directly, taking over 200,000 to safety. The wooden section was later lost in a storm, but the stone part of the Mole is one of the most evocative places to visit here: the beginning of the road home, and for many the last time they would see France until D-Day four years later.

423

Battle of Britain and the Blitz

LONDON, ENGLAND

The Battle of Britain began in July 1940 when Nazi Germany's air force targeted ports throughout the UK. However, it failed to gain the air superiority needed for Operation Sea Lion, a planned amphibious and airborne invasion of Britain. But what came next was worse. The Blitz: the eight-month saturation bombing of cities and towns throughout Britain that killed 43,000 people. The list of walks is endless, but the most iconic would be around St. Paul's Cathedral, which Winston Churchill ordered "must be saved at all costs."

424

Chemin de la Liberté

ARIÈGE, FRANCE

The Chemin de la Liberté is a four-day-long hiking trail that runs over the crest line of the Pyrenees mountains from France to Spain. The route is one of a number used by the Resistance during World War II to smuggle French Resistance fighters, Jews, and Allied airmen out of Nazi-occupied France and into Spain. Back then, people were unlikely to have paused to enjoy the scenery, but today this marked (and fairly strenuous) route starting from the village of Saint-Girons offers hikers the chance to combine spectacular Pyrenean mountainscapes with a sense of history.

425

The Wolf's Lair

GIERŁOŻ, MASURIA, POLAND

Adolf Hitler moved into this 45-acre complex of concrete bunkers in northeast Poland in June 1941 and stayed here for three and a half years. It was here that the most famous attempt was made on his life in July 1944, by Colonel Claus von Stauffenberg of the German resistance. The Allies knew nothing of the Wolf's Lair until 1945. There are pathways around the overgrown site that pass by a number of bunkers, including Hitler's (number 13) and Hermann Göring's (number 16).

426

Brest Fortress

BREST, BELARUS

The frontier stronghold of Brest was taken by Nazi Germany as it advanced into the Soviet Union in 1941. Two regiments of Soviet soldiers garrisoned inside the fortress faced eight days of heavy artillery fire that destroyed much of the structure, before the majority of the Soviet troops were captured and the remainder surrendered shortly after. The fortress has been left as it was after the war, and used as Soviet propaganda as a testament to the resilience of the Soviet people. Walk around the fortress and the ceremonial square.

ABOVE LEFT The outside of the 45-acre Wolf's Lair.

LEFT Inside the Wolf's Lair, where Hitler lived for three and a half years.

Attack on Pearl Harbor

PEARL HARBOR, HONOLULU, HAWAII

December 7, 1941, was described by U.S. President Franklin D. Roosevelt as "a date which will live in infamy." At 7:48 a.m., Japan attacked the U.S. naval base of Pearl Harbor despite having made no declaration of war against the United States. Two hours later, sixteen U.S. warships and 180 aircraft were damaged or destroyed; 2,400 Americans were dead and more than 1,000 were wounded. This attack, later judged a war crime, brought the United States into World War II. At the Pearl Harbor National Memorial, walk along the quayside to bring the events of that pivotal day to life and reflect at the memorials.

Fall of Hong Kong

HONG KONG, CHINA

The day after Japan's attack on Pearl Harbor in Hawaii in 1941, Japanese forces swept down from Guangzhou in China and into the British colony of Hong Kong. After two weeks of resistance, the British surrendered, beginning four years of Japanese occupation. Conditions were harsh, with indiscriminate massacres of Chinese civilians and incarceration of Europeans at Stanley Prison. Next to the prison is the Hong Kong Correctional Services Museum, which traces the history of incarceration in Hong Kong. Walk to the Stanley Military Cemetery, which contains a number of graves from the early 1940s.

Japanese Submarine Attack on Sydney Harbour

SYDNEY, AUSTRALIA

When a Japanese floatplane flew over Sydney Harbour, no alarms were raised; many mistook it for a training flight. The next night, May 31, 1942, three Japanese midget submarines entered the harbor. Their targets were the anchored Allied warships. The attack failed; two submarines were captured but the third disappeared off the radar, only to be discovered in 2006 by recreational divers. Take a walk on the cliffs of North Head for a great view of the harbor's topography.

Raid on St. Nazaire

LOIRE, BRITTANY, FRANCE

Described as "the Greatest Raid of All," as part of the Allied Operation Chariot on March 28, 1942, British Navy and Army commandos attacked the German Kriegsmarine base with HMS *Campbeltown* ramming the dock gates and later (intentionally) exploding. Start where the *Campbeltown*'s gun is found on the seafront, then walk to the massive U-boat bunkers in the docks. The roofs of the bunkers give panoramic views, then walk down to the port area where the commandos came in and on to the Normandie Dock where the HMS *Campbeltown* made its mark.

LEFT From the cliffs at North Head outside Sydney, you can get a feel for the topography of the harbor.

Battle of Crete (Operation Mercury)

MONI GOUVERNETOU, CRETE

Walk through the gorge in Crete that Allied servicemen used for evacuation after Hitler's invasion.

◆ **DISTANCE**
7.6 miles

◆ **START**
Village of Imbros

◆ **TYPE OF WALK**
Half-day hike

◆ **WHEN TO GO**
All year

After taking Greece, the ambitions of Nazi Germany turned to Crete as a means to control the Mediterranean. While the German army was occupied with Russia, the Luftwaffe commanders convinced Hitler that an airborne attack on the island would prove successful.

The first troops were dropped by parachute along the stretch of coast at Chania on May 20, 1941. Over the next ten days, 22,000 paratroopers and mountain troops were dropped from the skies above the north coast.

Still recovering from fighting in mainland Greece, the Allied defense efforts could not match the determination of the Germans. Evacuations began on May 28. The British, Commonwealth, and Greek forces embarked for Egypt from the south coast. Crete was surrendered to the Germans on June 1. Though this was a victory for Hitler, it was costly in terms of aircraft and men, and he never used the same strategy again.

Walk along the Imbros Gorge, the evacuation route taken by Australian and New Zealander troops, toward Hora Sfakion War Memorial, marking the embarkation point of the evacuation.

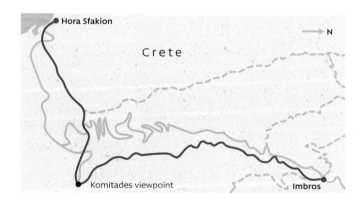

Dieppe Landings
UPPER NORMANDY, FRANCE

On August 19, 1942, the Allies launched a disastrous "hit and run" attack on German-held Dieppe. The beach at Puys became a killing ground, mainly of the Royal Regiment of Canada who landed here but whose tanks couldn't cope with the shingle. Walk along the pebbled beach with numerous monuments.

LEFT Hike through the Imbros Gorge to the point on the coast where the Allies were evacuated.

433

Dachau Concentration Camp

DACHAU, BAVARIA, GERMANY

Auschwitz was not the only Nazi death factory; the Germans and their collaborators set up 1,000 concentration camps between 1933 and 1945. These included the first at Dachau, a town ten miles northwest of Munich. Tours of the memorial site—both guided and individual—begin at the visitors' center.

The Holocaust

AUSCHWITZ-BIRKENAU (OŚWIĘCIM), POLAND

The horror of the Holocaust can be felt and never forgotten as you walk through Auschwitz.

◆ **DISTANCE**
4.5 miles

◆ **START**
Auschwitz Jewish Center

◆ **TYPE OF WALK**
Easy

◆ **WHEN TO GO**
Avoid winter

ABOVE LEFT Freight trains were used to transport more than a million people to Auschwitz.

LEFT The chilling sign over the gates of Auschwitz I.

The Nazis regarded many groups as *Untermenschen* (subhuman), including ethnic Slavs, Roma, and gay men, as well as Jews. But the term "Holocaust" generally refers to the genocide of European Jews during World War II. Most date the start of what is often called the *Shoah* (Hebrew for "catastrophe") from 1941 when paramilitary death squads, in conjunction with the German army, murdered around 1.3 million Jews in mass shootings and pogroms (riots incited to kill or expel Jews).

The Jews were to be eliminated completely. At first, they were segregated and confined in ghettos, then shipped off to concentration or extermination camps scattered around the country where inmates were either worked to death or exterminated outright in gas chambers.

The Holocaust ended in May 1945 with the liberation of Europe, but by then six million Jews, including Poland's entire Jewish population of three million, had been murdered.

No place is more evocative of the Holocaust than Auschwitz, a name synonymous with the largest attempt at genocide in human history. From the Auschwitz Jewish Center, walk southwest to Auschwitz I and the Auschwitz-Birkenau Memorial and Museum, where the infamous *Arbeit Macht Frei* (Work Brings Freedom) gate sign is kept. Then walk northwest to the huge, 430-acre Auschwitz II (Birkenau).

Bataan Death March

MARIVELES, PHILIPPINES

After the Battle of Bataan in 1942—when the Allied forces surrendered to the Japanese—American and Filipino prisoners of war were forced to march from Mariveles to Camp O'Donnell. Large numbers of prisoners died en route or on arrival. Impressive memorials can be visited at both Mariveles and Camp O'Donnell.

Battle of Manila

MANILA, PHILIPPINES

In 1945, American and Philippine forces reconquered Manila and ended the Japanese occupation. The fighting was some of the worst urban warfare of World War II and resulted in the loss of 100,000 civilian lives and the total devastation of the city. Today the Manila American Cemetery and Memorial covers 152 acres and contains 16,589 graves and 36,286 names of the missing. It is a peaceful site for a walk full of reflection.

Battle of Corregidor

CORREGIDOR ISLAND, PHILIPPINES

Walk between two iconic sites on the island of Corregidor, which was conquered by the Japanese in World War II.

◆ **DISTANCE**
3.1 miles

◆ **START**
Statue of General
Douglas MacArthur

◆ **TYPE OF WALK**
Along a quiet road

◆ **WHEN TO GO**
All year

ABOVE LEFT The Malinta Tunnel served as a bunker and a hospital for the wounded.

LEFT The skeleton of the Mile Long Barracks shows how heavily the site was bombed.

The 14th Japanese Imperial Army was intent on taking the island of Corregidor from Filipino and American soldiers. Its position and defenses in Manila Bay were key if Japan was to succeed in the war.

Nicknamed "The Rock," Corregidor was the largest fortified island in the bay, with a formidable defensive arsenal. For months it withstood the enemy bombardment, but in April 1942, the Japanese successfully took nearby Bataan, and were able to set up their batteries to launch a relentless attack on Corregidor, firing up to 16,000 artillery rounds in just one day.

Although the Filipino and American soldiers fought back, they were vastly outpowered, and on May 6, 1942, U.S. General Jonathan Wainwright was forced to surrender to the Japanese.

In the eastern part of the island is the Malinta Tunnel, a U.S.-built bunker that later served as a hospital for the wounded. Start here, then walk west to reach the Mile Long Barracks— today only the skeleton remains, although it's a striking site that serves as testament to the intensity of the Japanese bombardment. Finish your walk at the reconstructed Corregidor Island Lighthouse; you can climb the steep steps to the top to soak up peaceful views of the island and beyond.

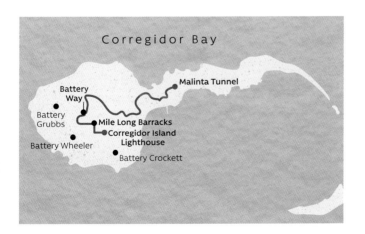

Corregidor Bay

Battery Way

Battery Grubbs

Malinta Tunnel

Mile Long Barracks

Corregidor Island Lighthouse

Battery Wheeler

Battery Crockett

Kokoda Campaign

PAPUA NEW GUINEA

This trail across Papua New Guinea, which Australia successfully defended from the Japanese, has become something of a patriotic pilgrimage for Australians.

◆ **DISTANCE**
60 miles

◆ **START**
Owers' Corner

◆ **TYPE OF WALK**
Multi-day hike

◆ **WHEN TO GO**
During the dry season of April–October

RIGHT The multi-day hike shows just how tough conditions were for fighters in these hills.

As the Japanese advanced across the Pacific, they were keen to capture Port Moresby, the capital of Papua New Guinea, which would enable them to bomb Allied bases in Australia. Their plan was to land in the north of the island and march through the Owen Stanley Range on the Kokoda Track to reach the capital.

The trail was heavily guarded by Papuan and Australian infantry battalions, and fierce fighting broke out as soon as the Japanese landed at Gona on July 21, 1942. The remote areas of Papua made the logistics for backup support difficult and the defending forces initially had to concede ground to the invaders.

This was the first time Australia felt directly threatened by the war. Poorly equipped and lacking supplies, the Australians weren't able to hold back the Japanese advance until they reached Imita Ridge, a natural obstacle close to Port Moresby. Here, the situation turned in favor of the Australians as supplies were able to come through from the capital and they were within artillery range from Owers' Corner. Suffering heavy losses against the defense, the Japanese retreated and fought their way back toward the north coast.

The campaign is considered a great achievement by the Australian military, and trekking the Kokoda Track has become something of a pilgrimage, commemorating the soldiers and the native Papuans who took part in the Australian campaign.

Papua
New Guinea

Gona
Buna

Kokoda

Efogi — The Kokoda Gap
Menari
Nauro

Port Moresby
Imita Ridge
Owers' Corner

Bombing of Darwin

DARWIN, NORTHERN TERRITORY, AUSTRALIA

The worst of the 111 Japanese World War II attacks on Australia was the first, the bombing on February 19, 1942, of the Northern Territory capital by 242 enemy planes that killed 235 people. Visit the waterfront Cenotaph where a ceremony is held every February 19, and then head east to the Oil Storage Tunnels, built in 1942, which exhibit wartime photos.

440

441

Battle of Stalingrad

VOLGOGRAD, RUSSIA

In order to advance the Eastern Front and to capture the Caucasus oil fields, Hitler ordered a major offensive to invade Stalingrad (now Volgograd) in August 1942. The city was destroyed by intense Luftwaffe bombing, and both sides fought a close house-to-house battle. After months of endless combat, the Soviet army fought through and surrounded the Germans in Stalingrad. After five months, as the Germans exhausted their supplies and continued battle became unsustainable, they became the first of Hitler's field troops to surrender in World War II. Walk among the monuments of Mamayev Hill.

Dam Busters Raid

RUHR VALLEY, NORTH RHINE-WESTPHALIA, GERMANY

On May 16, 1943, a Royal Air Force squadron nicknamed "the Dam Busters" dropped purpose-built "bouncing bombs" that could skip across water to attack a dam below water level as part of Operation Chastise. The bombs breached dams on the Möhne and Edersee reservoirs that were vital to German industry, causing catastrophic flooding of the Ruhr and Eder valleys. Some 1,600 civilians died, with 53 aviators killed. Today you can walk across the dam at Edersee and into the Kellerwald-Edersee National Park, which has well-marked tracks through ancient beech forest.

ABOVE Monuments on Mamayev Hill in Volgograd.

Bombing of Hamburg

HAMBURG, HAMBURG STATE, GERMANY

As a major industrial site, Hamburg was a prime target for Allied bombing during World War II, but until late July 1943 efforts had been largely unsuccessful. Then a sustained campaign of strategic bombing by British and American planes, code-named Operation Gomorrah, created one of the largest firestorms in the war, killing up to 37,000 civilians and incinerating the entire city. A 5.5-mile walk westward from the evocative Bunker Museum will lead you past St. Nicholas Church, which was gutted in the air raid and now houses a museum, and on to the U-Boat Museum, along the river in the St. Pauli district.

Air Battle of Berlin

BERLIN, GERMANY

The aerial Battle of Berlin, which began at the end of 1943 and continued for four months, was a series of attacks by the Royal Air Force (RAF) on Berlin and other German cities to keep German defenses dispersed. The bombardment caused huge loss of life and destroyed much of Berlin, 4,000 people were killed and 450,000 made homeless; the RAF itself lost upward of 2,700 crew. Walk around the husk of Kaiser Wilhelm Memorial Church, all that is left of a once-magnificent neo-Romanesque structure. It now stands quiet and dignified as an anti-war memorial.

ABOVE The remains of the Kaiser Wilhelm Memorial Church show how much of Berlin was destroyed.

Italian Resistance

APENNINES, ITALY

The Sentieri Partigiani (Partisan Trails) honor the partisans who fought in the Apennine Mountains of Reggio Emilia against Nazi occupation and Italian fascists.

◆ **DISTANCE**
8 miles

◆ **START**
Cerreto Alpi

◆ **TYPE OF WALK**
Mountain trail,
strenuous at times

◆ **WHEN TO GO**
All year

RIGHT The circular walking route
from Cerreto Alpi takes in some
beautiful scenery.

In September 1943, the first partisan units began to be active in the Apennine Mountains, organizing an armed resistance against Nazi Germany and the Italian fascists of the Republic of Salò.

The Gothic line, a German defensive line of the Italian Campaign, stretched from Cinquale to Pesaro along the summits of the northern Apennine Mountains. The line was the Germans' last line of defense in the fight against the Allied armies in Italy who were commanded by British General Sir Harold Alexander. The Germans set thousands of forced laborers and prisoners of war to work to build bunkers, observation posts, and artillery positions.

In the spring and summer of 1944, the Allies carried out an offensive, although no breakthrough occurred for months, forcing the Italians to fight throughout the last bitter winter of the war.

The circular Sentiero del Passo meanders through Apennine landscapes from Cerreto Alpi, passing two memorial stones that honor the fallen and the partisans of Sassalbo. Along the route, you'll pass areas that were the scene of intense fighting, with the ruins of German trenches and strongpoints.

Burma (Death) Railway

KANCHANABURI, KANCHANABURI PROVINCE, THAILAND

Japan used around 250,000 civilian laborers and 60,000 Allied prisoners of war to build a 258-mile-long stretch of railway between Bangkok and Rangoon. The center of the original 1,000-foot-long Death Railway Bridge in Kanchanaburi (of the 1957 movie *The Bridge on the River Kwai*, inspired by Pierre Boulle's novel of the same name) was destroyed by Allied bombs in 1945. From the bridge, follow the river Kwai (Khwae Yai) for around two miles to the Thailand–Burma Railway Centre, an excellent museum and research center.

Invasion of Sicily

REGIONE SICILIANA, ITALY

The Allied invasion of Italy began with Operation Husky in July 1943, when American, British, and Canadian troops landed on the island of Sicily. British Airborne forces were tasked with taking the Primosole Bridge over the Simeto River. Start west of the bridge where a Horsa glider landed, follow the attack route toward and over the modern bridge, and visit the nearby memorial and wartime bunkers. Battle damage can be seen on many buildings in the area. End with a visit to the Catania Commonwealth War Cemetery.

Salerno Landings

CAMPANIA, ITALY

Once Sicily was in Allied hands, it was possible to launch a strike on the Italian mainland and make a symbolic return to Europe. In Operation Avalanche, on September 9, 1943, American and British troops went ashore. On the seafront south of Salerno, walk past the towers covered with battle damage and up the road inland where British soldiers pushed forward. Then walk on to the Salerno War Cemetery, where the graves of British soldiers include press correspondents killed while reporting on the war.

ABOVE LEFT The bridge on the river Kwai, which inspired the book of that name.

LEFT Trains still use the railway today.

Battle of Ortona

CHIETI, ITALY

As the men of the multinational Eighth Army advanced up the Adriatic coast, crossing the Sangro Valley, Canadian troops attacked the coastal town of Ortona in December 1943. The Canadians captured the town but casualties were heavy on both sides. Starting at Piazza Porta Caldari, walk to the nearby war museum, and then down through the narrow streets to see battle damage and wartime signs, to the ruins of buildings destroyed in the battle; men fought from room to room here. At the far side of the town above the sea, visit the moving bronze memorial in the Moro River Canadian War Cemetery.

Battle of Rapido River

GARI RIVER, FROSINONE, ITALY

As the Allies advanced through Italy, American forces tried to cross the Gari River in January 1944, suffering terrible losses. Walk to the Bell of Peace Memorial close to the river at Sant'Angelo in Theodice. The bell is rung daily in memory of all those who died, and close by are American monuments. Walk back over the bridge to the town square where there is a memorial to the soldiers from Texas who died in the battle.

Albaneta Farm

CASSINO, FROSINONE, ITALY

With a stalemate on the Gustav Line at Cassino, the Allies looked for a way around the dominating position of the monastery. From the village of Caira take the Cavendish Road, built by Indian and New Zealander engineers to reach Monte Cassino. It is a long walk up, but the signs of battle are everywhere in the scrub. At Albaneta Farm, a knocked-out Polish Sherman tank remains as a memorial and the ruins of the farm show signs of the tank assault stopped by German paratroopers and the final advance in May 1944.

BELOW At Albaneta Farm, a Polish tank has been turned into a war memorial.

Cap de la Chèvre

BRITTANY, FRANCE

Guarding the Baie de Douarnenez in Brittany's storm-wracked Finistère region, the defensive works at the far end of the high cliffs of the Cap de la Chèvre were, in fact, constructed shortly before World War II, but served as defensive positions during it. There's a superb half-day, marked cliff-top walk that takes in these defensive positions as well as the moody Atlantic beaches on the western side of the headland and the limpid, almost Mediterranean blue waters on the sheltered eastern side. There's also a shorter 90-minute version of the walk.

Omaha Beach

NORMANDY, FRANCE

Omaha Beach was one of two American D-Day beaches, and was the deadliest with an estimated 2,400 casualties. From Les Moulins, walk along the beach to the monument where the original American burials were made in 1944; you'll soon arrive at the Dog Green sector depicted in *Saving Private Ryan*. The National Guard Monument sits on a German bunker with the original 88mm gun inside. The bronze figures here depict a GI dragging a wounded comrade across the beach. By walking the Vierville Draw, you can climb to the bluffs above the beach for the German viewpoint.

ABOVE The imposing cliffs of Omaha Beach that faced the Allied troops who landed here on D-Day.

Siege of Anzio

LAZIO, ITALY

Operation Shingle in January 1944 was meant to take the Allies to Rome, but instead resulted in static warfare for months. Walking up from Peter Beach where they landed, the Sicily–Rome American Cemetery and Memorial at Nettuno shows the cost of the longest siege in the Italian Campaign.

Monte Cassino

LAZIO, ITALY

Walk through Italian hill country to a monastery that
was captured by Polish troops.

◆ **DISTANCE**
2 miles

◆ **START**
Snakeshead Ridge,
Monte Cassino

◆ **TYPE OF WALK**
Marked footpaths

◆ **WHEN TO GO**
All year

ABOVE LEFT More than a
thousand Polish soldiers lost
their lives as they fought to
capture Monte Cassino.

LEFT The original monastery was
reduced to rubble during the
fighting; the current one was
built after the war.

For five months there had been a stalemate in front of the
monastery at Monte Cassino. Its position, as part of the German
line, overlooked the road to Rome, and stopped any Allied
advance. Free Polish troops under General Władysław Anders
were tasked with taking it in the final battle in May 1944.

Reached by a minor road, Snakeshead Ridge once marked the
front lines and there are traces of forward positions and gun pits
here, as well as the Doctor's House used as an aid post. Crossing
No Man's Land and climbing up to Hill 593, you can take in the
German view of the battlefield ground defended by their
parachute forces. Walking down, you find mortar pits and shell
holes among the brush. Crosses in the Polish Cemetery
remember over a thousand dead who fell here in the capture of
this ground, and a visitors' center explains the history.

From here, walk up to the highest point where the ancient
Benedictine monastery is located. It was largely destroyed but
was later rebuilt, although battle scars are still visible.

In 1944, the Polish flag was raised on the rubble so the men
on the battlefield below could
see it and know that Anders
and his men had finally
captured it. The views from
here are simply incredible
and show how the monastery
dominates the landscape.

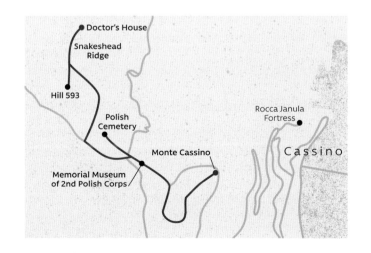

Pegasus Bridge

NEAR OUISTREHAM, NORMANDY, FRANCE

Cross the bridge that saw the first action of D-Day and stop in the café that helped the wounded.

◆ **DISTANCE**
1 mile

◆ **START**
Pegasus Bridge

◆ **TYPE OF WALK**
Largely urban

◆ **WHEN TO GO**
All year

ABOVE RIGHT The modern Pegasus Bridge is an almost identical copy of the original.

RIGHT The Café Gondrée helped treat the wounded on D-Day, and retains its bond as a living museum today.

D-Day was the largest invasion by sea in history, as Allied forces landed on the beaches of Normandy to begin their campaign to push the Nazis back into Germany.

It did, however, include airborne support which involved sending a glider force of 2nd Oxfordshire and Buckinghamshire Light Infantry to take and hold the bridges over the Caen Canal and Orne River just after midnight.

Starting by the markers denoting where three of the gliders landed near the canal, you can see how close they got to the objective of Pegasus Bridge. The lead glider had Major John Howard in it, and a bronze of him is here. Lieutenant Den Brotheridge then led the charge over the wire, into the trenches and bunkers. One of the original field guns can be seen, and while the original Pegasus Bridge is now in the nearby museum, the modern copy is almost identical. Walking to the far side, just outside the Café Gondrée, leads you to where Brotheridge received his fatal wound, becoming the first Allied battle fatality of D-Day. The Gondrées helped with the wounded and the café is now a living museum.

Walking up to the battle-damaged *mairie* (town hall), the 7th Parachute Battalion memorial reminds you that Howard took the bridge, and these men defended it. At the nearby church in Le Port you will find graves of some of the dead, including a priest who stood in the way of Nazi bullets to save the wounded.

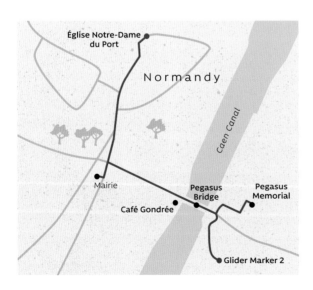

Église Notre-Dame du Port

Normandy

Caen Canal

Mairie

Pegasus Bridge

Pegasus Memorial

Café Gondrée

Glider Marker 2

Brécourt Manor Assault

SAINTE-MARIE-DU-MONT, NORMANDY, FRANCE

In a field near Brécourt Manor farmhouse, the Germans placed a gun battery that fired on Utah Beach. Major Richard Winters led the men of the U.S. Army's Easy Company into an assault that silenced the guns on D-Day. From the Richard Winters Memorial on the main road, walk down to the Easy Company Memorial overlooking the fields, and follow the hedgerow-lined roads to the farm, looking much like it did in 1944. Continue into Sainte-Marie-du-Mont and the square where the "Band of Brothers" were photographed.

BELOW The town of Sainte-Marie-du-Mont, where Easy Company helped win the war.

Operation Epsom

TOURMAUVILLE, NORMANDY, FRANCE

As the British pushed inland across France, tanks and infantry advanced as part of Operation Epsom on June 26, 1944. From the 15th (Scottish) Division memorial that stands near Tourmauville, take the road down into the wooden Odon River valley along the "Scottish Corridor" where these men attacked. As you pass through Baron-sur-Odon, you come to the open fields of Hill 112, the scene of bitter fighting and terrible shelling. Now a memorial site, there's a Churchill tank, a bronze statue of a British soldier, and an original monument to the 43rd (Wessex) Division, who were almost wiped out here.

Battle for the Bocage
SAINT LÔ, NORMANDY, FRANCE

American soldiers found themselves in a terrible battle for the *bocage*—the landscape, particularly hedgerows of Normandy—in July 1944. The advance took them through villages to the town of Saint Lô, which was almost destroyed. From Saint-Georges-d'Elle, walk south into the hedgerows and find "Purple Heart Draw," the scene of bitter fighting, and continue via the enclosed countryside and narrow lanes to Saint-André-de-l'Épine and into the outskirts of Saint Lô. Rebuilt as a modern town, the Chapelle de la Madeleine remembers the American sacrifice in the fighting with memorials, photographs, and artifacts.

Operation Goodwood
CAEN, NORMANDY, FRANCE

Once Caen had fallen to the Allies, over a month after D-Day, on July 18, 1944, the British then launched a massive tank assault on the German positions east of the city and against the Bourguébus Ridge. With the advantage of terrain, the Germans inflicted heavy losses in tanks and men. From the open fields near Caen, follow the route to Cagny. Here the ruined church has memorials to the Guards Armoured soldiers involved in the fighting. Take the road to Émiéville and find the memorial to John Gorman of the Irish Guards, who rammed a German King Tiger tank with his Sherman tank.

ABOVE The Chapelle de la Madeleine in Saint Lô has memorials to the American fighters.

460

The Falaise Pocket
NORMANDY, FRANCE

As the Normandy campaign brought success to the Allies, German forces were pushed into a pocket around Falaise. Near the church in Saint-Lambert-sur-Dive, information panels show photographs of German tanks left here in August 1944. Follow a track across the fields, walking the Corridor of Death, where men, horses, and vehicles all lay smashed, and continue into Chambois to just below the castle where American and British troops met up. Finishing on Mont Ormel, you can look back over the battlefield and see memorials to Polish troops who took this high ground.

461

Warsaw Uprising
WARSAW, POLAND

The uprising began in August 1944 as German forces retreated across Poland. The Polish army took back control of large parts of the city from the Germans and waited for Allied and Soviet support, which never came. Fighting raged for sixty-three days before the insurgents were forced to surrender. The German revenge was brutal—Warsaw was razed to the ground, with only 15 percent of the city left standing, and 200,000 Poles were killed. Walk from the main square in Warsaw's Stare Miasto (Old Town), which was flattened during the war, to the moving Monument to the Warsaw Uprising.

462

Massacre of Monte Sole
MARZABOTTO, BOLOGNA, ITALY

Between September 29 and October 5, 1944, 775 people were brutally massacred by Nazi troops in the Monte Sole area—including the entire village community of Marzabotto. Liberation came on April 16, 1945, following a fierce conflict between the Nazis and Allied troops. An 11-mile trail through the Parco Storico di Monte Sole follows paths once used by inhabitants and partisans during the war, meandering through fields and wooded areas, with ruins of abandoned, vegetation-covered buildings peppering the route.

ABOVE LEFT The Monte Sole Natural Historic Park.

LEFT A memorial trail with information and monuments winds for 11 miles through the park.

463

Market Garden
NEAR EINDHOVEN, THE NETHERLANDS

In September 1944, General Bernard Montgomery hoped Operation Market Garden would end the war before Christmas, dropping British Airborne troops behind enemy lines and sending ground forces up a narrow road into the Netherlands. On the Belgian border, walk onto "Joe's Bridge" outside Neerpelt, where the Irish Guards got a foothold to begin their advance, seeing their memorial before walking the road they followed up to Valkenswaard War Cemetery. Guardsmen and soldiers from Wales lie side by side, including some of the Irish Guardsmen killed in their tanks. Continue into Eindhoven, where the liberated Dutch population effectively stopped the advance.

Arnhem Bridge

ARNHEM, THE NETHERLANDS

Visit this bridge at the heart of an ambitious Allied plan that didn't quite pay off.

◆ **DISTANCE**
4.5 miles

◆ **START**
John Frost Bridge

◆ **TYPE OF WALK**
Urban walk

◆ **WHEN TO GO**
All year

ABOVE RIGHT The area around Arnhem Bridge was flattened in the bombing.

RIGHT The bridge has been rebuilt since the war, but on the old supports.

Dropped a long way from their objective, only 600 British Airborne troops, led by Lieutenant Colonel John Frost, made it to the north side of Arnhem Bridge, behind enemy lines, on September 17, 1944. Their objective was to take the south end of the bridge, with support from ground forces. The ground forces never arrived, and Frost's troops held on for four days, before being forced to pull back without ever taking the bridge.

The bridge was later destroyed in bombing. An identical replacement was built in 1948 using the original bridge supports that show signs of the battle. In 1977 this was officially renamed the John Frost Bridge (John Frostbrug). The nearby Bridge Visitors' Centre explains the story—which was later turned into the film *A Bridge Too Far*.

From here, walk into Oosterbeek via the former St. Elizabeth's Hospital. In Oosterbeek, the Hartenstein Hotel served as the British Airborne headquarters and is now a war museum. Follow the Stationsweg, the route of the perimeter, where Airborne troops defended the houses on the left while German battle groups attacked from the right. End at the Airborne War Cemetery where the dead from the battle, the "Airborne Carpet," now guard the drop zones where Airborne troops landed.

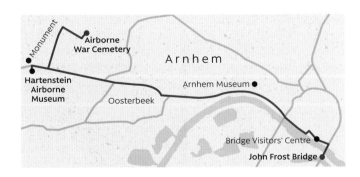

Operation Berlin
DRIEL, THE NETHERLANDS

The British Airborne, trapped at Arnhem, needed a means to get away. Canadian engineers took assault boats to rescue over 2,000 men. Walking the evacuation route from Oosterbeek Church along the Rhinebank, take the foot ferry to Driel and see the memorial to this remarkable event.

Battle of the Crossroads
RANDWIJK, THE NETHERLANDS

In October 1944, Major Richard Winters led the U.S. Army's Easy Company here. Their fight against the Germans is commemorated in the TV miniseries *Band of Brothers*. From Randwijk, walk east along the bank of the Rhine; the high-banked roads and flat ground beyond can easily be seen. Farther up the Crossroads, the spot where Winters fired his rifle is now marked by a memorial.

Battle of the Bulge

BASTOGNE, ARDENNES, BELGIUM

Explore the woods and fields from where the 101st American Airborne Division defended the town of Bastogne.

◆ **DISTANCE**
1.5 miles

◆ **START**
Band of Brothers
Memorial, Bastogne
Woods

◆ **TYPE OF WALK**
Forest walk

◆ **WHEN TO GO**
All year

ABOVE RIGHT The woods around Bastogne are full of hollows where soldiers dug in.

RIGHT The village of Foy was the scene of fighting in 1945.

The German offensive in the Ardennes in December 1944 was Hitler's last gamble in the west. When a massive armored force broke through the American lines—causing a bulge or "salient" in the German line—units of the 101st American Airborne Division were moved up from France to defend the key town of Bastogne, and very quickly found themselves besieged.

The old railway line northeast of Bastogne was used to evacuate the wounded in Jeeps during the fighting. Today there is a memorial to the "Band of Brothers," the men of Easy Company 506th Parachute Infantry, that overlooks the ground they defended during Christmas 1944. Walking up the road beyond, there are signs of positions among the trees where the Airborne troops dug in, and when you come to Bois Jacques, the very front line, more are found among the trees. While some date from later reenactments, many are original, and walking to the edge of the woodland looking down into the village of Foy, you get an idea of the ground they defended. Continue into the village, where you can see shrapnel and bullet damage on the walls. Ending at the church, this is where Easy Company went into the attack in January 1945, following the long period of static warfare in the woods.

468

Bombing of Dresden
DRESDEN, SAXONY, GERMANY

In mid-February 1945, British and American planes unleashed almost 4,000 tons of explosives on Dresden. The bombing and the resulting firestorm destroyed more than 1,600 acres of the city center and killed up to 25,000 people. Whether or not the attacks were justified has become one of the biggest debates of World War II. Walk around the 135-acre Städtische Heidefriedhof, a municipal forest cemetery on the northern outskirts of the city, where 18,365 victims of the bombings were buried.

469

Battle of Okinawa
NAHA, OKINAWA, JAPAN

Requiring a base in the Pacific for the war against Japan, the United States launched a large amphibious assault on the southwest coast of the island of Okinawa on April 1, 1945. The forces initially met with minimal resistance until Japanese troops arrived from inland and began a fierce defensive campaign. The war is described by the United States as the longest and bloodiest in the Pacific Theater. The islanders called the war "the typhoon of steel and bombs." Walk around the city of Naha, visiting Maeda Escarpment, Wana Ridge, and the Tomari International Cemetery.

470

Siege of Küstrin
GORZÓW COUNTY, POLAND

By early 1945, the Soviet advance reached Germany. The walled city of Küstrin (given to Poland after the war and now known as Kostrzyn) stood on the road to Berlin and was declared a *Festung*—a strongpoint, to be held at all costs. Bitter fighting raged as a small German force held on against overwhelming Russian numbers which eventually saw a Soviet victory. Walk from Germany across the Oder River into old Küstrin; you will see battle damage everywhere. Find the museum and literally touch the past.

ABOVE LEFT The fortress walls in Küstrin.

LEFT Many parts of old Küstrin have been left untouched since the war.

471

Rhine Crossing
NORTH RHINE-WESTPHALIA, GERMANY

By March 1945, the Allies had reached the Rhine. British troops crossed near Wesel in a massive river assault, Operation Plunder. From the ruins of an old fort south of the river, walk to the Wesel railroad bridge. Built before World War I, it carried men to the front in both world wars. Blown up by the Germans in 1945, it shows signs of heavy battle damage. Walk into Wesel on the new crossing, then to the north bank to find the remains of the bridge. From one of its supports you can view the area where the crossing took place.

Reichswald Forest

KLEVE, GERMANY

Wander among the tangled trees that Allies negotiated on their route to the Rhineland.

DISTANCE
2 miles

START
Kranenburger Strasse,
Reichswald Forest

TYPE OF WALK
Forest walk

WHEN TO GO
All year

RIGHT British forces navigated this dense and boggy forest as part of Operation Veritable.

After Operation Market Garden, the fighting settled down to allow the Allies to build up their forces over the winter for an offensive the following year. Known as Operation Veritable, this opened on February 8, 1945, with over a thousand guns firing in support.

From Kranenburger Straße, a road in the northern area of Reichswald Forest, you can take a path through the trees following the line of the British advance. It is as dense and tangled as it was in 1945, and the signs of positions, bomb craters, and shell holes are visible. Walking it gives an indication of the difficult nature of this as a battlefield, and while today you emerge onto a new fast road to Kleve, in 1945 these roads were thick with mud and hampered progress.

At the Reichswald Forest War Cemetery, the largest British and Commonwealth cemetery from World War II with over 7,500 graves, the burial ground is split between the services; on the left are Royal Air Force graves, and British Army graves are on the right. Many Commonwealth nations are represented among the dead, and every rank from ordinary soldier through to a general: Major-General Tom Rennie, who died in the Rhine crossing. To get some idea of scale, take the staircase up into the viewing platform.

473
Seelow Heights
BRANDENBURG, GERMANY

Once the Soviets crossed the Rhine near Küstrin in January 1945, the last defense before Berlin was the high ground at Seelow. For several months, a small force of German soldiers, many of them just boys, held back the Soviet attacks. At the Seelow Memorial site you can see tanks, artillery, and rocket launchers. Walking to Lindendorf, past where a German railway gun was in action, you come up onto the Seelow Heights and can see signs of trenches, mortar pits, and gun positions.

474
Berlin
BRANDENBURG, GERMANY

The fighting in Berlin in April 1945 was really a series of small, isolated battles. Cross the Spree River by the Bodestrasse to Museum Island and you can see signs of those final battles on almost every wall here. In Museum Island's Lustgarten (Pleasure Garden), German war trophies were once displayed. From the island head to the Neue Wache, which is now the Central Memorial for the Victims of War and Tyranny, featuring a statue by Käthe Kollwitz. Then walk to the Brandenburg Gate: the very symbol of Berlin, where the fighting raged. Close by is the site of Hitler's bunker, now a parking lot.

475
Bombing of Hiroshima
HIROSHIMA, HONSHU, JAPAN

With the war over in Europe by May 1945, the Allies called for Japan's unconditional surrender, which was ignored. On August 6, the United States dropped the world's first atomic bomb on Hiroshima. The blast and resulting firestorm killed 90,000 civilians and leveled five square miles of the city. Hiroshima is full of monuments and sites recalling the destruction. Walk from the Atomic Bomb Dome (Genbaku) south through the Peace Memorial Park and its memorial mound, cenotaph, and eternal Flame of Peace to the Hiroshima Peace Memorial Museum.

LEFT The Atomic Bomb Dome in Hiroshima's Peace Memorial Park.

476
Bombing of Nagasaki
NAGASAKI, KYUSHU, JAPAN

Three days after the Hiroshima bombing, an American B-29 flew toward Kitakyushu on Kyushu's northeastern coast, the site of a major munitions plant, to drop a second atomic bomb on Japan. But due to poor visibility, the crew diverted southwest to a secondary target. On August 9, 1945, a bomb with an explosive power twice that of the Hiroshima bomb was dropped on Nagasaki, killing a third of its 240,000 residents. Japan surrendered less than a week later. In Nagasaki, visit the Nagasaki Atomic Bomb Museum and adjacent Peace Memorial Hall, then walk north to the 10-ton bronze Nagasaki Peace Statue in Peace Park.

Liberation of Europe

LIBERATION ROUTE, EUROPE

An epic, long-distance, multi-country trail celebrates the liberation of Europe from Nazi Germany.

◆ **DISTANCE**
Over 6,200 miles

◆ **START**
Various starting points

◆ **TYPE OF WALK**
An epic long-distance trail

◆ **WHEN TO GO**
All year

RIGHT Begin at Utah Beach, one of the five beaches used for the D-Day landings.

The Liberation Route is an ongoing project across nine European countries to link important sites for Allied forces as they liberated Europe from the grip of the Nazis.

Many battle sites are included on the route, and there are 200 audio spots to allow walkers to stop and listen to stories from those locations and gain a perspective on the war from different nations.

The campaign to liberate Europe began when the Allies came to the conclusion that only an "unconditional surrender" by Hitler would end the war.

While the Red Army of Russia fought against the Nazis from the east, the Allies started their campaign from the west with the D-Day landings on June 6, 1944. Following a deception campaign providing false information to Germany, 156,000 American, British, and Canadian forces made amphibious landings across five beaches of the strongly fortified Normandy coast, coupled with airborne support. Four thousand Allied troops lost their lives on landing, with the remainder successfully breaching the defense line and fighting their way over the countryside to liberate France within two months. Months of fighting followed, and the Allies merged forces with the Soviet troops advancing from the east, as their lines met in Germany.

Arrogance, miscalculations of Allied advances, and mistrust among Hitler's close advisers led to the defeat and an unconditional surrender from Nazi Germany, liberating much of Europe from the regime of the Third Reich on May 8, 1945.

The Liberation Route brings together many of the individual walks covered on previous pages.

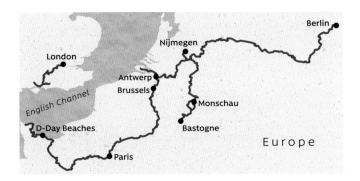

Sosabowski's Trail

DRIEL, THE NETHERLANDS

The 1st Polish Independent Parachute Brigade under General Sosabowski came to the Netherlands, marched across the river Rhine at Driel, and relieved the surrounded British troops near Oosterbeek. As part of the Liberation Route, follow the footsteps of the Poles around Driel on a short walk.

El Bogotazo

BOGOTÁ, COLOMBIA

On April 9, 1948, Jorge Eliécer Gaitán, leader of the left-wing Liberal Party and a popular candidate for the presidency, was murdered in his office in downtown Bogotá. The assassination of the "voice of the people" sparked the Bogotazo, a ten-hour riot that destroyed much of the city, left thousands dead, and plunged Colombia into a decade-long conflict, La Violencia. Walk from the corner of Carrera Séptima and Avenida Jiménez, where Gaitán's office was located, through the area worst affected by the violence—now a busy shopping district—to the Candelaria neighborhood. Here you'll find the Supreme Court, which was targeted by rioters.

BELOW The old part of Bogotá was beset by violence during the Bogotazo.

Battle of Guningtou

KINMEN, TAIWAN

Kinmen is a group of islands less than three miles from the shores of mainland China. In October 1949, after the Communist Party won control of mainland China, Chiang Kai-shek's Kuomintang fled to Taiwan, to which Kinmen belongs. Communist leader Mao Zedong invaded Kinmen but underestimated the defensive troops on the island. Overwhelmed by the surrounding Kuomintang troops, the Communist soldiers surrendered the next day. A walk around these heavily militarized islands is a testament to the resilience of the Taiwanese.

481

Korean War

SOUTH KOREA

The Korean War (1950–1953) reshaped Korea and the world stage, separated families, and cost millions of lives. The Demilitarized Zone (DMZ) remains one of the most heavily fortified borders on the planet. Visits are under tight supervision and one cannot enter the DMZ; to see things for yourself, head to the Goseong Unification Observatory Tower, where you can look across the DMZ to North Korea and the fabled Kumgang Mountains, and then find a spot to walk along the beach. You'll see plenty of barbed wire and blockades; no peace treaty has ever been signed, so technically a war is still going on.

482

Mau Mau Uprising

ABERDARE MOUNTAINS, KENYA

The 1952–1960 Mau Mau Uprising was an armed revolt against British colonial rule that took place in central Kenya. At least 11,000 people died during the uprising but, due in part to disunity among those opposing British rule, the uprising eventually failed to overthrow the British, although it did help set in motion the wheels that led to Kenyan independence in 1963. Much of the fighting took place in and around the high and bleak moorlands of the Aberdares Range. Today this area is a national park and offers some exciting hiking. You'll need an armed park guide, however, because buffalo are common and can be aggressive.

BELOW The Goseong Unification Observatory Tower allows you to look across to North Korea.

483

First Indochina War
VĨNH LINH DISTRICT, VIETNAM

Vietnam was part of French Indochina until World War II put a halt to France's control over the region. At the end of the war, France landed troops in Hai Phòng to push for a renewed inclusion of Vietnam in France. Fights broke out between the French and the Việt Minh, a communist and nationalist movement formed by Hồ Chí Minh, and the country would see battles for the next seven years. The French defeat at Điện Biên Phú in 1954 marked the end of the war. The consequence was a nation divided into communist North and pro-Western South Vietnam. Take a walk around the former Demilitarized Zone on the Bến Hải River.

484

Tibetan Uprising
CENTRAL TIBET, CHINA

Although Tibet had been under the effective control of China since 1951, things came to a head in the spring of 1959 when a revolt erupted in the Tibetan capital of Lhasa. It was caused over fear that the authorities were about to arrest the fourteenth Dalai Lama. Peaceful protest against the Chinese presence turned violent and the Dalai Lama was forced to flee to India. There are no official battle sites (the political atmosphere remains tense), but a three-to-five-day hike between the culturally and historically important monasteries of Ganden and Samye, a short way from Lhasa, offers stunning scenery.

485

Malayan Emergency
KUALA LUMPUR, MALAYSIA

The Malayan Emergency was a guerrilla war fought between Communists and British and Commonwealth armies. Britain created the Federation of Malaya in 1948, and while most Malays were pleased, many Chinese citizens felt betrayed. The Malayan Communist Party embarked on a twelve-year guerrilla war against the British. Almost 12,000 people died, more than a quarter of them civilians. The federation became independent in 1957, but fighting continued for three more years. From Merdeka (Independence) Square in Kuala Lumpur, where independence was declared, walk west to the National Monument.

486

Algerian War of Independence
ALGIERS, ALGERIA

The Battle of Algiers was an urban guerrilla campaign carried out by the Algerian National Liberation Front. It began in late 1956, after French colonials planted a bomb in the Casbah, killing seventy-three civilians. A year of fighting ended in French victory. But by 1962, Algeria was independent. From the atmospheric Casbah, scene of the fiercest fighting, walk to the hilltop Martyrs' Memorial, a 302-foot-tall colossus with views of the city and port.

TOP Ganden Monastery in Tibet.

ABOVE It's a stunning walk to the culturally and spiritually important Samye Monastery.

Cuban Revolution

SANTA CLARA, CUBA

This route whisks you back to the climax of the Cuban Revolution in the central city of Santa Clara.

◆ **DISTANCE**
2.5 miles

◆ **START**
Che Guevara's
mausoleum

◆ **TYPE OF WALK**
Easy walk, mostly along
sidewalks and paths

◆ **WHEN TO GO**
All year, although
November–April is the
coolest, driest period

ABOVE RIGHT The memorial park
commemorating the capture of
the Tren Blindado.

RIGHT Ernesto "Che" Guevara's
mausoleum in Santa Clara.

After a five-and-a-half-year uprising, Fidel Castro's 26th of July Movement finally ousted the dictator Fulgencio Batista in the Battle of Santa Clara, which has become synonymous with the Cuban Revolution.

After capturing the strategic Capiro Hill on the edge of the city, the revolutionary forces bulldozed the railway track to derail the Tren Blindado (armored train) carrying arms and reinforcements for Batista's forces, many of whom subsequently asked for a truce. Despite pockets of resistance, Castro's fighters had the momentum and went on to capture the whole of Santa Clara. Within hours, Batista's authoritarian regime collapsed and the dictator fled to Portugal, allowing the revolutionaries to claim the capital, Havana, unhindered.

Start your walk at the impressive mausoleum of Ernesto "Che" Guevara, who led the revolutionary forces during the Battle of Santa Clara (and was later killed in Bolivia in 1967). Then head east across the city center to a memorial park and museum marking the dramatic capture of the Tren Blindado. Finish your walk farther east at the summit of Capiro Hill, a hideaway and command center for Che's guerrillas.

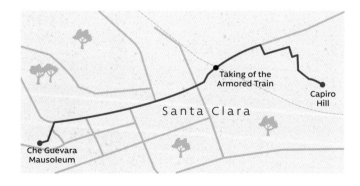

488

Bay of Pigs
PLAYA GIRÓN, CUBA

This beach was a landing site for the CIA-backed Bay of Pigs invasion in April 1961, in which Cuban exiles failed to overthrow Fidel Castro. Walk across the sand, via a small invasion-focused museum, to the Ciénaga de Zapata wetlands, where much of the fighting took place.

489

Hungarian Uprising

BUDAPEST, HUNGARY

This nationwide revolution against the Stalinist government began on October 23, 1956, when university students assembled in Budapest, demanding a new prime minister. When Imre Nagy formed a government and began making sweeping reforms, Soviet tanks crossed into Hungary and attacked Budapest. Twelve days later, 25,000 people were dead and 250,000 had fled to Austria. From the former Hungarian Radio headquarters on Bródy Sándor Street, where agents first fired on demonstrators, walk to Corvin Square where the heaviest fighting took place. There's a monument to the Pesti *srácok*, the heroic "kids from Pest" who fought and died here.

490

The Cold War

EASTERN AND WESTERN EUROPE

"From Stettin in the Baltic to Trieste in the Adriatic, an iron curtain has descended across the Continent" is how Winston Churchill described the political tension between the Western and Eastern blocs from 1947 until the dissolution of the Soviet Union in the early 1990s. Political tension—mostly expressed through implied actions and propaganda from both sides—led to the formation of NATO and the Warsaw Pact, and resulted in a divided Germany. This "iron curtain" has turned into a long-distance trail across twenty countries, most interestingly the former border between East and West Germany, which can be walked in small sections at a time.

491

Indo-Pakistani War

AMRITSAR, PUNJAB, INDIA

The partition of British India in 1947 into India and Pakistan has led to many issues since. When both countries claimed control over the disputed region of Kashmir in 1965, skirmishes between the two sides erupted into a full military battle that involved aerial, land, and naval assaults. The war lasted seventeen days and saw thousands of deaths on both sides. Relations between the two neighbors remain strained. After a visit to the Partition Museum, walk to the border and witness the dramatic closing of the borders ceremony, which takes place each day.

492

Killing of Che Guevara

LA HIGUERA, SANTA CRUZ, BOLIVIA

Che Guevara was killed on October 9, 1967, in the remote hamlet of La Higuera in Bolivia. From the village, walk down to a steep-sided ravine known as the Quebrada de Churo, where Che was captured by Bolivian soldiers, before climbing back up to the hamlet, which is filled with monuments and murals in tribute to the revolutionary. Finish in the *escuelita*, the old one-room school—now a museum—where Che was interrogated and then executed.

ABOVE RIGHT The monument to Che Guevara.

RIGHT A mural on a building in La Higuera pays tribute to Che Guevara.

493

Cambodian Civil War
PHNOM PENH, CAMBODIA

Political instability in Cambodia turned into a full-scale war in 1970 when the communist party of the Khmer Rouge, supported by North Vietnam and the Vietcong, rose up against the ruling government of the Kingdom of Cambodia led by Prince Sihanouk. Despite military assistance from the United States and South Vietnam, Prince Sihanouk was overthrown in 1975, and the Khmer Rouge, led by dictator Pol Pot, came to power, beginning a period of terror and genocidal campaigns. Walk the boulevards of Phnom Penh, lined with architecture that tells the story of the country's turbulent past.

494

Vietnam War
VIENG XAI, LAOS

In a valley in northeast Laos, this formidable network of karst caves was the headquarters of the Lao People's Liberation Army (or Pathet Lao), sheltering them from heavy U.S. bombing during the Vietnam War (1955–1975). After the war, it was turned into a "reeducation camp" for the army's political opponents. It is possible to explore a dozen of the caves, which were occupied by hundreds of people at their height. You'll see the remains of concert halls, classrooms, and workshops, as well as bunkers for use during chemical weapons attacks.

495

Prague Spring
PRAGUE, CZECH REPUBLIC

Alexander Dubček, elected First Secretary of the Communist Party of Czechoslovakia in 1968, was a reformist who wanted to grant additional rights to the citizens. However, Soviet Russia was not so keen. In August, troops and tanks of the Warsaw Pact rolled into Prague. The Soviets faced resistance for eight months before eventually occupying the country, ending the reform and beginning a period of "normalization" of Czechoslovakia. Take a loop walk between Legion Bridge and Charles Bridge and visit the Memorial to the Victims of Communism at the base of the castle.

ABOVE LEFT The valley in Laos, under which hundreds of people sheltered.

LEFT The caves were used as concert halls.

Battle of Huế

HUẾ, VIETNAM

Marvel at the restoration of this beautiful palace whose destruction contributed to the United States leaving the Vietnam War.

◆ **DISTANCE**
500 yards

◆ **START**
Entrance to Huế Palace

◆ **TYPE OF WALK**
Flat, paved walk, good for strollers or wheelchairs

◆ **WHEN TO GO**
All year

ABOVE RIGHT Bridges over Perfume River were attacked in the Battle of Huế.

RIGHT The Meridian Gate and moat at the Imperial Palace.

Of all the battles of the Vietnam War, the Battle of Huế may have been the most decisive. In an uprising that swept through the nation, the North Vietnamese attacked multiple positions all over the country, including Huế.

On January 31, 1968, the North Vietnamese attacked the city in force during the Tet Offensive. Key targets were the Imperial Palace, as well as the airfield and bridges over the Perfume River. They succeeded only temporarily and were driven back, with huge loss of life on both sides. But the real damage done was to U.S. and South Vietnamese morale. The fact that a force that had seemed inconsequential could mount such a fierce attack, massacre so many innocent people, and hold off the U.S. forces made this a Pyrrhic victory, one that deeply scarred the Vietnamese psyche, and ultimately contributed to the United States leaving the war.

Today, the city of Huế bears little resemblance to a battleground, and the Imperial Palace has been restored. A lovely walk takes you from inside the grounds around the picturesque moat that encircles the structure, then along the banks of the now-placid Perfume River nearby.

Cù Chi Tunnels

HÔ CHÍ MINH CITY, VIETNAM

Amid rusting Vietnam War weaponry are the Cú Chi Tunnels, vital to the Vietcong fighting against American troops. On a guided walk through the network, you'll see camouflaged trapdoors, mess areas, and learn about the various diseases that soldiers on both sides endured while in combat.

498

Battle of Khe Sanh

KHE SANH, VIETNAM

An embarrassing defeat for the United States, the Battle of Khe Sanh (1968) resulted in the evacuation of a key military base, with steep casualties on both sides in heavy fighting. Now a small museum, airfield, and walking trails are what remains.

Cordobazo

CÓRDOBA, ARGENTINA

During the military dictatorship of Juan Carlos Onganía, Argentina's second city of Córdoba was the site of a general strike in May 1969. This was met by brutal police repression, provoking a civil uprising that was put down violently by the military. The events became known as the *Cordobazo*. Walk from the campus of the National University of Córdoba—whose students were heavily involved in the uprising—to the Microcentro district, where protesters marched, erected barricades, and set regional government buildings on fire.

Pinochet's Military Coup

SANTIAGO, CHILE

The center of Santiago has numerous sites linked to General Augusto Pinochet's right-wing military coup on September 11, 1973. At the Palacio de la Moneda, the democratically elected socialist president Salvador Allende died during Pinochet's military assault. From here, head north to the elegant Ex Congreso Nacional, where congress met before being dissolved by Pinochet. Finally, loop around to the París-Londres neighborhood, where a nondescript house, Londres 38, was once one of Pinochet's main torture centers. Today it is a haunting museum and memorial to the thousands of victims of his dictatorship.

RIGHT The Palacio de la Moneda, where Salvador Allende died during Pinochet's military coup.

ARTURO
ALESSANDRI
PALMA

INDEX

CONTRIBUTORS

RAY BARTLETT

Ray Bartlett is a full-time travel writer, photographer, and novelist. His novels include *Sunsets of Tulum* and *Celadon* and he has worked on more than three dozen guidebooks about places as disparate as Canada, Japan, Mexico, Guatemala, Korea, Tanzania, Indonesia, and many parts of the United States. His novels are "destination fiction," designed to pull the reader to a particular part of the world and leave them wanting to go there. When not on the road, he lives on Cape Cod and can be found at www.kaisora.com or on social media at @kaisoradotcom.

STUART BUTLER

Stuart Butler is a writer and photographer who specializes in writing about hiking and conservation. Much of his work is focused on Africa, the Himalayas, and southwest Europe. He is the author of numerous guidebooks for Lonely Planet, Bradt, and Rough Guides, and a regular contributor to BBC radio, bbc.com, *Geographical* magazine, and major international newspapers and in-flight magazines. He has authored multiple hiking guidebooks to places as diverse as the Pyrenees, northern England, the Nepalese Himalayas, and the highlands of Ethiopia. Stuart is based in southwest France with his wife and two children. His website is www.stuartbutlerjournalist.com.

KIKI DEERE

Brought up bilingually in London and northern Italy, Kiki Deere writes about travel, culture, food, and history for major travel titles including *The Telegraph*, *Condé Nast Traveller*, Rough Guides, and DK Eyewitness. Her *Culture Trip* article on the history of La Serenissima, "When Venice Ruled the World," won Best Single Article at the Digiday Media Awards Europe. She can be found on Instagram at @kikideere.

STEVE FALLON

A native of Boston, Massachusetts, Steve Fallon can't remember a time when he was not obsessed with travel, other cultures, and languages. After graduating from Georgetown University with a degree in linguistics, he taught English in then-Communist Poland. The "new Asia" took him to Hong Kong where he worked as a journalist and travel writer for twelve years; the "new Eastern Europe" then enticed him to Budapest for another three. Based in London since 1994, Steve has written or contributed to more than a hundred guidebooks. He is also a qualified London Blue Badge Tourist Guide. Visit his website at www.steveslondon.com.

JULIAN HUMPHRYS

After gaining a degree in history at Emmanuel College Cambridge, Julian Humphrys joined the staff of London's National Army Museum where he curated numerous exhibitions and was spokesperson to the media on all matters of British Army history. He moved on to organize English Heritage's program of guided tours to historic sites and continues to lead battlefield walks for its members. An author of numerous books and articles on Britain's military history, he is a Fellow of the Royal Society of Arts and a Trustee of the UK Battlefields Trust.

AMY MCPHERSON

A travel writer based in London, Amy McPherson was born with a curious nature and is always on the lookout for new experiences and ways to travel. Having studied language and culture at university, Amy is particularly interested in how the past has shaped the present, and the stories associated with the histories of our cultures. An outdoor enthusiast, she is often found walking, running, or cycling around the world, looking out for a tale to tell. Amy writes for British and international publications. Follow her on Instagram at @amymcp_writer.

SHAFIK MEGHJI

Shafik Meghji is an award-winning journalist, travel writer, and author specializing in Latin America and South Asia. Over the last fifteen years he has worked on all seven continents, co-authoring more than forty guidebooks for Rough Guides and DK Eyewitness and writing about travel, history, culture, and sports for the likes of *BBC Travel*, *Wanderlust*, *Lonely Planet*, *the i*, and *Atlas Obscura*. A fellow of the Royal Geographical Society and a member of the British Guild of Travel Writers, his latest book, *Crossed off the Map: Travels in Bolivia*, was published in March 2022.

PAUL REED

Paul Reed is a professional military historian who has been visiting battlefields across the world since 1979 and working as a professional battlefield guide for over twenty-five years. The son of a World War II veteran, Paul has written ten books on the subject, lived on the Somme for over a decade, and has worked in the media and appeared in many TV history documentaries covering both world wars. Paul is the host of his own podcast, *The Old Front Line*, which he started in 2020. He can be found on Twitter at @sommecourt and online at www.oldfrontline.co.uk.

LIZZIE WILLIAMS

Lizzie Williams is originally from the United Kingdom but has lived in Cape Town, South Africa, for more than twenty years. She has authored or contributed to more than seventy guidebooks for DK Eyewitness, Footprint, Bradt, Rough Guides, Frommers, and Fodors and works for numerous magazines specializing in Africa and the Caribbean. While the hotels and restaurants are fabulous to research, she equally enjoys writing about fascinating history and culture. Visit her website at www. write-travel.com.

IMAGE CREDITS

t = top, b = bottom, l = left, r = right

123RF: Eric Middelkoop 10 b; Stormin1 17 t; Haim Magiura 17 b; okanakdeniz 22; Kaiskynet t; coffe72 278 t; Jesse Kraft 378 b.

Adobe Stock: Iza_miszczak 31; Nejdet Duzen 211 t; Progarten 291 b; Tynrud 312 t; Marko 373.

Alamy: REDA &CO srl 33 t, 259 t and b; Realy Easy Star / Toni Spagone 36–7; Hervé Lenain 56, 361 b; Hemis / Christian MARTELET 60, Hemis / Emmanuel BERTHIER 61, Hemis 104–5, 148, 149, 316; Hemis / Francis LEROY 205, Hemis / Franck GUIZIOU 227; John Alan Joyce 66; Wolfgang Diederich 73 t and b; Les Polders 79 t; Tudor Morgan-Owen / The National Trust Photolibrary 79 b; FredP 95 John Boud 110; EyeEm 111; Chris and Sally Gable / LatitudeStock 129; Ian Townsley 134; Colin Underhill 137; Holmes Garden Photos 143 t; eye35.pix 143 b; Jean Williamson 146; Danita Delimont 153; Richard Cummins 167 t; Keith Homan 168; Nik Taylor 177; Andrew Hasson 181; Jerry and Marcy Monkman / EcoPhotography.com 191; volkerpreusser 192 t; David Robertson 206; H. Mark Weidman Photography 217 b; Rafal Rozalski 221 b; Seth Lazar 241 t and b; MERVYN REES 247 t; Chris Hellier 255; Nikolay Mukhorin 257 t; robertharding 257 b; Don Mammoser 271 b; imageBROKER 277; Witold Skrypczak 283; Peter Jeffreys 286; DE ROCKER 287, 289; Arterra Picture Library 288, 307 t; Nature Picture Library 309 t; Niall Ferguson 309 b; JONATHAN EASTLAND / AJAX 319 t; Maurice Savage 320 t; Joris Kaper 335 t; David Hancock 340; Clive Downes 356; VerySmallPlanet 364 t; Pietersma 367 t; Marc Hill 367 b; Stuart Black 369 b; Mauritius images GmbH 370 t; Dennis MacDonald 377; Have Camera Will Travel / Asia 386 t and b.

Dreamstime: Sadık Güleç 18 b; Chun Ju Wu 28 b; Hao Wan 30; Jinfeng Zhang 39; Dudlajzov 67; Andrew Martin 69; Giulio Mignani 81 t; Wirestock 84; Rndmst 92–3; Pablo Boris Debat 99 t; Smithore 99b; Krisztian Juhasz 100; Vasily Iakovlev 101; Kateryna Levchenko 103; Sergei Afanasev 106 t; RIRFStock 114; Wirestock 115; Denis Kelly 127 t; Mihail Ivanov 130; Bernadett Pogácsás-Simon 140; Antonio Delluzio 147; Jesse Kraft 150; Akarawut Lohacharoenvanich 156 b; Victordenovan 158 b; Jesse Kraft 175; Bonandbon Dw 179; David Bright 184–5; Dudlajzov 188–9; Rui Baião 201; Bratty1206 214; Georgiy Golovin 230; Vladyslav Musiienko 233; Jesus Eloy Ramos Lara 261; Alacrityp 265; Supoj Buranaprapapong 273 b; Jeeaachen 280t; Giocalde 291 t; Cyclingscot 294, 295; Richard Billingham 297t; Lochstampfer 300 t; Pintxoman 330; Jackmalipan 332; Wirestock 339 b; Velishchuk 344 t; Emotionart 344 b; Walter Eric Sy 346t; Nuvisage 346 b; Mariohagen 351; Adamara26 353; Antonio Nardelli 358 t; Wolfmaster13 374; Sandra Foyt 383 t; Ngvliem 389 t; Diego Grandi 390–91.

Getty: HUSSEIN FALEH / AFP 14; Hulton Archive 15; Geography Photos / Universal Images Group 47; DEA / G. WRIGHT 47; Gary Tumilty 58–9; Gannet77 82–3; Hugh Sitton 88–9; Otto Stadler 90–91; Buena Vista Images 96–7, 112; ViewStock 182–3; Howard Pugh 187 b; Amit Basu Photography 223 t; Massimo Borchi / Atlantide Phototravel 225; Holgs 226; Scott E Barbour 238–9; Nigel Killeen 250; Tetra Images 267; Manuel Breva Colmeiro 329 b; Visual China Group 333; Andrew Peacock 349; Claudia Beretta / Mondadori 364 b; Matteo Colombo 381 t.

Istock: clubfoto 158 t; Libre de droits 319 b.

Pixta: Ken 165 t; ogurisu_Q 165 b.

Shutterstock: Cover images; Gary Saxe 4–5; Alexander Sorokopud 6–7; Anastasios71 8–9; Marco Tomasini 11; Ole Nesheim 12–13; Reimar 18 t; akimov Konstantin 21; Leventina 23; Oleg Znamenskiy 24; Lefteris Papaulakis 25; Tinnaporn Sathapornnanont 27; S.Borisov 28 t; Fabio Lamanna 33 b; zhu difeng 34–5; Essevu 40; Karl Allen Lugmayer 41; Guenter Albers 43; Oszibusz 45 t; Henk Vrieselaar 45 b; TLF Images 49; Roberto Destarac 51; alenfra 52; Christian Vinces 53; Danilo Strino 54; Anton_Ivanov 55; KiyechkaSo 63 t; Shinelu 63 b; Nikonov Vladimir 65 b; Odessa25 70, 71; Anastas Styles 75; Aberu.Go 76; Sergey Dzyuba 77; Phortun 81 b; Chris Dorney 86 t; 4kclips 86 b; Potapov Sergey 106 b; Chernyshev Dmitry 108–9; Gerhard Roethlinger 116–17; john paul slinger 118; SeraphP 119; Belikova Oksana 120; humphery 121; Andrew Mayovskyy 123; Aliaksandr Antanovich 123; Aanimesh 125; Heracles Kritikos 132; acsen 133; Peter Yeo 135; beibaoke 136; olrat 138; Matyas Rehak 141; Claudio306 144–5; Mark Pitt Images 155 t; Alan Falcony 155 b; Boris-B 156 t; Lana Kray 160–61; Nicholas Courtney 162 t; Milan Gonda 162; pxl.store 167 b; mihyang ahn 169; Tessa Bishop 171; beibaoke 172 t; OKAP 172 b; SGR Wildlife Photography 174; Andrej Privizer 192 b; Burhan Ay Photography 194 t; Dan Rata 194 b; Photosounds 197 t; www.filmotions.com 197 b; Jon Bilous 198–9; Alizada Studios 200; SvetlanaSF 202; Alice-D 203; TGP-shot 209 t; DronaVision 209 b; Nejdet Duzen 211 b, 324 b; Jay Yuan 213; Katkami 213; Matthew Herman 217 t; Pawel Kazmierczak 218–9; PRIYA DARSHAN 223 b; Alex Anton 224; alexilena 229; KlepachA 232; Mccallk69 235; Alexandros Michailidis 237 t; Arjan Kemeling 237 b; Alejo Miranda 243 t; Ecuadorpostales 243 b; Abdullah Durman 245; Sean Pavone 247 b; 2630ben 248–9; Centli 253; HelloRF Zcool 260; TYL Photography 262; Walt Bilous 263 b; TJ Brown 265 t; Bob Pool 266; Estebran 268; Javen 269; Rey Rodriguez 271 t; YingHui Liu 273 t; Joseph Sohm 274–5; Yoga Ardi Nugroho 277; OSTILL is Franck Camhi 279; superjoseph 280 b; Juan Carlos Munoz 284–5; Katerina Samsonova 292; Bodrumsurf 297 b; BeAvPhoto 299; Joaquin Ossorio Castillo 300 b; Madrugada Verde 302–3; Nikolay Tsyu 305; Melanie Hobson 307 b; Eric Valenne geostory 311; timsimages.uk 311 b; Ondra Vacek 312 b; Cortyn 314; Thomas Dekiere 315; Karavanov Lev 322–3; Birol Aydin 324 t; Pierre Jean Durieu 327; Christopher Cook 327; Angel L 329 t; Sara Glop 331; Maxim Lysenko 335 b; Audrey Snider-Bell 336, 369 t; MisterStock 337; Tartezy 339 t; Richard Whitcombe 343; Darksoul72 350; Sergey Colonel 354 t; TAMVISUT 354 t; Michael Mulkens 357; HungryBild 358 b; Kyrien 361 t; Kateafter 362; FotoFabrikHamburg 370 b; Oliver de la Haye 379; Vladimir Zhoga 381 b; Greta Gabaglio 383 b; Jess Kraft 385; Jess Kraft 385, 389 b.

Wikimedia Commons: CC BY-SA 3.0: Z thomas 176; Duca696 228; Heimlich 282; Xfigpower 363; CC BY-SA 4.0: FrDr 320 t.

Also: Library of Congress: cover map and endpapers; Unsplash: Aaron Thomas 50; Jeremy Jagger / Battlefield 1403 Farm Shop, Shrewsbury 127 b; Jenny Quiggin 187 t; Allison Ryder / VisitArklow.ie 221 t.

Every effort has been made to credit photographers and to obtain their permission for the use of copyright material. The publisher would like to apologize should there have been any omissions or errors, and would be pleased to make the appropriate corrections for future editions of the book..